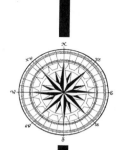

BASIC COASTAL
NAVIGATION

BASIC COASTAL NAVIGATION

An Introduction to Piloting

Second Edition

Frank J. Larkin

S

SHERIDAN HOUSE

Published by
Sheridan House Inc.
145 Palisade Street
Dobbs Ferry, NY 10522

First edition 1993
Second edition 1998
Copyright © 1993, 1998 by Frank J. Larkin

Library of Congress Cataloging-in-Publication Data

Larkin, Frank J.
    Basic coastal navigation : an introduction to piloting / Frank J.
        Larkin. — 2nd ed.
            p.   cm.
    Includes index.
    ISBN 1-57409-052-6 (alk. paper)
    1. Coastwise navigation. 2. Yachting. I. Title.
VK559.L34   1998
    623.89' 22—dc21   98–13057
                                                                             CIP

Production/Design: Lorretta Palagi
Composition: Kathleen Weisel
Printed in the United States of America

ISBN 1-57409-052-6

Author's Note

The warning statements shown in this book can be found on every nautical chart and in most navigational publications. They are not simple disclaimers, as the skeptic may think: instead, they reflect the reality of an environment that is hostile to human habitation—the sea. Navigation is a flawed science that requires knowledge, skill, and attention to many details while you pilot your boat. Read and heed these warnings.

CONTENTS

INTRODUCTION

Thanks to the great response to the first edition of *Basic Coastal Navigation,* I am now fortunate to have the opportunity to present a new edition and to share with you new experiences and knowledge gained on the subject of coastal navigation. It also gives me the excuse to further simplify the navigation processes which I am constantly researching and testing. Each time I take my boat out, I calculate a predicted run for a specific time on a predetermined course. The times obtained from these runs are checked by computer against the predicted times. Analyzing the results, I develop new techniques to improve my boat's predictability on the water.

The changes in the new edition result partly from my acquisition of a 25-foot boat and partly from the predicted log contests—a great way to add dimension to the boating experience. I discovered that navigation processes which work well for larger boats are not sufficient for smaller boats if you want to attain a high level of accuracy. I have acquired a new admiration for all small boat operators who are good navigators.

If you want to know why small boats are so unpredictable, this is the book for you. I have found that DR accuracy, boat base weight, weight loss, weight shift, current, depth of water, and wind are the critical parts in this navigational puzzle and I have provided easy-to-use solutions. Being able to solve these problems is critical to your ability to accurately predict your boat's speed. Omit one and your predictions will be off the mark. Most mariners use only one or two of these navigation elements—dead reckoning and current vectors—and eventually lose confidence in their ability to predict accurately. Unfortunately, many new mariners rely solely on electronic navigation devices but don't understand the basics of navigation. In Florida, 64 percent of boating accidents and 83 percent of boating deaths involved operators with no boating instruction. According to the Coast Guard, approximately 85 percent of boating fatalities involve such operators. These statistics alone should provide you with the incentive to become proficient in navigation, among other boating skills.

Nautical terminology can be confusing and is one of the greatest deterrents to the study of navigation. This book is written in simple, easy-to-understand terms. I wish such a publication had been available when I started out. Each navigational technique is explained in simple language with easy-to-follow, step-by-step instructions. I have focused on practical navigational techniques that should be used every time you go out on your boat, and have omitted those that I never use. Every novice can learn a lot from this book. Experienced boat owners will brush up on their navigational skills after extended periods away from their boat. Even old salts will learn a few new tricks that will help make them better navigators. If you are studying for your Captain's license, the information provided in the book will help you pass the piloting section of the exam.

Basic Coastal Navigation is written in a self-instruction format with exercises, questions, and answers included in each chapter. For those of you who teach navigation, a full set of lesson plans is available. This instructor package contains the black-and-white artwork necessary to make overhead transparencies for each lesson. Also available is a disk, *Computerized Basic Coastal Navigation,* that contains all of the navigation calculations needed for a twenty-leg trip. If you have Windows 95 with EXCEL on your IBM compatible personal computer, you can use this software. This disk performs many of the navigation calculations explained in this book and much more, such as dead reckoning, compensating for heading change due to current, compensating for speed change due to current, correcting planned speed for water depths under eighteen feet, correcting planned speed for wind, and calculating a Speed Curve Worksheet. For information on the lesson plan or the disk, contact Sheridan House at 1-888-SHERIBK or check out their web site at http://www.sheridanhouse.com.

Read This Warning Carefully

The sea is a hostile environment for the sailor so plan to use every care to safeguard your life. The aids to navigation depicted on nautical charts comprise a system of fixed and floating aids with varying degrees of reliability. Therefore prudent mariners will not rely solely on any single aid to navigation, particularly a floating aid. Read the introduction to the U.S. Coast Guard *Light List* and the *U.S. Coast Pilot* for the specific details of these problems. While the Coast Guard uses every modern technique to position buoys accurately, there are many reasons why a buoy may be off station. Sound signals may not function or lighted buoys may be extinguished. Charted depths can change due to shoaling, shifting of the seabed, and storms, or you may be using an out-of-date chart. The Coast Guard makes every effort to maintain aids to navigation in an operable condition. However, don't assume anything while on the water. Keep your charts updated to the latest Local Notice to Mariners, a free service offered by the Coast Guard. Double check everything when you transit unfamiliar waters—LORAN and GPS are not always infallible. Train yourself to become a rational skeptic about the sea.

Now that you have been warned, let's begin your journey to learn about basic coastal navigation.

ONE

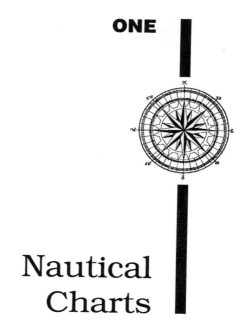

Nautical Charts

Your road map of the sea is the nautical chart. Without it, you are like a blind person. All it takes is one small rock or shoal to spoil a beautiful day and put a large dent in your bank account. The dangers are out there. I found a few the hard way before I learned to read a chart. In this chapter, we'll discuss the importance of nautical charts and explain the wealth of nautical information shown on them that can keep you and your family safer.

For the purpose of charting, the earth is considered to be a perfect sphere (a ball). In creating a chart, the cartographer or map maker must face the problem of presenting the features of the earth on a flat surface. From a practical point of view, it would be difficult to plot courses on a rounded surface. The chart maker uses a technique called *projection* to accomplish the transition from the sphere onto a flat plane or chart.

THE MERCATOR PROJECTION

Charts used aboard small boats are usually Mercator projections with the exception of the Great Lakes where polyconic projections are utilized. A Mercator projection is created by transferring the spherical surface of the earth onto a cylinder. This procedure is illustrated in Figure 1.1. A polyconic projection is made by transferring the earth's spherical surface onto a cone.

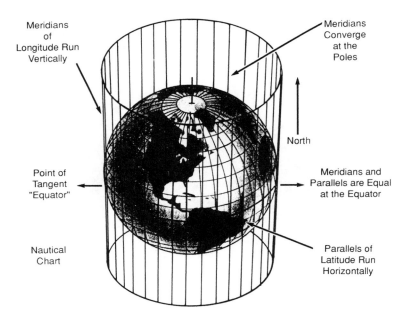

Fig. 1.1   The Mercator Projection. *(T. J. Larkin)*

The vertical lines on Mercator projections are called *meridians of longitude* and they are drawn so that they are equally distant from and parallel to each other. On a sphere or globe, meridians of longitude project distance accurately at only one location on the globe—the equator.

Refer to Figure 1.1 and observe how the meridians of longitude converge to meet at the North and South poles. Note how meridians of longitude become distorted as they approach the poles and, therefore, cannot be used for measuring distance on a nautical chart.

Longitude is measured 180 degrees east and west from the *prime meridian*, located at Greenwich, England, for a total of 360 degrees. These longitude lines meet at a point called the International Date Line on the opposite side of the globe. Longitude is labeled as either east (E) or west (W) of the prime meridian. Each degree of longitude has 60 minutes and each minute has 60 seconds.

The horizontal lines on nautical charts are called *parallels of latitude* because they are parallel to each other. Since they are parallel and not distorted like meridians, they are used to measure distance on a nautical chart. The parallel of latitude called the *equator* is labeled as zero (000) latitude. Parallels of latitude increase numerically northward and southward from zero (000) degrees at the equator to ninety (090) degrees at the poles for a total of 180 degrees for each hemisphere, which together equal 360 degrees. Each degree of latitude has 60 minutes and each minute has 60 seconds. One minute of latitude is equal to one nautical mile (nm). Latitude is labeled as either north (N) or south (S) of the equator.

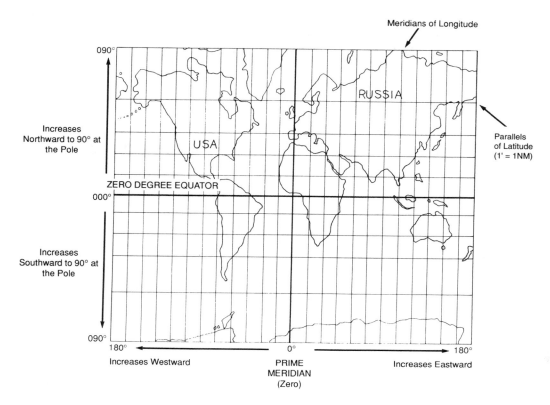

Fig. 1.2   Latitude and Longitude. *(T. J. Larkin)*

Study the graphic in Figure 1.2 until you fully understand how the numbering system for latitude and longitude works.

THE NAUTICAL CHART

Nautical charts contain a variety of information that is important to you as a boat operator. Charts show the depth of the water, lights, buoys, lighthouses, prominent landmarks, rocks, shoals, reefs, sandbars, and much more information that is essential for the safe operation of your boat.

Chart Orientation

Nautical charts are oriented with *true north* at the top, east on the right-hand side, west on the left-hand side, and south at the bottom. Review Figure 1.3, the Piloting Practice Chart, as an example of the design of a typical nautical chart.

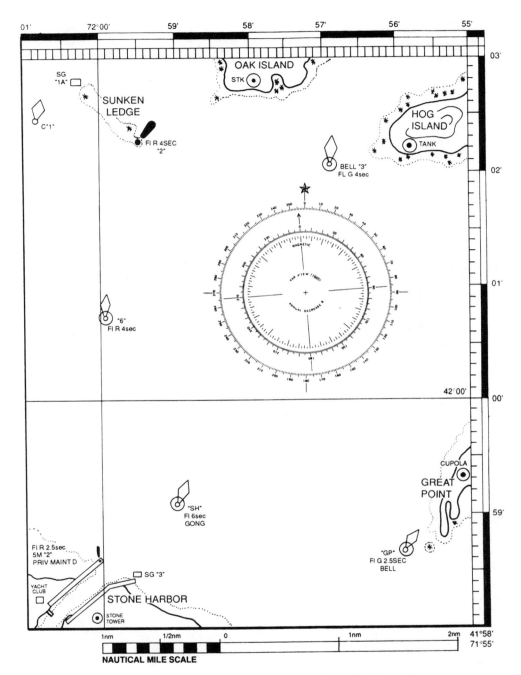

Fig. 1.3 The Piloting Practice Chart Orientation. *(T. J. Larkin)*

Small craft (SC) charts have a different orientation since they are made to follow a coast line and coastal bays. The area charted is more important on a SC chart than the location of true north. Figure 1.4 presents a sample section of a small craft chart. Note where true north is oriented on a SC chart and how this direction is different from a regular nautical chart. If you are not sure about the location of true north when using a small craft chart, you can make serious piloting errors very easily.

As mentioned in the previous section, the lines that run horizontally across the nautical chart are called the parallels of latitude. They are measured on the scales printed at the left and right margins of the chart. I use the phrase "LAT IS FLAT" as a memory aid.

One minute of latitude is equal to one nautical mile. The latitude scales on charts for areas in the northern hemisphere are numbered from the bottom of the chart toward the top. Review Figure 1.3 and observe the scale at the right-hand (easterly) side of the chart.

The lines that run vertically (up and down) on the nautical chart are the meridians of longitude. They are measured from scales located at the top and bottom margins of the chart. Note that these meridians of longitude scales are not as wide as the parallels of latitude scales found on the left- and right-hand sides of the chart. Stop here and measure the difference between a minute of longitude and a minute of latitude on the Piloting Practice Chart in Figure 1.3 so that you are convinced this is true. Never use the longitude scales on a nautical chart to measure distance. One degree of longitude does not equal a nautical mile.

Any position on a nautical chart can be expressed in terms of latitude and longitude. Review Figure 1.2 and study the numbering scheme. Your position will always be either north or south of the equator and east or west of the prime meridian.

In piloting, parallels, meridians, the equator, and the poles are all used as reference points to determine your boat's position; i.e., Boston is located at a latitude that is north of the equator and at a longitude that is west of Greenwich, England. Boston Light is positioned at 42 degrees, 19.7 minutes North and 70 degrees, 53.7 minutes West.

The Compass Rose

Every nautical chart has at least one *compass rose.* Figure 1.5 shows an example of a typical compass rose. Observe how the compass rose is similar to the card on your boat's compass. Each compass rose has two circles. The outer circle is aligned to true north on your nautical chart; the inner circle gives magnetic directions. Course directions can be measured by using the compass rose on your nautical chart. Study the following characteristics of a compass rose in Figure 1.5:

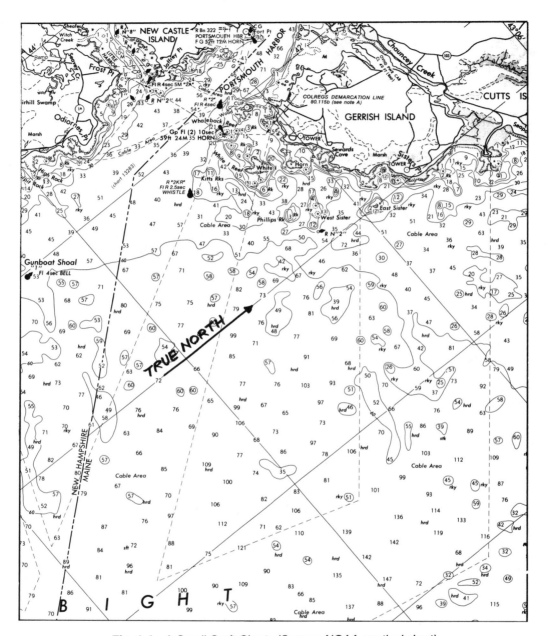

Fig. 1.4   A Small Craft Chart. *(Source: NOAA nautical chart)*

Magnetic Variation (example): 4° 15' W 1985 (8' E) *on magnetic north arrow means Magnetic Variation 4° 15' W in 1985, annual change 8' E (i.e. magnetic variation decreasing 8' annually).*

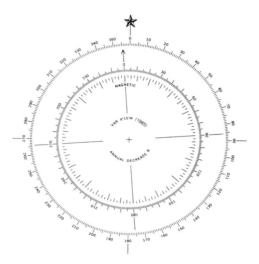

Fig. 1.5 A Compass Rose. *(Source: Nautical Chart No. 1)*

- True directions are printed around the outer circle of the compass rose.
- Magnetic directions are printed around the inner circle of the compass rose. This inner or magnetic scale is oriented toward magnetic north.
- Note that true north on the outer scale and magnetic north on the inner scale point to different directions.

In the Boston area, magnetic north (inner scale) is located approximately 15 to 16 degrees west of true north (outer scale). This difference between true north and magnetic north is called *variation.*

Variation will differ in relation to your location on the earth's surface. However, it is a predictable difference, and it is precalculated and printed for you in the center of each compass rose. Always use the variation printed on the compass rose nearest to your position on your nautical chart for course conversion calculations.

Find the variation in the center of the compass rose shown in Figure 1.5. It should read 4° 15' W, which is read as 4 degrees, 15 minutes West.

In piloting, variation is used to convert a compass course to a true course or vice versa. The formula for converting a true course to a compass course is covered in Chapter 10 of this book.

Soundings and Water Depth

Depth designations are depicted on a nautical chart with numbers, color codes, contour lines, and a system of standardized symbols and abbreviations. The NOAA publication Chart No. 1 contains all of the symbols and abbreviations used on nautical charts. This publication is explained in Chapter 2. Many of the figures used in this chapter are taken directly from Chart No. 1.

Water depths or soundings are the printed numbers on a nautical chart. These numbers can be expressed in feet, meters, or fathoms. A fathom is equal to six feet. The baseline measurement from which the chart's vertical or water depth measurements were made is found in the *general information block* on a nautical chart. Ordinarily this baseline reflects an average of the low water depth predictions for the area covered by the chart.

Figure 1.6 shows a sample general information block from a nautical chart. The depth in this example is expressed as "Soundings in Feet at Mean Low Water." This means that the depths on the chart are in feet and represent the average of the low water levels of the tides in the Boston Inner Harbor.

Remember that depths are averages and, therefore, can be lower or higher than the depth printed on the chart. Water depths can be affected by weather. Always allow yourself a margin of error when using the water depths shown on a nautical chart. Personally, I highlight every location on my charts that shows a depth of six feet or lower. This gives me a quick visual alarm when I get near shoal areas.

In the future, the new and revised NOAA charts will be metric. You will also see a progression toward "Lower Low Water" references on charts. These are more conservative predictions that use only the lowest of the daily low tide predictions to compute the average water depth. Usually tide cycles on the East Coast have two high tides and two low tides each day. The predicted depths of these tides will often be different on each tide cycle. Obviously, your greatest danger is at low tide, so it is important for you to understand that, since soundings or depths shown on your chart are averages, the depth of the water can at times be lower than the depth printed on your chart. Chapter 15 will explain how to determine the height of the tide at any time.

Contour Lines

Contour lines, also called *fathom lines,* connect points of roughly equal depth to provide a linear profile of the ocean's bottom. Contour lines can be numbered or coded to show depth. Figures 1.7 and 1.19 (see the section on "Other Charted Features") show some examples of contour lines. These codes are a series of lines, dots, or dashes. Figure 1.7 is

UNITED STATES – EAST COAST

MASSACHUSETTS

BOSTON INNER HARBOR

Mercator Projection
Scale 1:10,000 at Lat. 42°22′
North American 1927 Datum

SOUNDINGS IN FEET
AT MEAN LOW WATER

TIDAL INFORMATION

Place	Height referred to datum of soundings (MLW)			
	Mean High Water	Mean Tide Level	Mean Low Water	Extreme Low Water
	feet	feet	feet	feet
Castle Island	9.4	4.7	0.0	−3.5
Charlestown	9.5	4.7	0.0	−3.5

(1279)

ABBREVIATIONS   (For complete list of Symbols and Abbreviations, see Chart No 1):

Lights (Lights are white unless otherwise indicated.):

F. fixed	Mo. (A) morse code	OBSC. obscured	Rot. rotating
Fl. flashing	Occ. occulting	WHIS. whistle	SEC. sector
Qk. quick	Alt. alternating	DIA. diaphone	m. minutes
Gp. group	I. Qk. interrupted quick	M. nautical miles	sec. seconds
E. Int. equal interval			

Buoys: T.B. temporary buoy   N. nun   B. black   Or. orange   W. white
        C. can   S. spar   R. red   G. green   Y. yellow

Bottom characteristics:

Cl. clay	M. mud	hrd. hard	bk. black	gy. gray
Co. coral	Rk. rock	rky. rocky	br. brown	rd. red
G. gravel	S. sand	sft. soft	bu. blue	wh. white
Grs. grass	Sh. shells	stk. sticky	gn. green	yl. yellow

21,   Wreck, rock, obstruction, or shoal swept clear to the depth indicated.
(2)   Rocks that cover and uncover, with heights in feet above datum of soundings.

AERO. aeronautical   R. Bn. radiobeacon   C. G. Coast Guard station
Bn. daybeacon   R. TR. radio tower   D.F.S. distance finding station

AUTH. authorized; Obstr. obstruction; P.A. position approximate; E.D. existence doubtful.

HEIGHTS
Heights in feet above Mean High Water

AUTHORITIES
Hydrography and topography by the National Ocean Survey with
additional data from the Corps of Engineers and U.S. Coast Guard.

Fig. 1.6   The General Information Block from a Nautical Chart.
(Source: NOAA nautical chart)

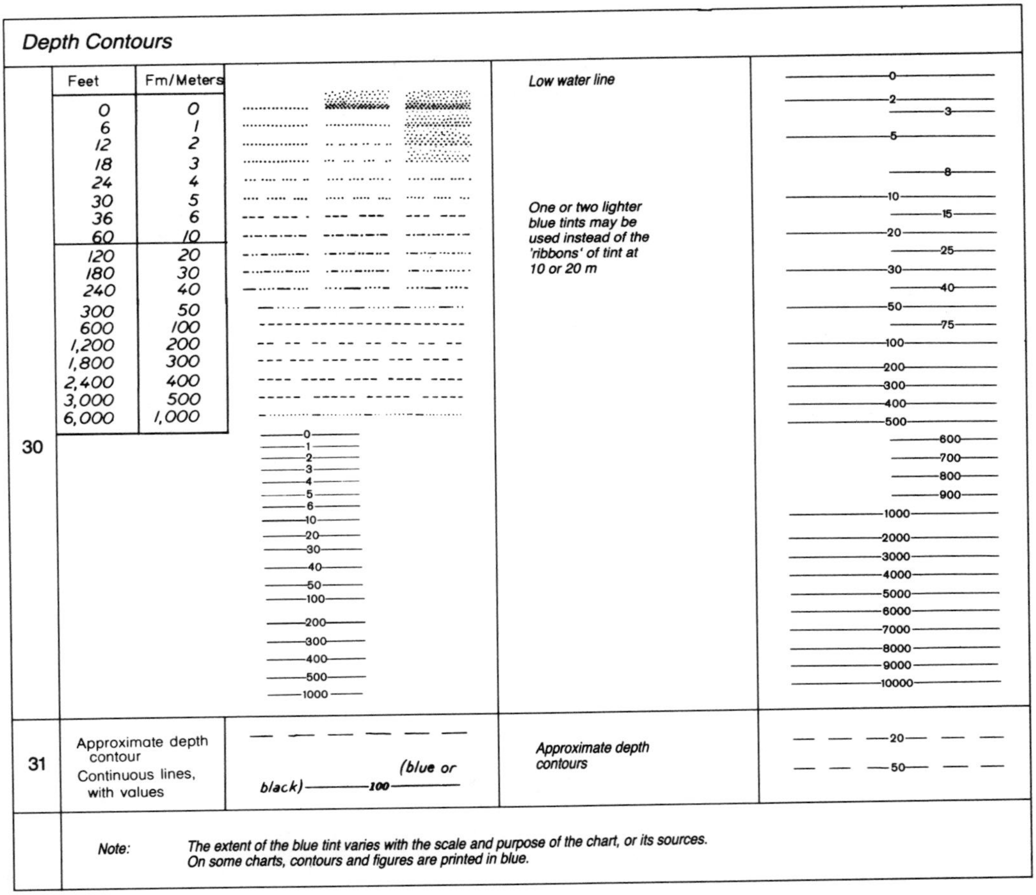

Depth Contours

	Feet	Fm/Meters			Low water line	
	0	0				0
	6	1				2
	12	2				3
	18	3				5
	24	4				
	30	5				8
	36	6			One or two lighter	10
	60	10			blue tints may be	15
	120	20			used instead of the	20
	180	30			'ribbons' of tint at	25
	240	40			10 or 20 m	30
	300	50				40
	600	100				50
	1,200	200				75
	1,800	300				100
	2,400	400				200
	3,000	500				300
	6,000	1,000				400
						500

(Depth contour scale markings: 0, 1, 2, 3, 4, 5, 6, 10, 20, 30, 40, 50, 100, 200, 300, 400, 500, 1000)

(Right column markings: 600, 700, 800, 900, 1000, 2000, 3000, 4000, 5000, 6000, 7000, 8000, 9000, 10000)

Row 30

31	Approximate depth contour Continuous lines, with values	black) ——— 100 ——— (blue or	Approximate depth contours	— — —20— — — — — — —50— — — —

Note: The extent of the blue tint varies with the scale and purpose of the chart, or its sources. On some charts, contours and figures are printed in blue.

Fig. 1.7   Depths. *(Source: Nautical Chart No. 1)*

taken from the NOAA publication Chart No. 1 and provides information that will help you interpret the meaning of the contour lines shown on nautical charts.

Shadings

Generally, the shallow water on a nautical chart is tinted a darker blue, while the deeper water is tinted a lighter blue or white. The meaning of these different shades is explained in Chart No. 1 in the section on "Depth Contours" (see Figure 1.7).

Place	Height referred to datum of soundings (MLW)			
	Mean High Water	Mean Tide Level	Mean Low Water	Extreme Low Water
	feet	feet	feet	feet
Castle Island	9.4	4.7	0.0	−3.5
Charlestown	9.5	4.7	0.0	−3.5

TIDAL INFORMATION

(1279)

Fig. 1.8 Tidal Information Block.
(*Source: NOAA nautical chart*)

Heights of Bridges

The clearance heights for bridges on a nautical chart are measured upward from the high water mark. The high water mark datum is found in the "Notes" section on your nautical chart. Turn back to Figure 1.6 and find the note "Heights." It states that heights on this chart are measured in feet above mean high water (MHW). Bridge height is measured to the lowest projection of the bridge over the navigable channel. Look at the tidal information block in Figure 1.8 and you will find that mean high water (MHW) is 9.4 feet at Castle Island and 9.5 feet at Charlestown. Always use the datum that is closest to your position.

Heights of Objects

The heights of objects such as a lighthouse are measured upward from the mean high water mark. This vertical datum is found in the tidal information block on your nautical chart along with a unit of measure. Again refer to Figure 1.8, which shows a sample tidal information block.

Note that lighthouses and other fixed lights are measured from the mean high water mark to the height of the focal plane of their light (the height of their light bulb).

BASIC CHART INFORMATION

It is important that you read all of the information printed on your nautical chart. Scan the complete chart for this information. You will be surprised at what you can learn about your boating area from your nautical chart. Figures 1.9(a) and (b) show the standard layout for the information shown on a nautical chart.

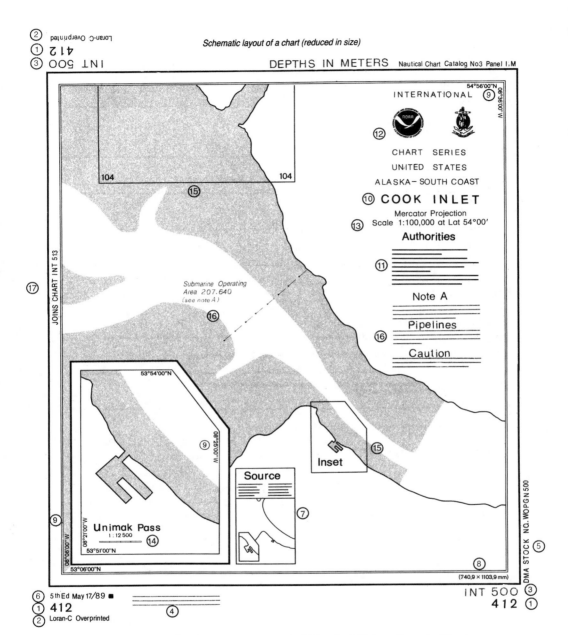

Fig. 1.9(a) Chart Number, Title, and Marginal Notes: Sample Chart.
(Source: Nautical Chart No. 1)

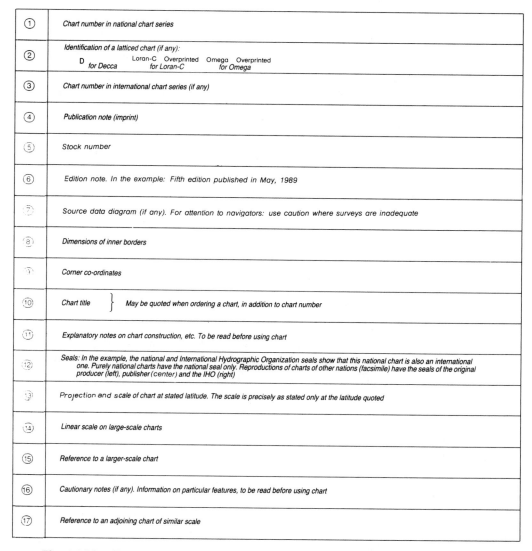

①	Chart number in national chart series
②	Identification of a latticed chart (if any): D for Decca Loran-C Overprinted for Loran-C Omega Overprinted for Omega
③	Chart number in international chart series (if any)
④	Publication note (imprint)
⑤	Stock number
⑥	Edition note. In the example: Fifth edition published in May, 1989
⑦	Source data diagram (if any). For attention to navigators: use caution where surveys are inadequate
⑧	Dimensions of inner borders
⑨	Corner co-ordinates
⑩	Chart title } May be quoted when ordering a chart, in addition to chart number
⑪	Explanatory notes on chart construction, etc. To be read before using chart
⑫	Seals: In the example, the national and International Hydrographic Organization seals show that this national chart is also an international one. Purely national charts have the national seal only. Reproductions of charts of other nations (facsimile) have the seals of the original producer (left), publisher (center) and the IHO (right)
⑬	Projection and scale of chart at stated latitude. The scale is precisely as stated only at the latitude quoted
⑭	Linear scale on large-scale charts
⑮	Reference to a larger-scale chart
⑯	Cautionary notes (if any). Information on particular features, to be read before using chart
⑰	Reference to an adjoining chart of similar scale

Fig. 1.9(b)   Chart Number, Title, and Marginal Notes: Explanation of Chart Notation.
(Source: Nautical Chart No. 1)

The General Information Block

The general information block on a nautical chart contains very important data about your chart. Reference the general information block shown in Figure 1.6 and identify the following items of information:

    1. The *chart title* is usually the name of the prominent navigational body of water in the area covered by the chart. When

ordering charts, the chart title may be quoted in addition to chart number.

2. A statement of the *type of projection* (Mercator or polyconic).

3. A statement of the *scale of the chart* at an indicated latitude; i.e., 1:10,000. This means that 1 inch on the chart represents 10,000 inches on the earth's surface. The scale is precisely as stated only at the latitude quoted. Chart scale is discussed in detail in the section on "The Scale of a Nautical Chart."

4. A statement of the *unit of measurement of soundings* for the chart. This measurement unit can be either meters, feet, or fathoms, i.e., "Soundings in Feet."

5. All *cautionary notes* should be read before using any nautical chart. Pay close attention to all notes that you find on your chart because they contain information that cannot be graphically presented on the chart. Look for notes that:

    - Explain the meaning of special abbreviations used on the chart.
    - Indicate the need for caution regarding dangers found on the chart.
    - Show special tidal and current information for the area.
    - Explain magnetic interference information in the area.
    - Refer to anchorage areas and special lighting regulations in anchorage areas.

Number and Edition of the Chart

The chart number, edition number, and the date of your chart are located in the margin at the lower left-hand corner of a chart. See Figure 1.10 for an example. The edition number and date indicate the last calendar date and year when information on your chart was updated by NOAA. This means that all essential corrections concerning lights, beacons, buoys, and dangers that were known by NOAA as of this date of issue are printed on the chart.

Also explained in this area is the identification of any lattice lines on the chart. This information may be coded as:

1. The letter "D" for Decca.

2. "LORAN-C Overprinted" for Loran-C.

3. "Omega Overprinted" for OMEGA.

Figure 1.9(a) shows an example of a "LORAN C Overprinted" note.

Corrections that occur after the date of issue of a chart are published in the "Local Notice to Mariners" (LNM). You must correct your chart

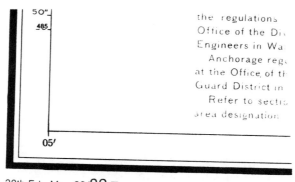

50"
485

the regulations
Office of the D...
Engineers in Wa...
Anchorage reg...
at the Office of th...
Guard District in...
Refer to secti...
area designation...

05'

38th Ed., Mar. 20/82 ∎

13272

Fig. 1.10 Number and Edition of a Nautical Chart.
(Source: NOAA nautical chart)

from this weekly publication. The LNM can be obtained free of charge from the local district office of the Coast Guard in your area. Appendix 8 carries a complete listing of the addresses and telephone numbers of all of the U.S. Coast Guard offices in the United States. Call the office in your district and get your name on this list today.

Another NOAA publication called the "Dates of Latest Editions" shows all nautical charts and their edition numbers and dates. This is a small white booklet and can usually be found at authorized chart dealers. This publication is explained in Chapter 2.

The Scale of a Nautical Chart

The scale of a nautical chart is found in the general information block. This scale is the ratio of a unit of distance on the chart to the actual distance on the earth's surface. On a chart with a scale of 1:2,500, 1 inch equals 2,500 inches (approximately 70 yards) on the earth's surface. Please note the following:

- Small-scale charts cover a large area of the earth's surface and show little detail. They will have high scale ratios, i.e., 1:150,000.

- Large-scale charts cover a small area and show more detail and features of the earth's surface. When navigating in an area, always use the largest scale chart available. Large-scale charts will have low scale ratios, i.e., 1:5,000.

- Coast charts are produced in scales of between 1:40,000 and 1:150,000. These charts are used for coastal navigation, for entering bays and harbors of considerable width, and for navigating large inland waterways.

- Harbor charts are produced at scales larger than 1:50,000 and are used in harbors, anchorage areas, and smaller waterways.
- Small craft charts are produced at scales of 1:40,000 and larger. They are special charts of inland waters, including the Intracoastal Waterway (ICW). These special editions of conventional charts are printed on lighter weight paper and are folded. The chart numbers on these charts will be suffixed with the letters "SC," for example, 11354SC. Small craft charts contain additional information of interest to small craft operators, such as data on facilities, tide predictions, weather broadcasts, ramps, marinas, repairs, fuel, etc. Figure 1.4 is a section taken from a small craft chart.

Chart Symbols and Abbreviations

Chart No. 1, published jointly by the Defense Mapping Agency Hydrographic Center and the National Ocean Survey, lists all of the standard symbols and abbreviations used on nautical charts. Often there are some symbols and abbreviations printed on your nautical charts in the "Notes" section. These symbols are a shorthand used to identify the physical characteristics of a charted area, the details of the available aids to navigation, and the significant landmarks on a nautical chart. Figures 1.5, 1.7, and 1.9(a) and (b) are pages from Chart No. 1 that show chart symbols and abbreviations.

Use of Color on a Nautical Chart

Color is used to distinguish various categories of information for the mariner, such as shoal water, deep water, and land areas. Red and green are used to color aids to navigation on a nautical chart so that they are easier to see and interpret.

A nautical purple or magenta-colored ink is used for some notes and to highlight lighted aids to navigation. This purple ink is easily read under a red light.

CAUTION: *The use of red lights in the bridge (steering) area of a vessel does not interfere with the night vision of the helmsperson and lookouts. Be aware that a sudden burst of white light impairs the night vision of a person for approximately 30 minutes. This is why you should not show bright white lights forward at night (running lights excluded) and never shine search lights at another boat's bridge area.*

Lettering on a Nautical Chart

The lettering on a nautical chart provides important information about aids to navigation. *Slanted lettering* is used to label all information about objects that are affected by tidal change and current (floating objects that can move about). Bottom soundings are the exception. All descriptive lettering for floating aids to navigation is slanted. *Vertical lettering* is used to label all information that is not affected by tidal changes or current. Lighthouses, ranges, and small lights are fixed navigational aids and are lettered vertically. Figure 1.11 illustrates this charting procedure.

The Accuracy of a Nautical Chart

A nautical chart is no more accurate than the survey on which it is based. Charting agencies make every effort to keep charts updated and accurate. However, hurricanes, earthquakes, and other major disturbances can cause sudden and extensive damage to a bottom contour or destroy floating and fixed aids to navigation. The everyday forces of wind and waves can erode or fill channels, creating uncharted shoals. As a prudent mariner you must be alert to these possibilities for change and for the potential inaccuracy of charted information.

The source and date of the survey used for a nautical chart are printed near the chart title in the general information block. On Figure 1.6, the North American 1927 Datum is indicated. With the use of the Global Positioning System (GPS) new charts will refer to more recent datums as they are updated by NOAA.

To judge the accuracy and completeness of a depth survey, use the following criteria:

1. The source and date of the survey are printed on your chart along with an indication of changes that have taken place since that date. Early surveys were often made under circumstances that precluded accuracy and detail. Except in often-frequented waters, few surveys have been so thorough as to make certain that all dangers have been found. The QE II grounding is a good example. Until a chart based on a survey is tested, you should regard it with caution.

2. Note the fullness of detail or lack of detail of the soundings within an area. Scant soundings are an indication of the lack of detail in the survey used to make the chart.

3. Large or rectangular blank spaces on your chart mean that no soundings were taken. Blank areas on nautical charts should be regarded with suspicion and be avoided by the mariner. The term "Dumping Ground" indicates that material was dumped in the area and that the soundings for the area are questionable.

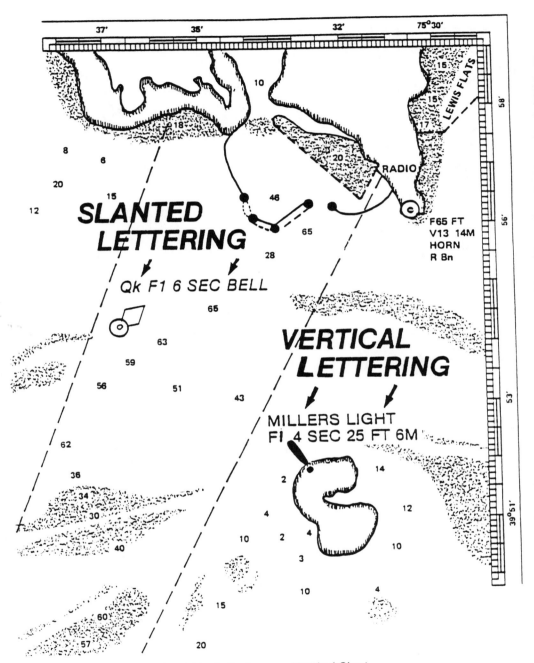

Fig. 1.11   Lettering on a Nautical Chart.
(Source: USCG Coxswain Training Manual)

THE NORTH AMERICAN DATUM OF 1983

A *datum* is a numerical quantity that serves as a reference for other quantities. On nautical charts, two datums are referenced:

1. *The tidal datum (or vertical datum):* This is the level from which all depths and heights on the chart are referenced, i.e., mean low water (MLW). The tidal datum is a depth or height reference.

2. *The horizontal datum:* The horizontal datum serves as a reference for the placement of lines of latitude and longitude on the nautical chart. The horizontal datum used on nautical charts of the United States and its territories is being changed to the North American Datum of 1983, abbreviated "NAD83." In the Pacific Island territories, the datum is being changed to the World Geodetic System of 1984, abbreviated "WGS84."

During the period of conversion, some charts will reference NAD83, while others will reference older datums. Use caution when moving between charts that have different datums. Differences of as much as 500 yards between geographic positions referenced to different datums may exist in some locales. In viewing nautical charts of an area that have different datums you cannot distinguish any changes to the charted features. A change in datum does not change the position of objects in relation to surrounding charted features. The difference will be a shift of the longitude and latitude grid. The latitude and longitude of a specific charted object will be different on charts referencing different datums.

In general, the range of the latitude and longitude shift varies in the United States from 15 yards in the Great Lakes, 35 yards along the Atlantic Coast and the Gulf of Mexico, 100 yards on the Pacific Coast, 500 yards in Hawaii, 200 yards in Alaska, to 240 yards in Puerto Rico.

By subscribing to the Local Notice to Mariners, you will stay informed about the latest editions of nautical charts. When a nautical chart is updated to the NAD83, all reports and corrections to objects shown on that chart will reference the corrected latitude and longitude, which will not plot correctly on your older chart. When the datum conversion process is not fully completed and a charted object appears on multiple charts, the latitude and longitude coordinates for both datums will be reported. Always use the latest edition of a nautical chart.

SYMBOLS FOR AIDS TO NAVIGATION

The basic symbol for a buoy is a diamond with a small circle. On older charts a dot is shown in place of the small circle. The diamond may be above, below, or alongside the circle. The small circle indicates the approximate position of the buoy's mooring. The diamond symbol is

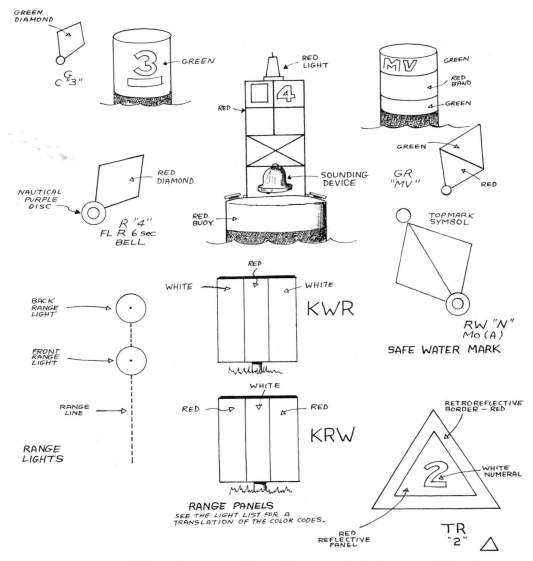

Fig. 1.12 Symbols for Buoys, Ranges, and Daymarks. *(F. J. Larkin)*

used to draw your attention to the position of the circle and to describe the aid to navigation on a chart. Figure 1.12 shows you some examples of buoy symbols.

Keep in mind that after the publication date of a chart, the Coast Guard may move the position of an aid to navigation. The Coast Guard alerts mariners when buoys are moved in the LNM. First, an intention to move the aid is published. Another message appears when the aid is physically moved. Future editions of *Light Lists* will show the latitude and longitude of the aid's new position. Be aware, however, that the

Coast Guard does not print the position of every aid in the *Light List*. Update your nautical charts and other nautical publications between printing editions by making corrections as they appear in the LNM. Otherwise, you risk the chance of missing a notification that an aid's position has changed. The *Light List* is explained in Chapter 2 and buoy symbols and markings are discussed in great detail in Chapter 3.

Abbreviations that Indicate Buoy Shape

When a buoy is unlighted (not rigged with a lantern by design), its shape is indicated by special letter abbreviations on your chart. An "N" indicates a *nun* or *cone-shaped* buoy. A "C" indicates a *can-shaped* buoy.

Check the shape abbreviations shown for the examples in Figure 1.12.

Abbreviations that Indicate Color

When an aid to navigation is painted red or green, the diamond symbol on the chart will be printed red or green. The abbreviations "R" for red and "G" for green appear with the symbol for the aid.

As a learning exercise, use red and green pens to color the aids and chart symbols depicted in Figure 1.12. This exercise will help fix the color of aids to navigation in your mind.

The diamond symbol for an aid is white when the aid is painted white or yellow. The abbreviations "Y" for yellow and "W" for white appear with the chart symbol for the aid on the chart.

The diamond symbol for a safe water aid remains white with a vertical line dissecting the diamond. The abbreviation "RW" for red and white appears with the chart symbol for the aid.

On preferred channel aids, the diamond symbol reflects the colors of the aid with a horizontal line dissecting the diamond. The abbreviations "GR" for green over red and "RG" for red over green appear with the chart symbol for the aid. Figure 1.12 shows an example of a preferred channel aid.

Symbols and Abbreviations for Lighted Buoys

When a buoy is lighted (fixed with a light), a nautical purple (magenta-colored) disk is printed over the small circle that marks the position of these aids on a nautical chart. The color of the light is indicated with special abbreviations:

- "R" indicates that the light is red.
- "G" indicates that the light is green.
- "Y" indicates that the light is yellow.

When there is no color abbreviation printed on a lighted buoy, the color of the light is assumed to be white.

Other Features on Buoys

Buoys may be fitted with sound signals, radar reflectors, numbers and letters, or any combination of these features. The existence of bells, whistles or horns on a buoy is printed near the buoy symbol on a chart. They are also noted in the *Light List*. The abbreviation for radar reflectors (Ra Ref) may not be shown on the chart. Consult your *Light List* for information on whether a buoy is fitted with a radar reflector.

Numbers and Letters

Numbers or letters that visibly show on the aid to navigation are printed on your nautical chart beside the chart symbol for the aid in quotation marks. For example, a can buoy with the number 3 on it would be identified as C "3" on a chart (see the upper left-hand corner of Figure 1.12).

Symbols for Lighthouses and Other Fixed Aids

The basic symbol for major and minor lights is a black dot with a nautical purple flare. On a chart, the flare looks like a large exclamation point. *Major lights* are named and described on the chart. *Minor lights* are described only. Figure 1.13 shows the symbol and description of a major light as it appears on a nautical chart.

Symbols for Ranges

A *range* consists of two beacons or daymarks positioned so that they appear in line when viewed from a specific line of position (LOP) or

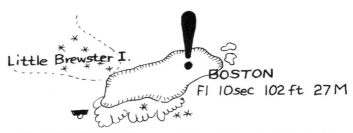

Fig. 1.13   Symbol, Name, and Description of a Major Light.
(F. J. Larkin)

direction referred to as the *range line*. Ranges are generally, but not always, lighted. Most ranges display rectangular daymarks with various colored panels. The *Light List* and Chart No. 1 contain a translation for the codes used to indicate the color of panels used on ranges.

Lighted ranges are identified on the nautical chart with symbols for their lights and with a dashed line to display the direction of the range.

Unlighted ranges are marked with symbols for their daymark shape and the directional dashed line. The *Light List* shows a series of codes utilized for the standard colors of range panels. Small triangles and squares are used for the symbols of the range. Unlike aids to navigation that mark channels, these symbols are not colored. Figure 1.12 shows some typical chart symbols used for ranges on a nautical chart.

CAUTION: *Remember that, when traveling on a range line, there is a point when you will go aground unless you turn away on a new course. It seems stupid to have to mention this but many novices ground their boats in this manner. Ranges are usually fixed on land or in shallow water. Don't make this mistake.*

Isolated Danger Marks

An isolated danger mark is an aid to navigation erected on, or moored above or near, an isolated danger that has navigable water around it. Isolated danger marks are horizontally banded black and red, and, when lighted, exhibit a white light. A top mark consisting of two black spheres, one above the other, may be fitted on lighted or unlighted isolated danger marks. These buoys are charted with the standard symbol that represents their type, but will also have two dots over the diamond symbol to identify them as an isolated danger mark. Figure 1.14 shows a drawing of a lighted isolated danger mark and its chart symbols and abbreviations.

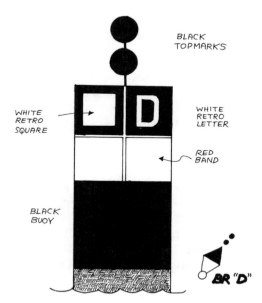

Fig. 1.14 Isolated Danger Mark.
(F. J. Larkin)

Day Beacons

Day beacons are structures that are permanently fixed to the earth's surface. They are fitted with panels that should be readily visible and easily identified against background conditions. During daylight hours the day mark conveys to the mariner the same information a light would convey at night.

CAUTION: *Vessels should not pass close aboard (near) fixed aids to navigation due to the danger of colliding with their structure, their foundations, or with the obstruction marked by these aids.*

Day beacons are indicated with small triangles or squares on a nautical chart. These symbols may be colored to match the color of the aid. Triangles, when colored red, have lateral significance (mark the edge of a channel) similar to nun buoys (Red on Right, Returning). Squares, when colored green, have lateral significance similar to can buoys. Refer to the example of a red triangle day beacon shown in Figure 1.12.

OTHER CHARTED FEATURES

Prominent Landmarks

Water towers, smoke stacks, church spires, flag poles, large public buildings, etc., are considered prominent landmarks and are often charted. You will find them marked with the chart symbol of a dot within a circle. The dot within the circle indicates that the position of the landmark is surveyed and it is usable for taking a position fix in piloting. Notation next to the chart symbol defines the landmark. Chart abbreviations such as "TWR" for tower, "STACK," and "CUPOLA" are typical.

The omission of the dot within the circle indicates that the position of this landmark is only an approximation and is subject to error when taking a position fix. Figure 1.15 shows some examples of symbols for landmarks.

Landmarks on private property are usually never plotted on a nautical chart.

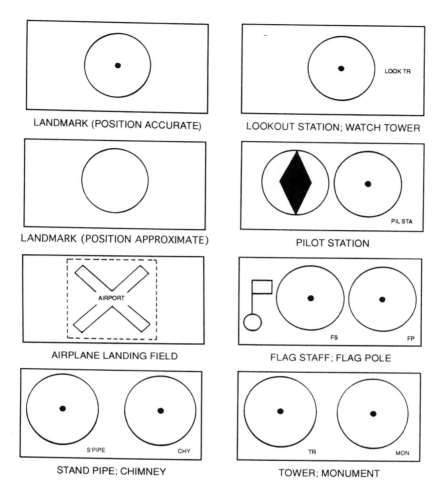

Fig. 1.15 Symbols for Landmarks on a Nautical Chart.
(T. J. Larkin)

Wrecks, Rocks, and Reefs

These obstructions are marked with standardized symbols that you should learn and memorize. A sunken wreck or rock may be shown with a symbol or by an abbreviation plus a number. This number indicates the depth of the obstruction at the low water datum for the nautical chart. A dashed or dotted line around any symbol calls special attention to its hazardous nature. Figure 1.16 illustrates the symbols for a group of common hazards. NOAA Chart No. 1 contains the chart symbol for every hazard that appears on a nautical chart.

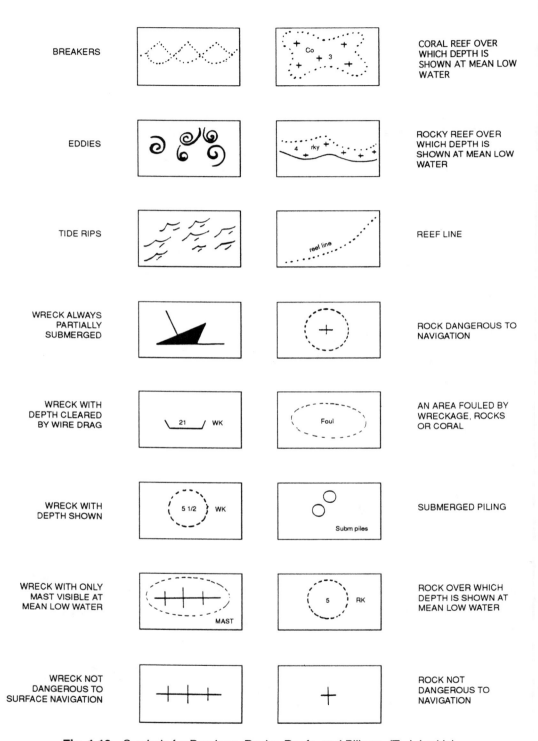

Fig. 1.16   Symbols for Breakers, Rocks, Reefs, and Pilings. *(T. J. Larkin)*

Bottom Characteristics

A system of abbreviations, used alone or in combination, describes the composition of the ocean bottom. Figure 1.17 lists a series of typical abbreviations that describe the seabed on a chart. Use this information for selecting the best holding ground when anchoring your boat.

Structures

Shorthand representations have been devised for low-lying structures such as jetties, docks, drawbridges, and waterfront ramps. These symbols are drawn to scale and are viewed from overhead on a nautical chart. Some docks will not appear on a nautical chart due to their size in relation to the scale of the chart. Figure 1.18 illustrates some examples of these charted features.

Coastlines

Coastlines are identified on nautical charts at both high and low water marks. Along a coastline, any prominent landmarks that can help you attain a position fix may be printed on your chart. Details located a short distance from the shoreline are often omitted from a nautical chart. Figure 1.19 displays some typical coastlines that you will find on a nautical chart.

METRIFICATION OF NAUTICAL CHARTS

The Metric Conversion Act of 1975 and the Omnibus Trade and Competitiveness Act of 1988 established the metric system of weights and measures as the preferred system for the United States. These acts require that all federal agencies move as fast as practical to convert to the metric system in all activities.

As a result of these acts, and to conform to international charting practices, NOAA's Coast and Geodetic Survey (C&GS) is planning to replace existing units of measure on its nautical charts with metric equivalents. This policy will not affect the use of the international nautical mile used for distances at sea.

In responding to this requirement, C&GS will adhere to the following general policies:

1. Safety of navigation will continue to be of primary importance.
2. Every effort will be made to convert charts in logical groupings

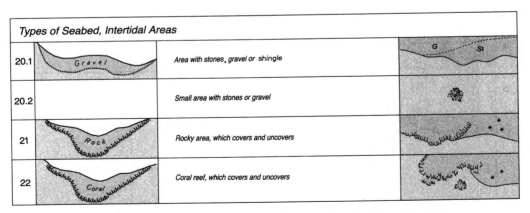

Types of Seabed			
Rocks → K			Supplementary national abbreviations: a-ag
1	S	Sand	S
2	M	Mud	M
3	Cy; Cl	Clay	Cy
4	Si	Silt	Si
5	St	Stones	St
6	G	Gravel	G
7	P	Pebbles	P
8	Cb	Cobbles	Cb
9	Rk; rky	Rock; Rocky	R
10	Co	Coral and Coralline algae	Co
11	Sh	Shells	Sh
12	S/M	Two layers, eg. Sand over mud	S/M
13.1	Wd	Weed (including Kelp)	Wd
13.2	Kelp	Kelp, Seaweed	
14	Sandwaves	Mobile bottom (sand waves)	
15	Spring	Freshwater springs in seabed	T

Types of Seabed, Intertidal Areas			
20.1	Gravel	Area with stones, gravel or shingle	G St
20.2		Small area with stones or gravel	
21	Rock	Rocky area, which covers and uncovers	
22	Coral	Coral reef, which covers and uncovers	

Fig. 1.17 Nature of the Seabed. *(Source: Nautical Chart No. 1)*

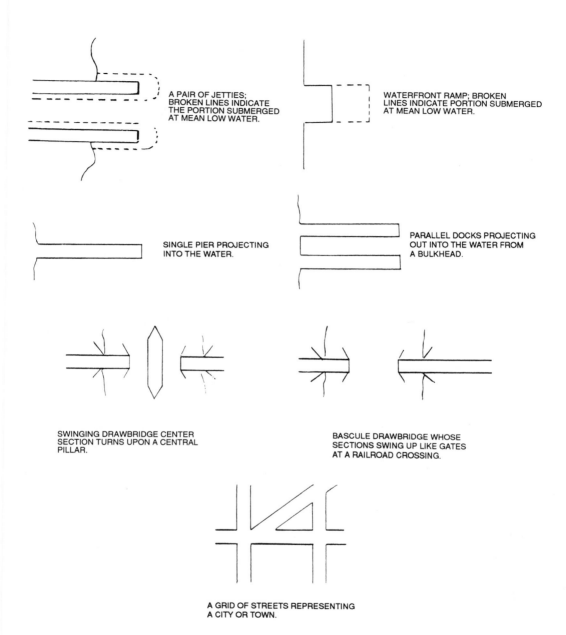

A PAIR OF JETTIES; BROKEN LINES INDICATE THE PORTION SUBMERGED AT MEAN LOW WATER.

WATERFRONT RAMP; BROKEN LINES INDICATE PORTION SUBMERGED AT MEAN LOW WATER.

SINGLE PIER PROJECTING INTO THE WATER.

PARALLEL DOCKS PROJECTING OUT INTO THE WATER FROM A BULKHEAD.

SWINGING DRAWBRIDGE CENTER SECTION TURNS UPON A CENTRAL PILLAR.

BASCULE DRAWBRIDGE WHOSE SECTIONS SWING UP LIKE GATES AT A RAILROAD CROSSING.

A GRID OF STREETS REPRESENTING A CITY OR TOWN.

Fig. 1.18 Chartable Structures. *(T. J. Larkin)*

so that travel on the water will require minimal shifting between the two measurements.

3. Conversion will be a multi-year effort with implementation expected in 10 to 15 years.

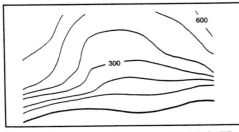

COASTAL HILLS; CONTOUR   LINES INDICATE
ELEVATIONS.

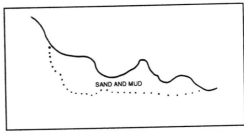

SAND AND MUD FLATS THAT ARE EXPOSED
AT MEAN LOW WATER.

STEEP INCLINED COASTLINE; HACHURES
(HATCH MARKS) ARE DRAWN IN THE
DIRECTION OF THE SLOPES

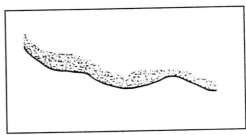

SANDY SHORE THAT IS EXPOSED AT MEAN
LOW WATER.

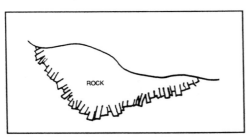

ROCK SHELF; UNCOVERS AT MEAN LOW
WATER.

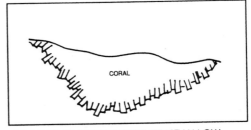

CORAL SHELF; UNCOVERS AT MEAN LOW
WATER.

Fig. 1.19   Symbols for Coastlines and Contour Lines.
(Source: Nautical Chart No. 1)

Things that will change on nautical charts:

- Depths.
- Depth curves intervals and labels.
- Depths over submerged objects, such as rocks, wrecks, reefs, ledges, obstructions, etc.
- Heights of objects, such as landmarks, fixed aids to navigation.
- Bridge clearances both vertical and horizontal.
- Overhead cables and pipeline clearances.

- Drying height of objects, such as rocks, piles, poles, etc.
- Elevations, such as summits, contours, etc.
- Land contour intervals and labels.
- Channel legend depths.
- Channel tabulation depths.
- Tide values (given in the tidal information block).
- Charted notes associated with depth, distances, heights, or elevations.

Radar sets and LORAN-C receivers will not become obsolete. Programmed waypoints will remain valid. Depth sounders will have to be calibrated in meters. However, many nautical publications provide metric conversion scales.

MULTIBEAM SURVEY MAPS

You may have heard about the new bottom contour maps being produced by NOAA. Blueprint copies of some maps are now available. There is no question about the accuracy and quality of these maps since they have been compiled from state-of-the-art multibeam survey data. The same precise positioning methods and standards used in conventional hydrographic surveying are used to collect data for these maps. Innumerable details and features that are ordinarily missed with narrow-beam fathometers are captured by the new multibeam system. The Department of Defense (DOD) has approved the distribution of these multibeam maps to the general public.

Multibeam maps are produced at 1:100,000 scale and they carry a 20-meter contour interval throughout, which means that a contour line is drawn at each 20 meters of depth.

Presently, 29 partial and complete multibeam maps are available and can be ordered for $10.00 each from:

National Ocean Service
Distribution Branch (N/CG33)
6501 Lafayette Avenue
Riverdale, Maryland 20737
Telephone: (301)436-6990

Additional information about bathymetric products may be obtained by contacting:

NOAA, National Ocean Service
Graphic Mapping (N/CG2241)
Rockville, Maryland 20852
Telephone: (301)443-8855

Reader Study Note

Spend some time reviewing what you have just read and try to interpret the symbols that you find on a nautical chart. Read the general information block carefully. Always read every note on your chart. Find the symbols for the aids to navigation and try to visualize how these would look on the water.

Using a red and green pen or pencil, color the aids to navigation drawn in Figure 1.12, which shows the symbols for buoys, ranges, and day marks in this chapter. This exercise will help you understand the color patterns of aids to navigation and fix them in your mind.

Answer the review questions. Test your understanding and knowledge by trying to find the answer in the text before you look up the answers provided at the end of the chapter. If you do poorly, reread the chapter.

Reader Progress Note

You should be familiar with the makeup of a nautical chart and some of the more important symbols and abbreviations that are used to describe aids to navigation, depths, objects and structures. You should also have a basic knowledge of where and how to find the explanations of symbols with which you are not familiar. Chapter 2 explains the common nautical publications in greater detail while Chapter 3 discusses interpretation of buoy colors, shapes, markings, etc., in more detail.

REVIEW QUESTIONS

1.1   A Mercator projection is made by transferring the spherical surface of the earth onto a _____.

1.2   Parallels of latitude increase numerically northward and southward from the _____ to 90 degrees at the earth's _____.

1.3   Any position on a nautical chart can be expressed in terms of _____ and _____.

1.4   True directions are printed on the outer circle of the _____ _____.

1.5   _____ is a known difference so it is printed in the center of the compass rose.

1.6   The _____ of the water can, at times, be lower than the depth printed on a nautical chart.

1.7   The NOAA publication, Chart No. 1, shows all the _____ and _____ used on a nautical chart.

1.8   The chart title, the type of projection, the scale of a chart, and the unit of measurement for soundings are all information found in the _____ _____ _____ on a nautical chart.

1.9   The _____ and _____ of a nautical chart are printed on the lower left-hand corner of the chart.

1.10 A large-scale chart covers a _____ area and shows more details and features of the earth's surface.

1.11 Nautical purple ink is used for notes and to highlight _____ aids.

1.12 The prudent mariner must be alert to the possibilities of _____ and the possible _____ of charted information.

1.13 The basic chart symbol for an aid to navigation is a _____ with a small circle.

1.14 _____ and letters appear with a chart symbol for a buoy.

1.15 The symbol for a _____ and other fixed lights is a black _____ with a nautical purple _____.

1.16 _____ are indicated on a nautical chart with small triangles or squares.

1.17 The omission of the dot within a landmark circle indicates that the position of the landmark is only an _____ position.

1.18 Coastlines are identified on a nautical chart at both _____ and _____ water.

1.19 Vessels should not pass close aboard (near) fixed aids to navigation due to the danger of _____ with structure foundations, or with the _____ marked by the aid.

1.20 _____ day marks, when colored green, have lateral significance similar to _____ buoys.

Answers

1.1   A Mercator projection is made by transferring the spherical surface of the earth onto a CYLINDER.

1.2   Parallels of latitude increase numerically northward and southward from the EQUATOR to 90 degrees at the earth's POLES.

1.3   Any position on a nautical chart can be expressed in terms of LATITUDE and LONGITUDE.

1.4 True directions are printed on the outer circle of the COMPASS ROSE.

1.5 VARIATION is a known difference so it is printed in the center of the compass rose.

1.6 The DEPTH of the water can, at times, be lower than the depth printed on a nautical chart.

1.7 The NOAA publication, Chart No. 1, shows all the SYMBOLS and ABBREVIATIONS used on a nautical chart.

1.8 The chart title, the type of projection, the scale of a chart, and the unit of measurement for soundings are all information found in the GENERAL INFORMATION BLOCK on a nautical chart.

1.9 The NUMBER and EDITION of a nautical chart are printed on the lower left-hand corner of the chart.

1.10 A large-scale chart covers a SMALL area and shows more details and features of the earth's surface.

1.11 Nautical purple ink is used for notes and to highlight LIGHTED aids.

1.12 The prudent mariner must be alert to the possibilities of CHANGE and the possible INACCURACY of charted information.

1.13 The basic chart symbol for an aid to navigation is a DIAMOND with a small circle.

1.14 NUMBERS and letters appear with a chart symbol for a buoy.

1.15 The symbol for a LIGHTHOUSE and other fixed lights is a black DOT with a nautical purple FLARE.

1.16 DAYBEACONS are indicated on a nautical chart with small triangles or squares.

1.17 The omission of the dot within a landmark circle indicates that the position of the landmark is only an APPROXIMATE position.

1.18 Coastlines are identified on a nautical chart at both HIGH and LOW water.

1.19 Vessels should not pass close aboard (near) fixed aids to navigation due to the danger of COLLISION with structure foundations, or with the OBSTRUCTION marked by the aid.

1.20 SQUARE day marks, when colored green, have lateral significance similar to CAN buoys.

TWO

Navigational
Reference Publications
and Almanacs

NAUTICAL CHART CATALOGS

Nautical chart catalogs provide a graphical presentation of all of the nautical charts available for U.S. waters. You will often find these publications displayed at chandleries and nautical chart stores. Their purpose is to help you choose the correct chart based on your cruising plans. Figure 2.1 is a small section of Nautical Chart Catalog 1, which shows the area and charts available for the Boston, Massachusetts, area. Nautical chart catalogs are published by the National Oceanic and Atmospheric Administration (NOAA), National Ocean Service (NOS), and are available free of charge. The following types of information are printed on these catalogs:

- A list of nautical publications published and issued by NOS with their retail prices.

- A list of authorized nautical chart agents who sell NOAA charts and related publications of the NOS. This listing is presented by state.

- A list of all nautical chart numbers, chart titles, and chart scales for all charts graphically presented in the catalog.

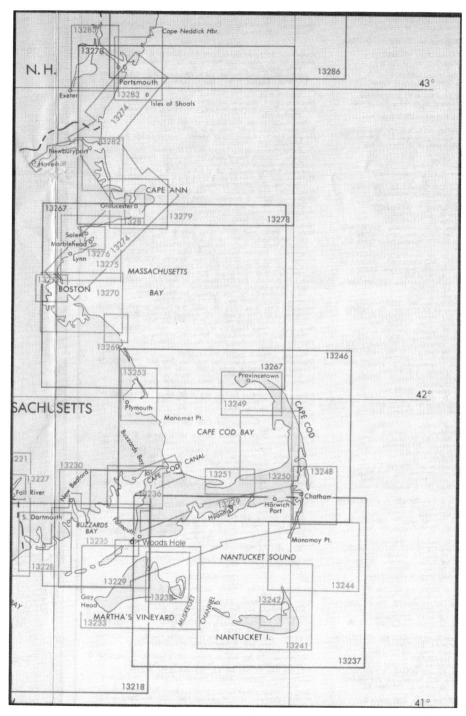

Fig. 2.1   Nautical Chart Catalog 1, Boston Area.
(Source: Nautical chart catalog)

Nautical chart catalogs are available in five versions:

- *Nautical Chart Catalog 1:* Atlantic and Gulf Coasts including Puerto Rico and the Virgin Islands
- *Nautical Chart Catalog 2:* Pacific Coast including Hawaii, Guam, and Samoa Islands
- *Nautical Chart Catalog 3:* Alaska
- *Nautical Chart Catalog 4:* Great Lakes and Adjacent Waterways
- *Nautical Chart Catalog 5:* Bathymetric Maps and Special Purpose Charts

DATES OF LATEST EDITIONS

The NOAA publication "Dates of Latest Editions, Nautical Charts & Misc. Maps" contains the latest information on the edition number and date of last publication for each nautical chart. Authorized nautical chart stores receive copies of this document quarterly. Read this publication to be sure that you are buying the latest edition of a chart. Each chart is listed by:

- Chart number,
- Chart scale,
- Price,
- Edition number,
- Edition date, and
- Printing revision date.

NOAA publishes the Dates of Latest Editions quarterly. Free copies may be obtained from:

National Ocean Service
Distribution Branch N/CG33
6501 Lafayette Avenue
Riverdale, Maryland 20737

Figure 2.2 shows the cover and Figure 2.3 shows a sample page from the Dates of Latest Editions. This is a white 5-in. × 8.5-in. booklet.

CHART NO. 1

If you are serious about navigation, you will own a copy of "Chart No. 1, USA: Nautical Chart Symbols, Abbreviations, and Terms." The 1997 price is $2.50 and it is a great bargain for the amount of information

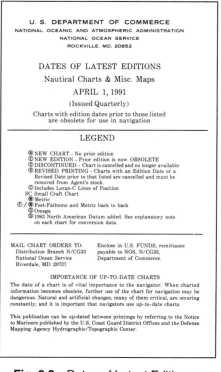

Fig. 2.2 Dates of Latest Editions, Cover. *(Source: Dates of Latest Editions)*

4

CHART NUMBER	SCALE	PRICE	EDITION NUMBER	EDITION DATE	LATEST REVISED DATE
11492	40,000	13.25	16	Apr 7 1990	
11495	40,000	13.25	12	Apr 21 1990	
11502	80,000	13.25	23	Dec 8 1990	
11503	20,000	13.25	34	Dec 15 1990	
11504	40,000	13.25	13	Jan 26 1991	
11506	40,000	13.25	34	Oct 6 1990	
11507 SC	40,000	13.25	24	Aug 11 1990	
11508	40,000	13.25	18	Oct 15 1988	
11509	80,000	13.25	22	Jul 21 1990	
11510	40,000	13.25	14	Jan 13 1990	
11511	40,000	13.25	13	Jun 9 1990	
11512	40,000	13.25	50	Jan 13 1990	
11513	80,000	13.25	19	May 19 1990	
11514 SC	20,000	13.25	22	Oct 20 1990	
11515 SC	20,000	13.25	14	Jul 21 1990	
11516	40,000	13.25	25	Oct 21 1989	
11517	40,000	13.25	13	Mar 17 1990	
11518 SC	40,000	13.25	25	Jun 9 1990	
11519	40,000	13.25	9	Oct 6 1990	
11520	432,720	13.25	31	Sep 15 1990	
11521	80,000	13.25	19	Jun 30 1990	
11522	40,000	13.25	13	Oct 22 1988	
11523	20,000	13.25	13	Jan 20 1990	
11524	20,000	13.25	37	Aug 18 1990	
11526	20,000	13.25	9	Jul 21 1990	
11527	20,000	13.25	13	Apr 7 1990	
11531	80,000	13.25	16	Oct 22 1990	
11532	40,000	13.25	16	Aug 11 1990	
11534 SC	40,000	13.25	25	Oct 6 1990	
11535	80,000	13.25	9	Apr 9 1988	
11536	80,000	13.25	11	Nov 18 1989	
11537	40,000	13.25	26	Jan 7 1989	
11539	80,000	13.25	15	Nov 21 1987	
11541 SC	40,000	13.25	25	Sep 29 1990	
11542	40,000	13.25	13	Jul 14 1990	
11543	80,000	13.25	19	Nov 28 1987	
11544	80,000	13.25	31	Mar 24 1990	
11545	40,000	13.25	54	Dec 8 1990	
11547	12,500	13.25	28	Jan 19 1991	
11548	80,000	13.25	32	Sep 2 1989	
11550	40,000	13.25	24	May 26 1990	
11552	40,000	13.25	16	Aug 11 1990	
11553 SC	40,000	13.25	23	Aug 5 1989	
11554	40,000	13.25	14	Aug 5 1989	
11555	80,000	13.25	32	May 12 1990	
12200	419,706	13.25	38	Jan 13 1990	
12204	80,000	13.25	30	Jun 23 1990	
12205 SC	40,000; 80,000	13.25	21	Aug 4 1990	
12206 SC	40,000	13.25	25	Apr 28 1990	
12207	80,000	13.25	17	Aug 18 1990	
12210	80,000	13.25	30	Aug 25 1990	
12211	80,000	13.25	33	Jun 9 1990	
12214	80,000	13.25	36	Feb 24 1990	
12216	40,000	13.25	22	Oct 14 1989	
12220	200,000	13.25	33	Nov 17 1990	
12221	80,000	13.25	58	Sep 15 1990	
12222	40,000	13.25	32	Aug 18 1990	
12224	40,000	13.25	19	Feb 9 1991	
12225	80,000	13.25	43	May 19 1990	
12226	80,000	13.25	12	Mar 17 1990	
12228	40,000	13.25	24	Feb 3 1990	
12230	80,000	13.25	46	Jul 28 1990	
12231	40,000	13.25	22	Sep 2 1989	
12233	40,000	13.25	30	Jun 30 1990	
12235	40,000	13.25	25	Sep 2 1989	
12237 SC	40,000	13.25	22	Jan 19 1991	
12238	40,000	13.25	30	Dec 1 1990	
12241	20,000	13.25	17	Dec 1 1990	
12243	40,000	13.25	11	Jul 14 1990	

Fig. 2.3 Sample Page from Dates of Latest Editions. *(Source: Dates of Latest Editions)*

that it contains. Chart No. 1 contains all the symbols and abbreviations that have been approved for use on nautical charts published in the United States. A glossary of terminology used on the charts of various other nations is also included. Every good nautical chart store stocks this publication.

Figure 2.4 is a reprint of the cover of Chart No. 1 and Figure 2.5 shows a sample page. You have already seen multiple page samples from this publication in Chapter 1.

Chart No. 1 is published by NOAA and the Department of Defense's Defense Mapping Agency (DMA). The DMA stock number is WOBZC1. Notices of corrections for this publication appear in the weekly "Local Notice to Mariners" (LNM).

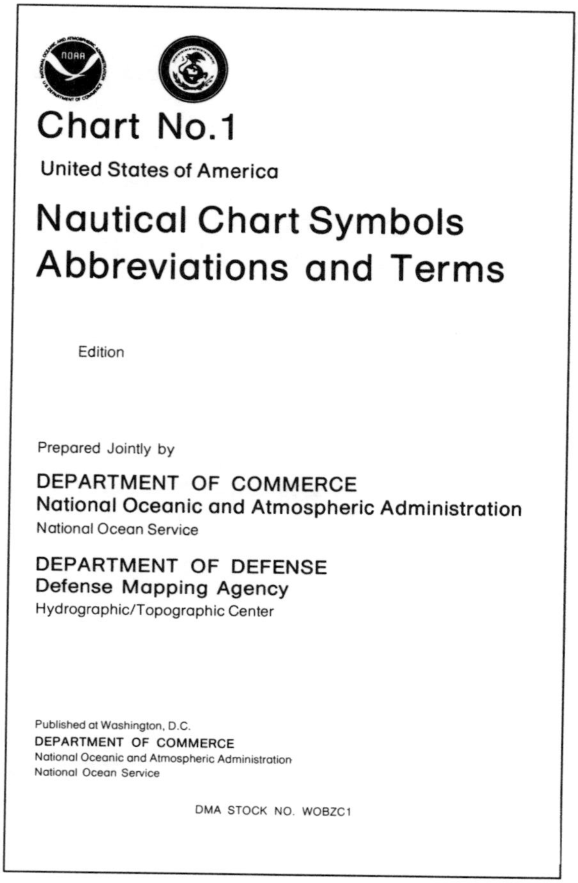

Chart No.1

United States of America

**Nautical Chart Symbols
Abbreviations and Terms**

Edition

Prepared Jointly by

**DEPARTMENT OF COMMERCE
National Oceanic and Atmospheric Administration**
National Ocean Service

**DEPARTMENT OF DEFENSE
Defense Mapping Agency**
Hydrographic/Topographic Center

Published at Washington, D.C.
DEPARTMENT OF COMMERCE
National Oceanic and Atmospheric Administration
National Ocean Service

DMA STOCK NO. WOBZC1

Fig. 2.4 Cover of Chart No. 1.
(Source: Nautical Chart No. 1)

LIGHT LIST

The *Light List* is published to provide mariners with more complete details about aids to navigation (ATONs) than can be printed on a nautical chart. The *Light List* is a catalog of all aids to navigation, their lights, sound signals, color, type, radio beacons, and LORAN stations. It is published annually by the U.S. Coast Guard. The *Light List* is printed in seven volumes:

- *Volume I:* St. Croix River, ME, to Toms River, NJ
- *Volume II:* Toms River, NJ, to Little River, SC
- *Volume III:* Little River, SC, to Econfina River, FL
- *Volume IV:* Econfina River, FL, to Rio Grande, TX
- *Volume V:* Mississippi River System

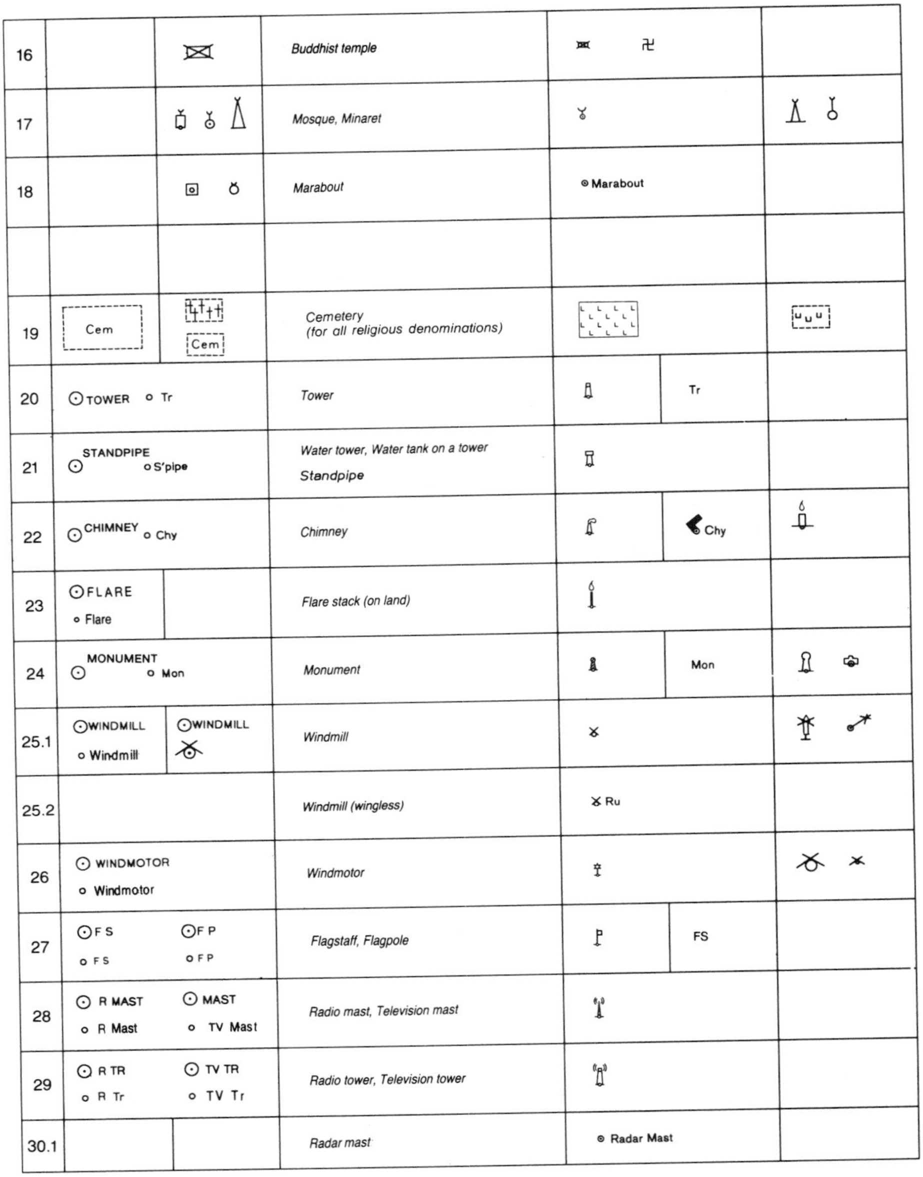

#	Symbol 1	Symbol 2	Description	Symbol 3		Symbol 4
16		⋈	*Buddhist temple*	⋈ 卍		
17		Ŏ ŏ Λ	*Mosque, Minaret*	ŏ		Λ ŏ
18		⊡ ŏ	*Marabout*	⊚ Marabout		
19	⌐ Cem ¬	Cem	*Cemetery (for all religious denominations)*	L L L L L L L L		ᴜ ᴜ ᴜ
20	⊙ TOWER ∘ Tr		*Tower*	⌷	Tr	
21	STANDPIPE ⊙ ∘ S'pipe		*Water tower, Water tank on a tower* *Standpipe*	⌷		
22	⊙ CHIMNEY ∘ Chy		*Chimney*	⌷	◀ Chy	⌷
23	⊙ FLARE ∘ Flare		*Flare stack (on land)*	⌷		
24	MONUMENT ⊙ ∘ Mon		*Monument*	⌷	Mon	⌷ ⊚
25.1	⊙ WINDMILL ∘ Windmill	⊙ WINDMILL ⊗	*Windmill*	✗		⚓ ⤴
25.2			*Windmill (wingless)*	✗ Ru		
26	⊙ WINDMOTOR ∘ Windmotor		*Windmotor*	⚐		⊗ ✗
27	⊙ F S ∘ F S	⊙ F P ∘ F P	*Flagstaff, Flagpole*	⌐	FS	
28	⊙ R MAST ∘ R Mast	⊙ MAST ∘ TV Mast	*Radio mast, Television mast*	⌷		
29	⊙ R TR ∘ R Tr	⊙ TV TR ∘ TV Tr	*Radio tower, Television tower*	⌷		
30.1			*Radar mast*	⊚ Radar Mast		

Fig. 2.5   Typical Page from Chart No. 1, Landmarks.
(Source: Nautical Chart No. 1)

- *Volume VI:* Pacific Coast and Pacific Islands. Also includes some lighted aids to navigation on the coast of British Columbia, which are maintained by Canada.

- *Volume VII:* Describes the aids to navigations in U.S. waters of the Great Lakes. Also includes some lighted ATONs on the Great Lakes and the St. Lawrence River above the St. Regis River, which are maintained by Canada.

DEPARTMENT OF TRANSPORTATION, U.S. COAST GUARD

LIGHT LIST

Volume I

ATLANTIC COAST

St. Croix River, Maine to
Toms River, New Jersey

1991 EDITION

This publication contains a list of lights, sound signals, buoys, daybeacons, radiobeacons, and LORAN stations

Includes:
First Coast Guard District Local Notices to Mariners through No. 15, April 10, 1991
and
Weekly Notice to Mariners No. 18, May 4, 1991

IMPORTANT

THIS PUBLICATION SHOULD BE CORRECTED EACH WEEK FROM THE LOCAL NOTICES TO MARINERS OR NOTICE TO MARINERS AS APPROPRIATE.

COMDTPUB P16502.1

U.S. GOVERNMENT PRINTING OFFICE
WASHINGTON, DC: 1991

For sale by Superintendent of Documents, U.S. Government Printing Office, Washington, DC 20402
Stock number: 050–012–00303–3

Fig. 2.6 Cover of Volume I of the *Light List.* *(Source: Light List)*

Figure 2.6 shows the cover of Volume I of the *Light List* and Figure 2.7 shows a typical page. Note that each entry on this sample page contains the following information:

1. A *Light List number:* Each aid to navigation is assigned a special number. The abbreviation for this number is "LLNR." The LLNR for an aid is changed from time to time by the Coast Guard.
2. *Name of the aid to navigation:* Each ATON has a unique name. The name for the section under which the aid is listed is included as part of the name of the aid. For example, Buoy SC is listed in the section labeled "Squantum Channel." The proper name of this aid is "Squantum Channel Buoy SC."
3. *Geographic position of the aid:* The latitude and longitude is not shown for every ATON in the *Light List.* If you plan to use these positions for LORAN waypoints, be sure you have updated all corrections published in the Local Notice to Mariners for your edition of the *Light List.* The Coast Guard

(1) No.	(2) Name and location	(3) Position	(4) Characteristic	(5) Height	(6) Range	(7) Structure	(8) Remarks
			MASSACHUSETTS – First District				
	BOSTON INNER HARBOR (Chart 13272)	N/W					
	Bird Island Flats						
10720	– Buoy 1	42 21.5 71 01.9				Green can.	
10725	– Buoy 2					Red nun.	
10730	– Buoy					Red and green bands; nun.	
10735	Jeffries Point Wreck Buoy WR	42 21.7 71 01.9				Red and green bands; nun.	
10736	EAST BOSTON DOCK LIGHT SE	42 21.6 71 02.0	F Y			On pile.	Private aid.
10737	EAST BOSTON DOCK LIGHT NW		F Y			On pile.	Private aid.
	BOSTON HARBOR (Chart 13270)						
	Dorchester Bay						
10740	– Buoy 2	42 19.6 71 00.1				Red nun.	
10745	– Buoy 3					Green can.	
10750	– Buoy 4	42 19.3 71 00.8				Red nun.	
10755	– Lighted Buoy 5	42 19.0 71 01.3	Fl G 4s		4	Green.	Replaced by can from Dec. 1 to Mar. 15.
10760	– Buoy 6					Red nun.	
10765	– Buoy 8	42 18.8 71 01.6				Red nun.	
10770	– Buoy 10	42 18.6 71 01.8				Red nun.	
10775	– Lighted Buoy 12	42 18.5 71 02.0	Fl R 4s		3	Red.	Replaced by nun from Nov. 15 to Mar. 15.
10780	PLEASURE BAY JETTY LIGHT	42 19.8 71 00.9	Fl W 2.5s	25	6	NR on skeleton tower.	
10781	COLUMBIA POINT LIGHT	42 18.9 71 02.0	Fl W 5s			On post at northeast corner of dike.	Private aid.
	Squantum Channel						
10785	– Buoy SC	42 18.5 71 01.9				Green and red bands; can.	
10790	– Buoy 2					Red nun.	
	Dorchester Bay Basin						
10795	– Channel Buoy 1	42 18.3 71 03.0				Green barrel.	Maintained from May 1 to Dec. 1. Private aid.
10796	– Channel Buoy 2					Red barrel.	Maintained from May 1 to Dec. 1. Private aid.
10797	– Channel Buoy 3					Green barrel.	Maintained from May 1 to Dec. 1. Private aid.

Fig. 2.7 Sample Page from the *Light List. (Source: Light List)*

moves the position of buoys from time to time and publishes the new position in the LNM.

4. *Light characteristics for all lighted aids.*

5. *Height above water:* For all floating ATONs, the height of a light is measured from the focal plane (the height of the light bulb) to the water line. On all fixed ATONs, the height is

measured from the mean high water mark to the focal plane of the light. Height is currently listed in feet on most charts. However, this will change as charts are converted to the metric system.

6. *Nominal range of lighted aids:* The nominal range is defined as the maximum distance at which a light can be seen in clear weather expressed in nautical miles. The nominal range is listed for all Coast Guard lighted aids except for range and directional lights.

7. *Structural characteristics of the aid:* Special construction characteristics or materials are indicated.

8. *General remarks:* This section may include information on radio beacon signals and characteristics, a light sector's arc of visibility, radar reflectors, emergency backup lights, seasonal ATON deployment schedules, and information about private aids to navigation.

The *Light List* is sold by Government Printing Office bookstores located in many cities, by Government Printing Office agents located in principal ports, or you can purchase it directly from:

U.S. Government Printing Office
Superintendent of Documents
Washington, DC 20402

The stock number for the *Light List* is 050-012-00303-3. Corrections to the *Light List* appear in the weekly LNM.

UNITED STATES COAST PILOT

The *Coast Pilot* is published annually by NOAA. This document supplements the information shown on nautical charts. It contains data that cannot be coded or abbreviated on a nautical chart. The sources for updating the *Coast Pilot* include, but are not limited to, field inspections conducted by NOAA, information published in the Local Notice to Mariners, reports from hydrographic vessels and field parties, and information from other government agencies, state and local governments, maritime and pilotage associations, port authorities, and mariners like yourself. Figure 2.8 reprints the cover of Volume 1 of the *Coast Pilot*.

The *Coast Pilot* is published in nine volumes:

- *Coast Pilot 1—Eastport to Cape Cod:* This edition covers the Massachusetts Bay side of Cape Cod.

- *Coast Pilot 2—Cape Cod to Sandy Hook:* Covers the Nantucket Sound side of Cape Cod.

- *Coast Pilot 3—Sandy Hook to Cape Henry.*

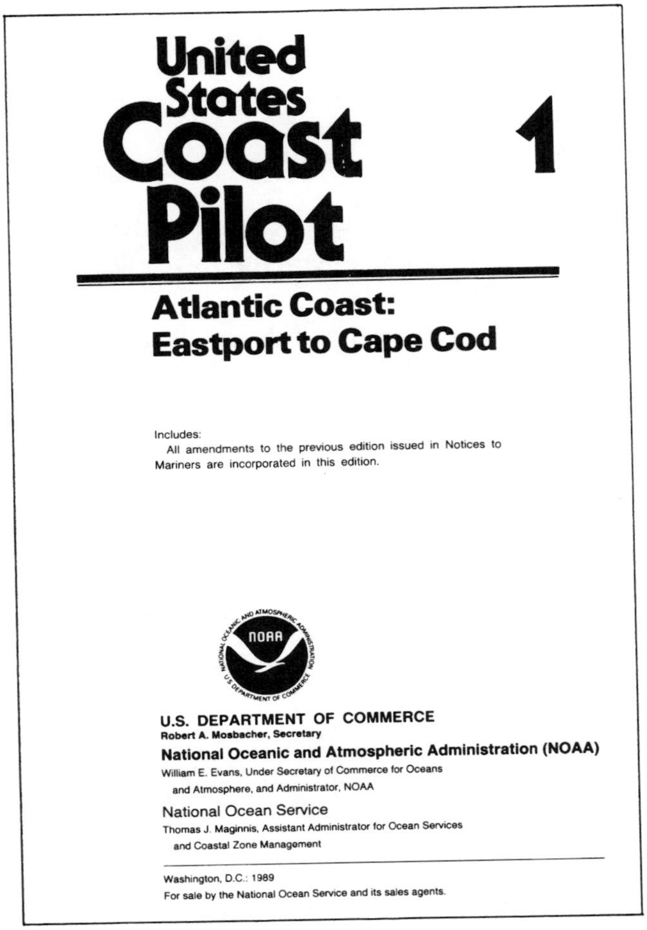

United States Coast Pilot 1

Atlantic Coast: Eastport to Cape Cod

Includes:
All amendments to the previous edition issued in Notices to Mariners are incorporated in this edition.

U.S. DEPARTMENT OF COMMERCE
Robert A. Mosbacher, Secretary
National Oceanic and Atmospheric Administration (NOAA)
William E. Evans, Under Secretary of Commerce for Oceans and Atmosphere, and Administrator, NOAA
National Ocean Service
Thomas J. Maginnis, Assistant Administrator for Ocean Services and Coastal Zone Management

Washington, D.C.: 1989
For sale by the National Ocean Service and its sales agents.

Fig. 2.8 Cover of Volume 1 of the United States Coast Pilot. *(Source: United States Coast Pilot)*

- *Coast Pilot 4—Cape Henry to Key West.*
- *Coast Pilot 5—Gulf of Mexico, Puerto Rico, and the Virgin Islands.*
- *Coast Pilot 6—Great Lakes and connecting waterways.*
- *Coast Pilot 7—California, Oregon, Washington, and Hawaii.*
- *Coast Pilot 8—Alaska: Dixon Entrance to Cape Spencer.*
- *Coast Pilot 9—Alaska: Cape Spencer to the Beaufort Sea.*

Most of the information contained in the *Coast Pilot* cannot be shown graphically on standard nautical charts and it is not readily available elsewhere. The typical subject matter contained in the *Coast Pilot* includes:

- Channel descriptions.
- Anchorages.

- Bridge and cable clearances and bridge regulations and opening signals.
- Currents.
- Tide and water levels.
- Prominent features.
- Pilotage.
- Towage.
- Weather.
- Ice conditions.
- Wharf descriptions and usage.
- Dangers.
- Routes.
- Traffic separation schemes.
- Small craft facilities.
- Federal regulations applicable to the mariner in the area.
- Locks and dams regulations and signals.

The *Coast Pilot* has seven major sections:

1. General information.
2. Navigational regulations.
3. General information about the overall area covered by the particular volume.
4. Specific information about individual areas.
5. Appendix.
6. Tables:
   - Climatological tables.
   - Meteorological tables.
   - Mean surface water temperature and densities.
   - Determination of wind speed by sea conditions.
   - National Weather Service coastal warning displays.
   - Nautical miles between two points.
   - Radio bearing conversion table.
   - Distance of visibility of objects at sea.
   - Conversion table—degrees to points and vice versa.
   - Conversion tables.
   - Table for estimating time of transit.
7. Index.

Corrections to the *Coast Pilot* appear in the weekly Local Notice to Mariners. A *Coast Pilot* report form is included in the back of each *Coast Pilot*. You can use this form to report errors and discrepancies as well as suggestions for increasing the usefulness of the *Coast Pilot*. Send your reports to:

> National Ocean Service, NOAA
> Director,
> Charting and Geodetic Services (N/CG2223)
> Rockville, Maryland 20852-3806

NOTICE TO MARINERS

The Weekly Notice to Mariners is the Coast Guard's method for communicating nationally concerning the establishment, the changing, and the discontinuance of aids to navigation. It also reports on channel conditions and depths, obstructions, hazards to navigation, danger areas, special events related to marine safety and other important information. These notices are essential to each mariner for updating nautical charts, *Light Lists, Coast Pilots*, and other nautical publications.

The Local Notice to Mariners is published weekly by the local Coast Guard District Office in your area at no charge. The information contained in each LNM is current as of 10:00 A.M. on the printing date. Keep in mind printing and mailing delays. Figure 2.9 shows a sample cover from a Coast Guard District 1 LNM. The LNM is arranged in sections as discussed in the following subsections.

Section I: Special Notices

Includes information that affects a wide segment of the maritime public or is otherwise noteworthy with regard to particular events and general development in navigation.

Section II: Discrepancies—Discrepancies Corrected

Lists all ATONs that are listed in the *Light List* but not currently operating. Discrepancies that are expected to be fixed before press time are not shown. Discrepancies that have been corrected since the publication of the last edition are listed as corrected. Discrepancies to private aids to navigation are also listed.

Section III: Temporary Changes—Temporary Changes Corrected

Lists the ATONs that have been changed on a temporary basis.

Temporary changes that have been corrected since their publication in the previous LNM will also be listed. Once listed as corrected, the entry for the ATON does not appear in a subsequent LNM unless the problem reoccurs. Where ATONs are temporarily relocated for dredging, a temporary correction will be listed in Section V, which will give the aid's new position.

Section IV: Index of Waterways

This section provides an index of waterways and chart numbers that are affected by chart corrections (Section V), coded "C," advance notice

Fig. 2.9 Cover of a Sample Local Notice to Mariners.
(Source: Local Notice to Mariners)

of changes (Section VI), coded "A," and proposed notice of changes (Section VII), coded "P."

Section V: Chart Corrections

Chart corrections include information about actual work performed, whether temporary or permanent, on federal or private ATONs that should be reflected on a nautical chart. New editions of nautical charts are listed in this section as well as NOS chart corrections.

Special codes are used in Section V:

- The letters "TEMP" below the chart number indicate that the chart correction is only temporary in nature.
- The letter "M" immediately following the chart number indicates that the corrections should be applied to the metric side of the chart only.
- Courses and bearings are given in degrees clockwise from 000 True.
- Bearings of light sectors are toward the light from the sea.
- The nominal range of lights is expressed in statute miles (St M).

Section VI: Advance Notice of Scheduled Changes in Aids to Navigation

This section contains advance notice of approved projects that are scheduled to be completed by a certain date. There may also be notices of future temporary changes, such as dredging. The notice is written in the same manner as a regular notice except for the statement that the change to the aid will take place in the future.

Advance notice must be given for significant changes that are planned to be made to aids used by the mariner engaged in trans-oceanic trade. The timing of these notices is prescribed by law. Major changes to important seacoast aids require four months notice, with the information repeated monthly until the change is completed. Other major changes require two months notice with the change notice appearing every two weeks until the change is completed. If the change cannot be accomplished within one week of the announced date, a postponement notice is issued. For important aids, the postponement notice will be broadcast by the Coast Guard twice daily on VHF Channel 22A.

Section VII: Proposed Changes in Aids to Navigation

Periodically the Coast Guard evaluates its system of aids to navigation in an area to determine whether the conditions for which the aids were established have changed. When changes are contemplated, the feasibility of improving, relocating, replacing, or discontinuing the aid(s) is considered. Section VII contains notices of projects conceived and in the planning stage, but which have not been approved or scheduled. Comments are requested from mariners on these proposed changes.

Section VIII: General

This general section contains information about navigational publications, channel conditions, obstructions, hazards to navigation, dangers, anchorages, restricted areas, bridge information, regattas, and other matters of marine information that do not fit into any of the other sections in the LNM. Each entry is first entered in paragraph form showing all of the pertinent information. If the discrepancy lasts for more than one week, the entry is placed on a summary list in subsequent publications of the LNM and will remain on the summary list until the approximate completion or repair date. You must retain your copies of the weekly LNM as a reference if you want to refer back to the details for an entry at a future date.

Section IX: Light List Corrections

This section contains tabulations of all current discrepancies and those corrected since the publication of the last LNM. Discrepancies that have occurred and have been corrected during this period are not published in the LNM. These corrections include:

- Proposed changes.
- General information of concern to the mariner.
- Summary of dredgings still in effect.
- Bridges with discrepancies.
- Applications received for permits for bridge reconstruction.
- OMEGA status.
- Discrepancies in LORAN chains.
- *Light List* corrections.
- Approved marine events and regattas. Includes information and restrictions on local regattas, marine parades, races, and other marine events in your area.

The LNM is issued weekly, at no cost to the user, by the U.S. Coast Guard. Questions about this publication, including requests to be placed on the mailing list, should be directed to your local U.S. Coast Guard district office. The addresses and telephone numbers for all of the district offices of the Coast Guard are included in Appendix 8.

TIDE TABLES

Tide tables contain predictions of the times and heights of high and low water for every day in the year for many of the important harbors (reference stations). It also shows the differences for numerous other places (substations). Chapter 15 explains how to utilize these tables for calculating the depth of water at any time and for determining the height available under a bridge at a specific point in time. Under license from NOAA, International Marine publishes four versions of the *Tide Tables:*

1. East Coast of North and South America, including Greenland.

2. West Coast of North and South America, including the Hawaiian Islands and the Alaskan Supplement.

3. Central and Western Pacific Ocean and Indian Ocean.

4. Europe and West Coast of Africa, including the Mediterranean Sea.

Figure 2.10 shows the inside cover of the *Tide Tables.*

The *Tide Tables* have a wealth of additional nautical information including:

- Astronomical data showing both lunar and solar information. This chart is printed on the inside of the back cover.

- An important notice that advises the mariner on the importance of outside forces on the predicted data in this publication. Mariners are cautioned about using only a single source of information in their piloting decisions.

- Listings of reference stations for Tide Table 2, Tidal Differences for Substations.

The tide tables included in the publication are as follows:

Table 1—Daily Tide Predictions for Reference Stations: Figure 2.11 shows a sample page from Table 1. The heights and times for the high and low water at reference stations are furnished in Table 1. Data in this table change from year to year. There are many available almanacs and calendars that provide Table 1 information—often at no

Tide Tables 1989
HIGH AND LOW WATER PREDICTIONS

East Coast of North and South America

Including Greenland

Issued

U.S. DEPARTMENT OF COMMERCE
C. William Verity, Secretary

National Oceanic and Atmospheric Administration
William E. Evans, Under Secretary

National Ocean Service
Paul M. Wolff, Assistant Administrator

Fig. 2.10 Cover of the *Tide Tables.*
(Source: Tide Tables)

charge as a promotional device at bait shops and chandleries.

Table 2— Tidal Differences for Substations: Table 2 lists a series of substations associated with the reference stations in Table 1. Table 2 shows the time and height difference from the reference station to the substation. Data in this table remain relatively constant from year to year. A sample of Table 2 is provided for you in Chapter 15.

Table 3— Height of Tide at Any Time: Table 3 provides a correction factor for determining the height of the tide at specific points of time. This table is constant and is included for you in Chapter 15.

Table 4— Local Mean Time of Sunrise and Sunset.

BOSTON, MASS.

Times and Heights of High and Low Waters

JANUARY

Day	Time h m	Height ft	Height m	Day	Time h m	Height ft	Height m
1 Su	0537	8.9	2.7	16 M	0556	10.3	3.1
	1154	1.7	0.5		1223	0.2	0.1
	1805	8.0	2.4		1838	8.7	2.7
2 M	0006	1.9	0.6	17 Tu	0035	0.9	0.3
	0627	9.0	2.7		0657	10.3	3.1
	1249	1.5	0.5		1328	0.2	0.1
	1902	7.9	2.4		1942	8.6	2.6
3 Tu	0057	1.9	0.6	18 W	0135	1.1	0.3
	0716	9.2	2.8		0758	10.3	3.1
	1344	1.2	0.4		1430	0.0	0.0
	1954	8.0	2.4		2045	8.6	2.6
4 W	0148	1.8	0.5	19 Th	0235	1.1	0.3
	0805	9.5	2.9		0856	10.4	3.2
	1435	0.8	0.2		1528	-0.1	0.0
	2045	8.2	2.5		2142	8.7	2.7
5 Th	0237	1.5	0.5	20 F	0328	1.0	0.3
	0853	9.9	3.0		0949	10.4	3.2
	1522	0.3	0.1		1617	-0.2	-0.1
	2135	8.5	2.6		2231	8.9	2.7
6 F	0325	1.2	0.4	21 Sa	0417	0.9	0.3
	0939	10.4	3.2		1036	10.5	3.2
	1609	-0.2	-0.1		1703	-0.3	-0.1
	2221	8.9	2.7		2317	9.0	2.7
7 Sa	0413	0.8	0.2	22 Su	0503	0.8	0.2
	1026	10.8	3.3		1121	10.5	3.2
	1654	-0.6	-0.2		1744	-0.3	-0.1
	2307	9.2	2.8		2358	9.1	2.8
8 Su	0500	0.4	0.1	23 M	0549	0.7	0.2
	1112	11.1	3.4		1203	10.3	3.1
	1740	-1.0	-0.3		1822	-0.2	-0.1
	2353	9.6	2.9				
9 M	0549	0.1	0.0	24 Tu	0036	9.2	2.8
	1200	11.3	3.4		0631	0.7	0.2
	1826	-1.2	-0.4		1242	10.1	3.1
					1901	0.0	0.0
10 Tu	0039	9.9	3.0	25 W	0113	9.2	2.8
	0637	-0.2	-0.1		0712	0.8	0.2
	1249	11.3	3.4		1324	9.8	3.0
	1912	-1.3	-0.4		1938	0.3	0.1
11 W	0126	10.2	3.1	26 Th	0151	9.2	2.8
	0727	-0.3	-0.1		0754	0.9	0.3
	1338	11.3	3.4		1404	9.4	2.9
	1958	-1.2	-0.4		2018	0.6	0.2
12 Th	0215	10.4	3.2	27 F	0231	9.2	2.8
	0822	-0.3	-0.1		0839	1.1	0.3
	1431	10.7	3.3		1448	9.0	2.7
	2049	-0.9	-0.3		2057	1.0	0.3
13 F	0305	10.5	3.2	28 Sa	0313	9.1	2.8
	0918	-0.2	-0.1		0924	1.3	0.4
	1527	10.2	3.1		1534	8.5	2.6
	2141	-0.4	-0.1		2140	1.3	0.4
14 Sa	0401	10.5	3.2	29 Su	0356	9.0	2.7
	1017	0.0	0.0		1014	1.4	0.4
	1628	9.6	2.9		1625	8.1	2.5
	2237	0.1	0.0		2227	1.7	0.5
15 Su	0457	10.4	3.2	30 M	0445	8.9	2.7
	1119	0.1	0.0		1108	1.6	0.5
	1730	9.1	2.8		1718	7.8	2.4
	2335	0.6	0.2		2318	2.0	0.6
				31 Tu	0537	8.9	2.7
					1205	1.5	0.5
					1816	7.7	2.3

FEBRUARY

Day	Time h m	Height ft	Height m	Day	Time h m	Height ft	Height m
1 W	0014	2.0	0.6	16 Th	0118	1.5	0.5
	0630	9.1	2.8		0745	9.7	3.0
	1302	1.3	0.4		1419	0.5	0.2
	1915	7.7	2.3		2037	8.3	2.5
2 Th	0109	1.9	0.6	17 F	0221	1.4	0.4
	0726	9.4	2.9		0846	9.8	3.0
	1358	0.9	0.3		1515	0.4	0.1
	2011	8.0	2.4		2131	8.6	2.6
3 F	0205	1.6	0.5	18 Sa	0317	1.2	0.4
	0821	9.9	3.0		0938	10.0	3.0
	1451	0.3	0.1		1603	0.2	0.1
	2106	8.5	2.6		2219	8.8	2.7
4 Sa	0258	1.1	0.3	19 Su	0405	1.0	0.3
	0914	10.4	3.2		1024	10.1	3.1
	1542	-0.3	-0.1		1643	0.1	0.0
	2154	9.0	2.7		2257	9.1	2.8
5 Su	0351	0.4	0.1	20 M	0448	0.7	0.2
	1005	11.0	3.4		1106	10.1	3.1
	1630	-0.9	-0.3		1720	0.1	0.0
	2242	9.7	3.0		2334	9.3	2.8
6 M	0440	-0.2	-0.1	21 Tu	0529	0.5	0.2
	1052	11.4	3.5		1143	10.1	3.1
	1716	-1.4	-0.4		1756	0.1	0.0
	2329	10.3	3.1				
7 Tu	0529	-0.7	-0.2	22 W	0008	9.5	2.9
	1142	11.6	3.5		0608	0.4	0.1
	1802	-1.6	-0.5		1220	9.9	3.0
					1829	0.2	0.1
8 W	0015	10.8	3.3	23 Th	0042	9.6	2.9
	0619	-1.1	-0.3		0645	0.4	0.1
	1231	11.6	3.5		1257	9.7	3.0
	1848	-1.7	-0.5		1904	0.4	0.1
9 Th	0101	11.1	3.4	24 F	0117	9.6	2.9
	0710	-1.2	-0.4		0725	0.5	0.2
	1322	11.3	3.4		1335	9.4	2.9
	1935	-1.4	-0.4		1941	0.7	0.2
10 F	0149	11.2	3.4	25 Sa	0153	9.5	2.9
	0802	-1.1	-0.3		0806	0.7	0.2
	1415	10.8	3.3		1415	9.0	2.7
	2023	-0.9	-0.3		2018	1.0	0.3
11 Sa	0239	11.1	3.4	26 Su	0231	9.4	2.9
	0857	-0.8	-0.2		0848	0.9	0.3
	1510	10.1	3.1		1458	8.6	2.6
	2116	-0.3	-0.1		2100	1.4	0.4
12 Su	0332	10.8	3.3	27 M	0311	9.2	2.8
	0956	-0.4	-0.1		0935	1.1	0.3
	1608	9.4	2.9		1545	8.1	2.5
	2211	0.4	0.1		2145	1.7	0.5
13 M	0430	10.4	3.2	28 Tu	0358	9.1	2.8
	1057	0.1	0.0		1027	1.4	0.4
	1712	8.7	2.7		1639	7.8	2.4
	2310	1.0	0.3		2237	2.0	0.6
14 Tu	0533	10.0	3.0				
	1204	0.4	0.1				
	1821	8.3	2.5				
15 W	0014	1.4	0.4				
	0638	9.8	3.0				
	1313	0.6	0.2				
	1932	8.2	2.5				

MARCH

Day	Time h m	Height ft	Height m	Day	Time h m	Height ft	Height m
1 W	0453	9.0	2.7	16 Th	0619	9.4	2.9
	1123	1.4	0.4		1253	1.0	0.3
	1736	7.7	2.3		1913	8.2	2.5
	2335	2.1	0.6				
2 Th	0549	9.1	2.8	17 F	0102	1.8	0.5
	1223	1.3	0.4		0728	9.3	2.8
	1838	7.8	2.4		1400	0.9	0.3
					2017	8.4	2.6
3 F	0035	1.9	0.6	18 Sa	0206	1.6	0.5
	0651	9.4	2.9		0827	9.4	2.9
	1323	0.9	0.3		1453	0.8	0.2
	1938	8.2	2.5		2109	8.7	2.7
4 Sa	0135	1.5	0.5	19 Su	0259	1.3	0.4
	0750	9.9	3.0		0920	9.6	2.9
	1421	0.3	0.1		1538	0.7	0.2
	2035	8.8	2.7		2153	9.0	2.7
5 Su	0233	0.8	0.2	20 M	0346	1.0	0.3
	0849	10.5	3.2		1003	9.7	3.0
	1512	-0.4	-0.1		1615	0.5	0.2
	2126	9.6	2.9		2231	9.3	2.8
6 M	0328	0.0	0.0	21 Tu	0427	0.7	0.2
	0941	11.0	3.4		1044	9.8	3.0
	1603	-1.0	-0.3		1650	0.5	0.2
	2215	10.4	3.2		2303	9.6	2.9
7 Tu	0420	-0.8	-0.2	22 W	0506	0.4	0.1
	1033	11.5	3.5		1120	9.8	3.0
	1649	-1.4	-0.4		1724	0.5	0.2
	2303	11.1	3.4		2335	9.8	3.0
8 W	0510	-1.4	-0.4	23 Th	0543	0.3	0.1
	1122	11.7	3.6		1155	9.7	3.0
	1736	-1.7	-0.5		1757	0.6	0.2
	2348	11.6	3.5				
9 Th	0600	-1.8	-0.5	24 F	0009	9.9	3.0
	1213	11.6	3.5		0620	0.2	0.1
	1823	-1.6	-0.5		1231	9.5	2.9
					1832	0.7	0.2
10 F	0034	11.8	3.6	25 Sa	0042	9.9	3.0
	0650	-1.9	-0.6		0658	0.3	0.1
	1304	11.2	3.4		1309	9.2	2.8
	1909	-1.2	-0.4		1909	1.0	0.3
11 Sa	0123	11.8	3.6	26 Su	0117	9.8	3.0
	0742	-1.6	-0.5		0737	0.4	0.1
	1356	10.6	3.2		1346	8.9	2.7
	1959	-0.7	-0.2		1946	1.2	0.4
12 Su	0212	11.5	3.5	27 M	0155	9.7	3.0
	0836	-1.1	-0.3		0819	0.6	0.2
	1451	9.9	3.0		1428	8.6	2.6
	2051	0.0	0.0		2028	1.5	0.5
13 M	0308	10.9	3.3	28 Tu	0237	9.5	2.9
	0934	-0.4	-0.1		0903	0.9	0.3
	1549	9.2	2.8		1516	8.3	2.5
	2147	0.8	0.2		2114	1.8	0.5
14 Tu	0406	10.3	3.1	29 W	0324	9.3	2.8
	1035	0.2	0.1		0956	1.1	0.3
	1654	8.6	2.6		1608	8.0	2.4
	2249	1.4	0.4		2206	2.0	0.6
15 W	0512	9.8	3.0	30 Th	0419	9.3	2.8
	1143	0.7	0.2		1051	1.2	0.4
	1804	8.2	2.5		1706	8.0	2.4
	2354	1.7	0.5		2305	2.0	0.6
				31 F	0519	9.3	2.8
					1152	1.0	0.3
					1806	8.2	2.5

Time meridian 75° W. 0000 is midnight. 1200 is noon.
Heights are referred to mean lower low water which is the chart datum of soundings.

Fig. 2.11 Sample Page Showing Table 1 of the *Tide Tables*.
(Source: *Tide Tables*)

Table 5— Reduction of Local Mean Time to Standard Time.

Table 6—Moonrise and Moonset for Eight Locations.

Table 7—Conversion of Feet to Meters.

The *Tide Tables* also include a glossary of terms and an index of stations, which gives you the page number for reference station data within the *Tide Tables.*

Corrections to Tide Tables

Like every other government publication, errors may occur in the *Tide Tables.* Corrections are summarized in the national Weekly Notice to Mariners each quarter. The numbers of these quarterly LNM summaries that contain *Tide Tables* corrections are 13, 26, 39, and 52. Corrections may also appear in the Local Notice to Mariners published weekly by the various Coast Guard district commanders.

TIDAL CURRENT TABLES

The annual *Tidal Current Tables*, published by International Marine under license from NOAA, provide advance information relative to currents. These data include daily predictions of the times of slack water and the times and velocities (speed) of maximum flood and ebb currents for a number of major waterways (reference stations). Tables are also provided for obtaining current predictions for numerous other locations (substations). There are two versions of the *Tidal Current Tables:* (1) Atlantic Coast of North America and (2) Pacific Coast of North America and Asia.

The *Tidal Current Tables* also have a wealth of nautical information, including

- An informative introduction on currents.
- A list of reference stations.
- Rotary currents.
- Information on the Gulf Stream.
- Wind-driven currents.
- A section on how to use current diagrams.
- A glossary of terms.

The current tables included in the publication are:

Table 1— Daily Current Predictions. The times of maximum and slack water are furnished in Table 1. Data in this table change from year to year.

Table 2—Current Difference and Other Constants and Rotary Tidal Currents. Table 2 lists a series of substations associated with the reference stations and shows the time differences for maximum and slack current from the reference station. Data in this table remain constant from year to year.

Table 3—Speed of Current at Any Time. This table provides a correction factor for determining the speed of the current at any time.

Table 4—Duration of Slack.

Table 5—Rotary Tidal Currents.

TIDAL CURRENT CHARTS

The *Tidal Current Charts,* published by the National Ocean Service, consists of a set of 11 charts, which depict, by means of arrows and figures, the direction (set) and velocity (drift) of the tidal current for each hour of the tidal cycle. These charts, which may be used for any year, present a comprehensive view of the tidal current movement in the respective waterway and provide a quick method for determining the direction and speed of the current at any point in time throughout the waterway covered by the charts.

Tidal Current Charts are produced for the following areas:

- Boston Harbor.
- Narragansett Bay to Nantucket Sound.
- Narragansett Bay. (The *Narragansett Bay Tidal Current Chart* is used with the annual *Tide Tables.* All other tidal current charts require the use of the annual current tables.)
- Long Island Sound and Block Island Sound.
- New York Harbor.
- Delaware Bay and River.
- Upper Chesapeake Bay.
- Charleston Harbor, SC.
- Tampa Bay.
- San Francisco Bay.
- Puget Sound—Northern Part.
- Puget Sound—Southern Part.

TIDAL CURRENT DIAGRAMS

The *Tidal Current Diagrams*, published by the National Ocean Service, are a series of 12 monthly diagrams that are used with the *Tidal Current Charts* to give you a convenient method for determining the flow of the current on a particular day. *Tidal Current Diagrams* are produced for the following areas:

- Long Island Sound and Block Island Sound.
- Boston Harbor.
- Upper Chesapeake Bay.
- New York Harbor.

The *Tidal Current Diagrams* may be ordered from the National Ocean Service Distribution Division.

RULES OF THE ROAD

The so-called "Rules of the Road" publication, officially called *Navigation Rules: International—Inland*, contains all of the inland and international rules for prevention of collisions between vessels (see Figure 2.12). These rules apply to all vessels regardless of size, method of propulsion, whether a private or commercial vessel, or national origin of registry of the vessel. This publication is divided into several sections:

U.S. Department of Transportation
United States Coast Guard

NAVIGATION RULES
INTERNATIONAL—INLAND

Fig. 2.12 Cover from *Rules of the Road.*
(Source: Rules of the Road)

    I. Introduction.
   II. Navigation Rules and Regulations.
      A. General Rules.
      B. Steering and Sailing Rules.
      C. Lights and Shapes.

D. Sound Signals.
E. Exemptions.
III. Interpretative Rules.
IV. Lines of Demarcations.
V. Penalty Provisions.
VI. Alternative Compliance—International and Inland.
VII. Vessel Bridge to Bridge Radiotelephone Regulations.
VIII. Legal Citations.
IX. Conversion Tables (Feet to Meters).

Requests to change the navigational rules are published in the Federal Register with requests for comment from the boating industry and the general public. Actual changes to these rules are published in the Weekly LNM.

Reader Study Note

The purpose of this chapter is to familiarize you with various navigational publications and provide a brief explanation of the types of information they contain. You are not expected to become an expert on the data by reading this chapter. You should acquire some of these publications for your nautical reference library. Most of them provide clear instructions on their use.

Reader Progress Note

You should be familiar with the nautical chart and most of the navigational publications that support and enhance the data provided on nautical charts. You are now at least a mile ahead of the average boat owner. You still have a lot to learn, so don't give up just yet.

REVIEW QUESTIONS

2.1   Nautical chart catalogs show all of the _____ _____ for a given geographical area.

2.2   The list of charts for the Great Lakes and Adjacent Waters is found in Nautical Chart Catalog ____.

2.3   The latest edition number, edition date, and printing revision date for a nautical chart are found in the publication _____.

2.4   A glossary of terminology used on nautical charts of various nations is found in the publication _____.

2.5   The _____ and _____ that have been approved for use on nautical charts published in the United States are found in the publication Chart No. 1.

2.6   The nautical publication that contains a catalog of aids to navigation is called the _____.

2.7   The aids to navigation for the Great Lakes are found in Volume _____ of the *Light List.*

2.8   Data that cannot be coded or abbreviated on a nautical chart are found in the _____.

2.9   The publication used by the Coast Guard to communicate with mariners concerning the establishment, changing, and the discontinuance of aids to navigation is called the _____.

2.10 The publication that contains predictions of the times and heights of high and low water for every day in the year is called the _____.

2.11 The local mean time of sunrise and sunset is found in the _____.

2.12 A listing of approved marine events and regattas is found in the _____.

2.13 A table showing the distance of visibility of objects at sea is found in the _____.

2.14 Federal regulations applicable to the mariner in a particular area are found in the _____.

2.15 Corrections to the *Tide Tables* are published in _____ summaries of the Local Notice to Mariners.

ANSWERS

2.1   Nautical chart catalogs show all of the NAUTICAL CHARTS for a given geographical area.

2.2   The list of charts for the Great Lakes and Adjacent Waters is found in Nautical Chart Catalog FOUR (4).

2.3   The latest edition number, edition date, and printing revision date for a nautical chart are found in the publication DATES OF LATEST EDITIONS.

2.4   A glossary of terminology used on nautical charts of various nations is found in the publication CHART NO. 1.

2.5   The SYMBOLS and ABBREVIATIONS that have been approved for use on nautical charts published in the United States are found in the publication Chart No. 1.

2.6   The nautical publication that contains a catalog of aids to navigation is called the LIGHT LIST.

2.7   The aids to navigation for the Great Lakes are found in Volume VII of the *Light List.*

2.8   Data that cannot be coded or abbreviated on a nautical chart are found in the COAST PILOT.

2.9   The publication used by the Coast Guard to communicate with mariners concerning the establishment, changing, and the discontinuance of aids to navigation is called the LOCAL NOTICE TO MARINERS.

2.10   The publication that contains predictions of the times and heights of high and low water for every day in the year is called the TIDE TABLES.

2.11   The local mean time of sunrise and sunset is found in the TIDE TABLES.

2.12   A listing of approved marine events and regattas is found in the NOTICE TO MARINERS.

2.13   A table showing the distance of visibility of objects at sea is found in the COAST PILOT.

2.14   Federal regulations applicable to the mariner in a particular area are found in the COAST PILOT.

2.15   Corrections to the *Tide Tables* are published in QUARTERLY summaries of the Local Notice to Mariners.

THREE

The IALA-B Aids to Navigation System

The term *aid to navigation* refers to a device outside of a vessel used to assist the mariner in determining his or her position or course, or to warn of dangers and obstructions. Several aids to navigation (ATONs) are used together to form a local ATON system that helps the mariner follow natural or improved channels. These aids provide a continuous system of charted marks for coastal piloting.

In April 1982, the United States agreed to conform to the International Association of Lighthouse Authorities System B (IALA-B). This system applies to buoys and beacons that indicate the lateral limits (edges) of navigable channels, obstructions, dangers, and other areas of importance to the mariner.

Aids are numbered according to a prescribed method. The lowest numbered aids are farthest out to sea. The numbers on aids increase as you approach the shore. The channels around islands are numbered in a clockwise direction. Aids on rivers are numbered from the mouth of the river upward. Even-numbered aids mark the right side of a channel as you progress from seaward. The memory aid "Red on Right, Returning from the Sea" is something you should memorize. The right side of a channel on a river is the bank that is on your right-hand side as you drift with the flow of the river current.

PORT SIDE MARKS OR LATERAL MARKS

When returning from seaward, the aids to navigation that mark the port (left) side of the navigable channel will have the following characteristics:

1. **Green** in color.

2. **Odd** numbered. Numbers increase from the farthest point at sea toward the land.

3. **Can** or pillar-shaped or **square** day marks.

4. Lighted with **green** lights.

5. **Green** retroreflective panels.

6. Light characteristics can be:

   - *Flashing:* The total duration of light is shorter than the total duration of darkness.

   - *Occulting:* The total duration of light is longer than the total duration of darkness.

   - *Quick flashing:* Light flashes are emitted at a rate of 60 flashes per minute.

   - *Isophase (ISO):* Duration of light and darkness are equal.

See Figure 3.1 for an illustration of a port side mark.

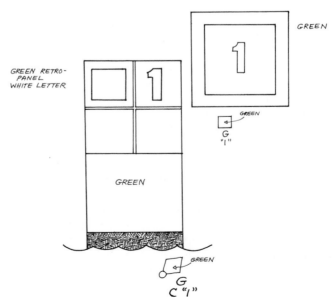

Fig. 3.1   Port Side Mark. *(F. J. Larkin)*

STARBOARD SIDE MARKS OR LATERAL MARKS

When returning from seaward, the aids to navigation that mark the starboard (right) side of the channel will have the following characteristics:

1. **Red** in color.

2. **Even** numbered. Numbers increase from seaward.

3. **Nun** or conical-shape or **triangular** day marks.

4. Lighted with **red** lights.

5. **Red** retroreflective panels.

6. Light characteristics may be flashing, occulting, quick flashing, or isophase (ISO), as explained earlier.

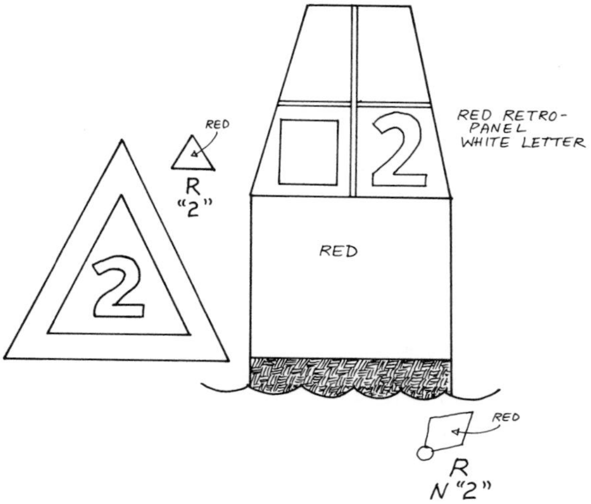

Fig. 3.2 Starboard Side Mark. *(F. J. Larkin)*

See Figure 3.2 for an illustration of a starboard side mark.

> MEMORY AID: *"Red on Right, Returning."*

SAFE WATER MARKS

Safe water marks are used to mark fairways, midchannels, and offshore approach points. They will have unobstructed water on all sides. They are also known as *midchannel marks* or *fairway marks*. Pass these aids to starboard. The aid will be off your port, or left side, to help separate incoming traffic from outgoing traffic and avoid collisions. Always enter on the red side of the channel and depart on the green side. Safe water marks have the following characteristics:

1. **Red and white** vertical stripes.

2. No numbers but may be **lettered.**

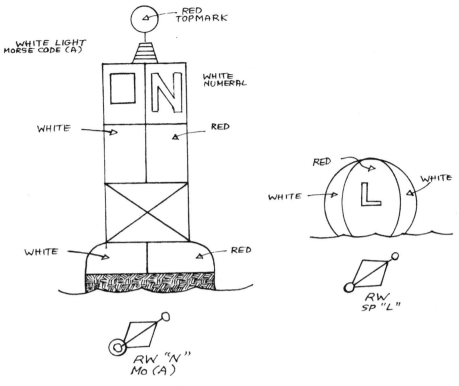

Fig. 3.3 Safe Water Mark. *(F. J. Larkin)*

3. **Spherical** in shape when not lighted. When lighted, buoys will be fitted with a round red ball topmark.

4. Lighted with **white** lights only.

5. **White and red** retroreflective panels.

6. Light characteristic will be **Morse Code A** (short-long flash). If the aid is fitted with a radio beacon, it will transmit a Morse Code A (dot-dash).

Figure 3.3 illustrates a safe water mark.

PREFERRED CHANNEL MARKS

At a point where a main channel divides or a side channel meets a main channel, when you are proceeding in the conventional (lateral) direction of buoyage, a preferred or main channel may be marked with a modified port or starboard lateral mark. Figure 3.4 illustrates this special marking scheme.

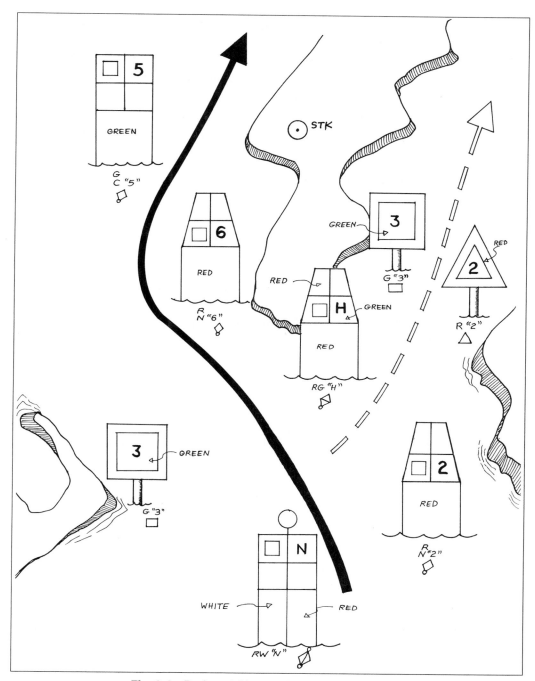

Fig. 3.4 Preferred Channel Scheme. *(F. J. Larkin)*

Preferred Channel to Starboard (Right)

Remember "red on right, returning," so green goes on your left.

1. *Color:* Green with one broad red horizontal band. The green band will be at the top.
2. *Shape:* Can or pillar shaped.
3. *Day mark:* Green square, lower half is red.
4. *Light color:* Green.
5. *Light characteristic:* Composite group flashing (2 + 1).
6. *Markings:* Preferred channel aids are never numbered, but may be lettered.
7. *Retroreflective panel color:* Green.

Figure 3.5 shows an illustration of this aid.

> CAUTION: *When proceeding toward the sea, it may not always be possible to pass on either side of a preferred channel aid to navigation. Always check the appropriate nautical chart for the area.*

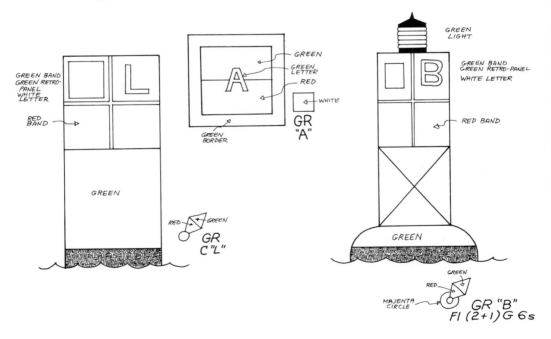

Fig. 3.5 Preferred Channel Mark to Starboard. *(F. J. Larkin)*

Preferred Channel to Port (Left)

Again, "red on right, returning."

1. *Color:* Red band on top with one broad green horizontal band below. The top color indicates the preferred or main channel.
2. *Shape:* Conical or nun-shaped.
3. *Day mark:* Red triangle, lower half is green.
4. *Light color:* Red.
5. *Light characteristic:* Composite group flashing (2 + 1).
6. *Markings:* Preferred channel buoys are never numbered but may be lettered.
7. *Retroreflective panel color:* Red.

Figure 3.6 shows an illustration of this aid.

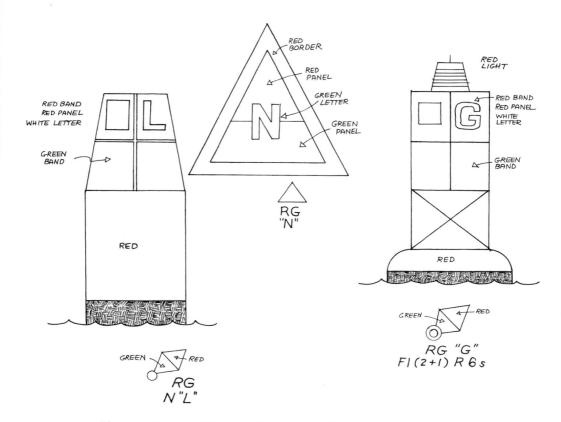

Fig. 3.6 Preferred Channel Mark to Port. *(F. J. Larkin)*

> CAUTION: *When proceeding toward the sea, it may not always be possible to pass on either side of a preferred channel aid to navigation. Always check the appropriate nautical chart for the area.*

Figure 3.7 shows more examples of the IALA-B system of buoyage.

LATERAL AIDS AS SEEN ENTERING FROM SEAWARD

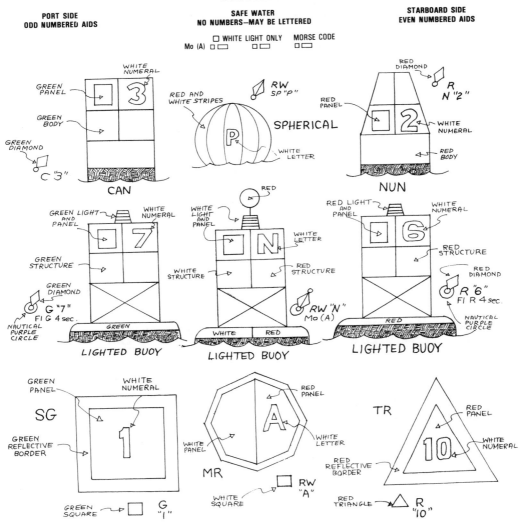

Fig. 3.7   IALA-B Buoyage System. *(F. J. Larkin)*

SPECIAL MARKS

These marks are not intended to assist in navigation but rather to alert the mariner to a special feature or area. The feature will be described in a nautical document such as a nautical chart, the *Light List,* the *Coast Pilot,* or the Local Notice to Mariners.

Some items marked by special marks are spoil areas, pipelines, traffic separation schemes, jetties, or military exercise areas.

Special marks are yellow in color and, if lighted, will show a yellow light.

INTRACOASTAL WATERWAY AIDS TO NAVIGATION SYSTEM

The Intracoastal Waterway runs parallel to the Atlantic and Gulf coasts from Manasquan Inlet, New Jersey, to the Mexican border. Aids marking these waters have some portion marked with a small yellow panel. Otherwise, the coloring and numbering of buoys and day marks follow the IALA-B System.

While the lateral buoyage system is numbered from seaward toward the shore ("red on right, returning"), the direction of buoyage in the Intracoastal Waterway system is generally south along the Atlantic Coast and generally west along the Gulf Coast.

When an intracoastal route joins another marked waterway, special yellow markings are applied to the ATONs that already mark this waterway for another purpose or direction, for example, a channel returning from the sea. These special marked aids are referred to as *dual-purpose* aids to navigation.

An example of this situation would be a channel with standard lateral buoys numbered low to high from seaward ("red on right, returning") where an intracoastal route uses a section of this channel. The intracoastal route enters at an inland point and heads toward the sea for a distance and then turns off out of the channel. Figure 3.8 illustrates the special yellow marking.

Dual-purpose aids that should be kept or passed on your port (left) side (heading generally southward on the Atlantic Coast) are marked with small yellow squares. The yellow squares indicate that you are to pass the aid as if it were a can buoy while you are operating on this section of the Intracoastal Waterway.

Dual-purpose aids that should be kept or passed on your starboard (right) side (heading generally southward on the Atlantic Coast) are marked with small yellow triangles. The yellow triangles indicate that you are to pass the aid as if it were a nun buoy while you are operating on this section of the Intracoastal Waterway. Again, see Figure 3.8 for an example of this type of dual-purpose aid.

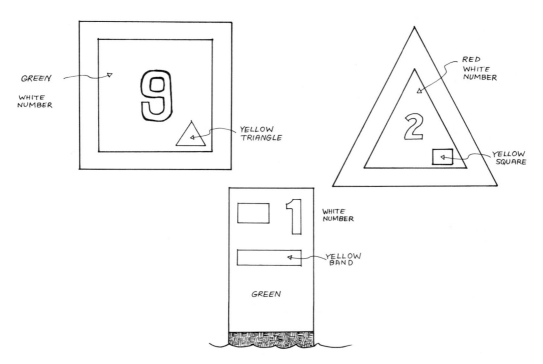

Fig. 3.8 Intracoastal Waterway Aids to Navigation. *(F. J. Larkin)*

When operating on the Intracoastal Waterway (ICW) where dual-purpose aids are used, the mariner must disregard the lateral significance of the color, number, and shape of the aid and be guided solely by the shape of the yellow square or triangle. This can become a problem during nighttime operations since the lighting for dual-purpose ICW aids reflects the channel direction as if you were returning from seaward. Use extra caution and follow your chart carefully in this situation.

THE UNIFORM STATE WATERWAY MARKING SYSTEM

The Uniform State Waterway Marking System (USWMS) was developed in 1966 to provide an easy-to-understand navigational system for small boats on state waterways. The port and starboard markings for USWMS aids to navigation are similar to the federal system except that the lateral colors are red and black. The regulatory buoys in the USWMS are colored white with orange stripes. The standard regulatory markings are outlined in the following subsections.

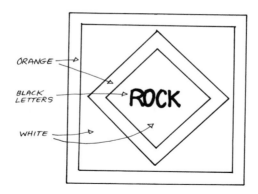

Fig. 3.9 USWMS Diamond Shape. *(F. J. Larkin)*

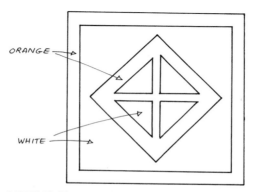

Fig. 3.10 USWMS Diamond Shape with Cross Inside. *(F. J. Larkin)*

Diamond Shape

A diamond-shaped display on a buoy is an indication of a dangerous area. The nature of the danger may be indicated inside the diamond shape. Messages such as *Rock, Wreck, Shoal,* or *Dam* are typical (see Figure 3.9). You should be alerted by the diamond shape that there is a danger nearby.

Diamond Shape with Cross Inside

A diamond-shaped display with a cross inside is an indication of a prohibited or boat exclusion area (see Figure 3.10). The explanation for the exclusion may be shown outside of the crossed diamond. Messages such as *Dam, Rapids,* and *Swimming Area* are typical. The diamond shape and the cross should alert you that you should not operate your boat in this area.

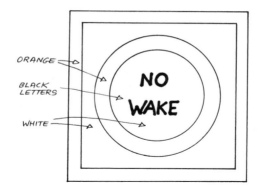

Fig. 3.11   USWMS Circle Shape. *(F. J. Larkin)*

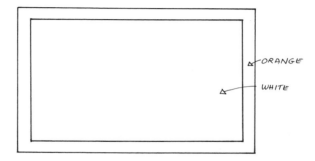

Fig. 3.12   USWMS Rectangle Shape. *(F. J. Larkin)*

Circle Shape

A circular-shaped display indicates a controlled area (see Figure 3.11). This means that a vessel operated in this marked area is subject to certain restrictions or rules. The classification of the regulation is indicated within the circle. *No Wake, Slow,* and *No Anchoring* are typical messages found within a circular-shaped display on a buoy.

Rectangular or Square Shape

General information is shown within rectangular displays. This could include directions, distances, and locations (see Figure 3.12).

All of these regulatory buoys may be lighted with white lights and may be lettered.

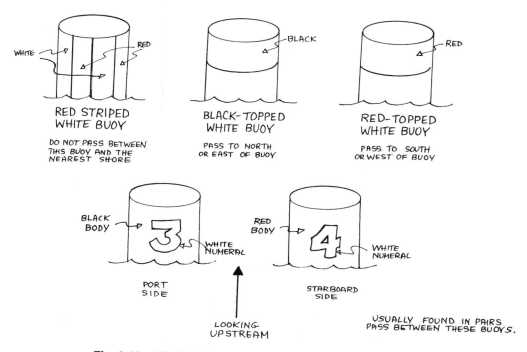

Fig. 3.13 USWMS Buoyage System. *(F. J. Larkin)*

Other USWMS Variations

The rules for passing buoys is different with the USWMS. The buoys are said to have cardinal significance. That is, they are passed from specific directions of north, south, east, or west. These variations are illustrated in Figure 3.13.

A **white** buoy with a **red** top indicates an obstruction. Pass the buoy to the south or west.

> MEMORY AID: *Think of the red top as warm and that warmth comes from the south and west.*

A **white** buoy with a **black** top also indicates an obstruction. Pass this buoy to the north or east.

> MEMORY AID: *Think of the black top as a storm such as a Nor'easter.*

A **red and white** vertically striped buoy indicates that an obstruction exists between the buoy and the nearest shore, so do not pass between them.

> CAUTION: *Sometimes it's hard to distinguish which shore is indicated when this type of buoy is placed near the center of a channel. Use local knowledge to find out the correct side before you put your boat and passengers in jeopardy by passing it on the wrong side. Report all position problems to the local harbormaster or to the officials of the town or county where the waterway is located.*

> EXTRA CAUTION: *Don't confuse this state waterway buoy with the center channel buoy used in the IALA-B buoyage system. I have seen this vertically red and white buoy incorrectly deployed in inland waterways. If you become confused, use local knowledge. Ask around before you transit such an area.*

Mooring Buoys

A standard color scheme for mooring buoys was also established in 1966. Mooring buoys should be white with a horizontal blue band. Mooring buoys have no lateral significance in navigation. I suggest that you stay out of mooring areas because you can catch a painter (a pick-up line for, say, a dinghy) in your props. Some inexperienced boat owners use polypropylene line for this purpose and polypro floats.

Lobster Trap Buoys

Lobster trap buoys are painted in the various colors authorized by the license of the lobster fisherman. Lobster trap buoys have no lateral significance in navigation except that they should be avoided.

Sailboats seem to have the worst problem with lobster buoys. They usually snag the buoy's line between their keel and their rudder. Prudent mariners keep a constant lookout for lobster buoys especially when backing their boats.

Bridges

Bridges that open usually have a clearance gauge installed to minimize the number of times they are opened. These gauges should be located at the right side of the channel facing an approaching vessel. Clearance gauges indicate the lowest vertical clearance under the span over the navigable channel.

Certain bridges may be equipped with sound signals, racons, and radar reflectors where unusual geographic or weather conditions exist. Check your *Coast Pilot* for information about bridges and the federal regulations concerning the bridge openings.

Private Aids to Navigation

Some aids to navigation are maintained by local municipal organizations or private citizens and are termed *private aids.* As of December 31, 1995, private aids are required by federal law to conform to the standard U.S. system for federal aids to navigation. Private aids may only be established, changed, or discontinued with the permission of the local Coast Guard district commander.

> CAUTION: *While federal aids are serviced by the Coast Guard and are usually kept in fine repair, private aids are serviced by their owner. Use caution when operating your boat in areas marked by private aids. Private aids can be off station, missing, or worse, misleading, that is, the wrong shape, color, or number.*

REPORTING DEFECTS AND DISCREPANCIES TO AIDS TO NAVIGATION

As a boater, you should be aware that the Coast Guard cannot keep the thousands of aids to navigation that comprise the federal ATON system under continuous surveillance. Add to this total the thousands of private aids and the lighting on all the bridges. It is virtually impossible for the Coast Guard to guarantee that every aid is operating properly, or is on its assigned position at all times. This situation worsens after any large storm in your area.

Therefore, for the general safety of all mariners, any person who recognizes that an aid to navigation is not on its assigned position or is not exhibiting its advertised light characteristic should promptly notify the nearest Coast Guard station about the problem.

Reader Study Note

Using red, green, and yellow pencils, color all the figures that have drawings of aids to navigation in this chapter. This will help you become familiar with the color and shape of these aids.

Reader Progress Note

Add the aids to navigation system to your basic navigation knowledge. You should be able to recognize these aids on nautical charts as well as on the water.

REVIEW QUESTIONS

3.1   Returning from seaward, a starboard side mark is _____ in color, has _____ numbers, and is _____ in shape.

3.2   Returning from seaward, a port side mark is _____ in color, has _____ numbers, and is _____ shaped.

3.3   Returning from seaward, port side marks have _____ lights, while starboard side marks have _____ lights.

3.4   In the IALA-B system, midchannel marks are also known as _____ or _____.

3.5   Returning from seaward, the starboard preferred channel mark is _____ with one broad _____ horizontal stripe.

3.6   The light characteristic of a preferred channel mark is _____.

3.7   When proceeding toward the sea, it may not always be prudent to _____ on _____ side of a preferred channel aid to navigation.

3.8   In the ICW, dual-purpose marks that should be kept on your port side consist of a yellow _____.

3.9   In the USWMS, diamond shapes are an indication of _____.

3.10   In the IALA-B system, a red and white vertically striped aid is called a _____ and can be _____ close aboard on either side.

3.11   In the USWMS, a red and white vertically striped buoy indicates that an _____ exists between the buoy and the nearest _____.

3.12   When returning from the sea, toward the shore, the numbers on the buoys will _____ and the red-colored buoys are kept on the _____ side of your boat.

ANSWERS

3.1　Returning from seaward, a starboard side mark is RED in color, has EVEN numbers, and is TRIANGULAR in shape.

3.2　Returning from seaward, a port side mark is GREEN in color, has ODD numbers, and is CAN shaped.

3.3　Returning from seaward, port side marks have GREEN lights, while starboard side marks have RED lights.

3.4　In the IALA-B system, midchannel marks are also known as SAFE WATER MARKS or FAIRWAY MARKS.

3.5　Returning from seaward, the starboard preferred channel mark is RED with one broad GREEN horizontal stripe.

3.6　The light characteristic of a preferred channel mark is COMPOSITE GROUP FLASHING (2 + 1).

3.7　When proceeding toward the sea, it may not always be prudent to PASS on EITHER side of a Preferred channel aid to navigation.

3.8　In the ICW, dual-purpose marks that should be kept on your port side consist of a yellow SQUARE.

3.9　In the USWMS, diamond shapes are an indication of A DANGEROUS AREA.

3.10　In the IALA-B system, a red and white vertically striped aid is called a SAFE WATER MARK and can be PASSED close aboard on either side.

3.11　In the USWMS, a red and white vertically striped buoy indicates that an OBSTRUCTION exists between the buoy and the nearest SHORE.

3.12　When returning from the sea, toward the shore, the numbers on the buoys will INCREASE and the red-colored buoys are kept on the STARBOARD (RIGHT-HAND) side of your boat.

FOUR

How to Use the Basic Navigational Instruments

THE MAGNETIC COMPASS

The *magnetic compass* is the most important instrument you can use for determining your boat's course. Prudent navigators will check the accuracy of their compass frequently because they know that the magnetic compass is influenced not only by the earth's magnetic field, but also by magnetic fields radiating from metallic materials aboard their boat. The compass is also subject to unforeseen error resulting from the violent motion of the boat in stormy weather. Figure 4.1 depicts a typical compass used on a small boat. A few important things you should know about a compass are discussed in this section.

The Compass Card

The compass card is the round disk on your compass that looks like a compass rose. The arc of the compass card is divided into 360 degrees. Most compass cards are only marked in 5- and 10-degree increments, which limits small boat owners in their ability to steer a course. The compass card is aligned to magnetic north by a magnet that is usually attached to the underside of the compass card. When the boat turns, the compass card swings on a pivot point and continues to align itself with the earth's magnetic field.

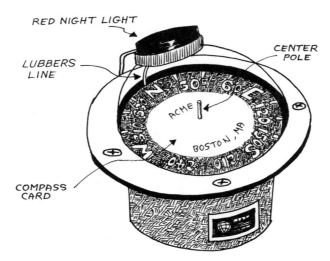

Fig. 4.1   A Typical Small Boat Compass. *(F. J. Larkin)*

A compass, unaffected by local magnetic influences, will point toward magnetic north. When a compass does not point to magnetic north, the error is called *deviation.* Mariners correct for the deviation error by using a deviation table. Procedures for developing a deviation table for your boat are found in Appendixes 3 and 4.

The Lubber Line

The *lubber line* is a mark scribed into the compass housing to indicate the direction in which the boat's bow is heading. When installing a compass, you need to align the lubber line and the center pole of the compass card with the keel line of your boat. Appendix 1 describes and illustrates this procedure. Failure to achieve this alignment will result in a built-in steering error on your boat.

Direction

Direction is measured clockwise from 000 degrees around the compass card to 360 degrees. Always use three digits when writing or expressing direction in degrees. Direction can be stated in true degrees, magnetic degrees, or compass degrees. Note that each is a different point of the compass:

   1. *True directions* or headings use the North Pole (top of the nautical chart) as its reference.

2. *Magnetic directions* use magnetic north as its reference. Magnetic north is located at a different point on the earth than the true North Pole. While true north is fixed, magnetic north moves around and this movement is predictable.

3. *Compass direction* is the point of the compass in which your boat is heading or should be heading. A compass heading is a calculated direction that is found by correcting a magnetic direction for all magnetic influences that are unique to your boat (the error called deviation). Each boat has different deviation error. Chapter 10 explains the formula for correcting a course for deviation.

DIVIDERS

A set of *dividers* is a two-armed pointed instrument that is used in navigation to measure distance on a nautical chart. Distance is measured from the "Nautical Mile Scale" or from the latitude scales, which are located at the left- and right-hand margins on a nautical chart. **Never** use the longitude scales at the top and bottom of a chart for measuring distance.

A good set of dividers will have an adjusting screw to tighten the tension of the divider's arms (see Figure 4.2). You will also want to add a small screwdriver to your navigation kit. Any good chart store sells dividers. You can get a suitable screwdriver at electronics stores.

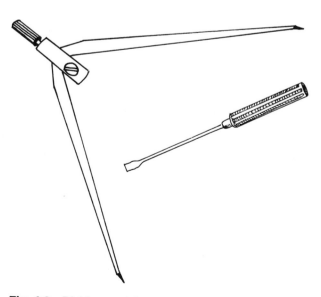

Fig. 4.2 Dividers and Small Screwdriver. *(F. J. Larkin)*

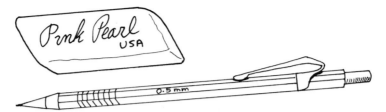

Fig. 4.3   Automatic Pencil and Eraser. *(F. J. Larkin)*

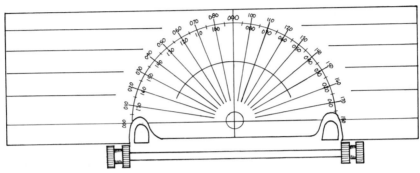

Fig. 4.4   Paraglide Plotter. *(F. J. Larkin)*

PENCILS

Fine-pointed automatic pencils using 2H or 3H 0.5 leads are the best for plotting courses. Add extra leads and erasers that fit your automatic pencil to your navigation kit (see Figure 4.3). If you use wooden pencils, you will need to add a pencil sharpener.

PARAGLIDE PLOTTERS

Figure 4.4 shows a *paraglide plotter.* I have found this type of plotter to be the most convenient instrument for measuring courses (directions) from a chart on a small boat. The paraglide plotter is easily rolled across a nautical chart without losing the course angle. The technique for reading a course angle with a paraglide plotter is explained in detail in Chapter 6. Here is a quick procedure:

Step 1.   Place the edge of your plotter along your course line.

Step 2.   Roll the plotter carefully and firmly so that the bull's-eye is directly over a meridian of longitude (the vertical lines).

Step 3.   Let your eye follow along the meridian toward the outer scale on the plotter. Read the course in degrees from the outer scale. Note that there are two scales that provide reciprocal (opposite) readings.

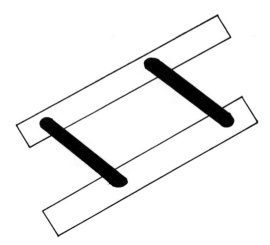

Fig. 4.5 Parallel Rules. *(F. J. Larkin)*

PARALLEL RULES

Parallel rules are also used to measure courses (directions) on a nautical chart (see Figure 4.5). I find this practice somewhat unreliable since the rules can easily slip and give an erroneous heading when used on a rocking boat. However, many navigators swear by them. Measure your course with a parallel rule as follows:

Step 1. Place the edge of the parallel rules along your course line.

Step 2. Carefully walk the parallel rules to the nearest compass rose so that the edge of the parallel rules intersects the center of the compass rose.

Step 3. Read your true course from the outer scale of the compass rose. Read your magnetic course from the inner scale of the compass rose. Keep your intended direction in mind so that you will avoid reading a reciprocal (opposite) course.

Chapter 6 explains this procedure in greater detail.

A STOPWATCH

A good stopwatch is an integral part of a navigation kit. You will need a watch to time the various legs of your trips and to develop your boat's speed curve. Your timepiece should be able to measure individual trip legs while tracking the total time for your entire trip. There are many inexpensive digital watches available that offer the multiple features required for navigation.

Reader Study Note

Try to get familiar with navigational instruments while reading this chapter. It is not necessary to master them at this time. There will be extensive coverage of the use of these instruments throughout this book as well as many practical exercises to develop your skill and confidence with navigation instruments.

Reader Progress Note

In addition to becoming familiar with the nautical chart, nautical publications, and the different aids to navigation that you will encounter on your chart and while under way on your boat, you are now aware of the basic navigational tools and ready to use them in piloting.

REVIEW QUESTIONS

4.1   The _____ _____ is a mark scribed into the compass housing to indicate the direction in which the boat is heading.

4.2   The _____ is aligned with the boat's centerline or keel.

4.3   Distance on a nautical chart is measured with _____ .

4.4   Direction is measured _____ from ____ degrees to ____ degrees.

4.5   The _____ or the _____ are used to measure course angles on a nautical chart.

ANSWERS

4.1   The LUBBER LINE is a mark scribed into the compass housing to indicate the direction in which the boat is heading.

4.2   The LUBBER LINE is aligned with the boat's centerline or keel.

4.3   Distance on a nautical chart is measured with DIVIDERS.

4.4   Direction is measured CLOCKWISE from 000 degrees to 360 degrees.

4.5   The PARAGLIDE PLOTTER or the PARALLEL RULES are used to measure course angles on a nautical chart.

FIVE

Measuring and Plotting Latitude and Longitude

In Chapter 1 you learned that your position or location on the earth's surface is measured in terms of latitude and longitude. In order to assist you in determining your position, latitude and longitude lines are drawn on nautical charts. The purpose of this chapter is to show you how to measure and plot your position on a nautical chart using latitude and longitude terminology. Remember that all positions determined on a nautical chart are referenced to true north and must be oriented to your compass before you can use them for a heading on your boat.

LATITUDE

> MEMORY AID: *"Lat is Flat."*

The horizontal or flat lines on your nautical chart are called *parallels of latitude.* The equator is a parallel of latitude and is labeled as zero (000) degrees. All parallels of latitude are the angular measurement of distance north and south of the equator. Boston, Massachusetts, is approximately 42 degrees or 2,520 miles north of the equator. Because Boston is north of the equator, write the letter "N" for north after an expression of latitude. If your position is south of the equator, write the letter "S" for south.

  Latitude measurements are read from the margin scales on the left-

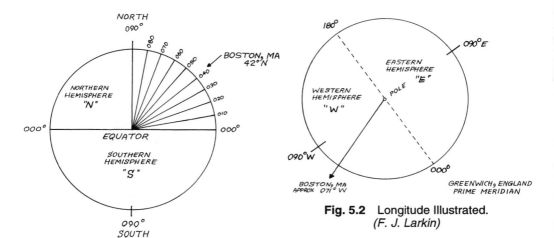

Fig. 5.1 Latitude Illustrated.
            (F. J. Larkin)

Fig. 5.2 Longitude Illustrated.
            (F. J. Larkin)

and right-hand sides of a nautical chart. Latitude increases from zero degrees at the equator to ninety degrees at the north and south poles. Study Figure 5.1, which is a graphic illustration of latitude.

EXERCISE: Pause for a minute and look at a nautical chart. Note that (in the northern hemisphere) the latitude designations in the margin scale on the left- and right-hand sides of your chart increase from the bottom of the chart toward the top.

Latitude is expressed in degrees, minutes, and tenths of minutes or seconds.

- One-tenth of a minute equals 6 seconds.
- One degree of latitude equals 60 minutes.
- One minute of latitude equals 1 nautical mile or 6,071.1 feet.

LONGITUDE

The vertical lines on your nautical chart are called *meridians of longitude.* Meridians of longitude are the angular measurement of distance east or west of the prime meridian. The prime meridian is located at Greenwich, England, and is assigned the value of zero degrees of longitude. Longitude is measured east and west from Greenwich, England, to meet at 180 degrees in the Pacific Ocean. As an example, Boston is located at approximately 71 degrees or 4,260 miles west of the prime meridian. Take a minute to review Figure 5.2, which graphically depicts longitude.

Before continuing, notice that a degree of longitude on a nautical chart (Mercator projection) is smaller than a degree of latitude. Since a degree of latitude is equal to a nautical mile, longitude is less than a nautical mile and, therefore, can never be used to measure distance on a nautical chart.

Longitude is expressed in degrees, minutes, and tenths of minutes or seconds. Since the United States is located west of the prime meridian, write the letter "W" for west after an expression of longitude; for example, 71° 40.5' W.

On a nautical chart, longitude measurements are read from the scales at the bottom and the top of the chart. Longitude increases westerly in the United States. Therefore, on a nautical chart, longitude increases from east to west or from the right-hand side of the chart toward the left.

EXERCISE: Look at the Piloting Practice Chart in Figure 5.3 and scan the margin scale at the top so that you are sure that the longitude increases toward the left.

TECHNIQUE FOR MEASURING LATITUDE ON A NAUTICAL CHART

Use a Piloting Practice Chart found in Appendix 7 to perform this exercise. Measure the latitude for Bell "3", southwest of Hog Island. Figure 5.3 illustrates the technique. Follow this step-by-step procedure for measuring latitude.

Step 1. Align the edge of your paraglide plotter along a meridian of longitude or at the left or right edge line of the chart. (Note: The left and right edge line will not work on a small craft chart.) Use a meridian of longitude line only. Don't be confused by any LORAN lattice lines on your chart.

Step 2. Roll the paraglide plotter to the object (Bell "3") you are measuring so that the object falls along the edge of your plotter. Using the edge of your plotter as your guide, draw a light pencil line on the nearest parallel of latitude (horizontal line) or on the margin scale at the top or bottom of the chart.

Step 3. Using your dividers, measure the distance from the object to the nearest parallel of latitude. In Figure 5.3, I placed the first point of the dividers on the pencil mark and laid the second point of the dividers downward to the 42 degree parallel line.

Step 4. Move your dividers to the latitude scale at the left- or right-hand side of the chart. Being careful not to disturb the opening of the dividers, place one point at the parallel (42 degrees) and lay the other point along the scale, in this case, upward toward the object.

Step 5. Read the latitude scale by starting at the bottom right-hand edge of the chart and reading upward.

- First find the degree reading. In Figure 5.3, the degree reading is 42 degrees. Notice that latitude begins as 41 degrees at the bottom of the chart and that you pass the 42 degree line as you read up the scale.

- As you read up the latitude scale, stop at the last whole minute before the second point of the dividers. In Figure 5.3, the minute reading is 02'.

- Continue reading up the scale to the second point of the dividers to find the seconds reading. In Figure 5.3, the correct reading is 0.1 minutes or 6 seconds. Notice that the divider's second point falls between two minute lines. When this happens, select the minute reading that is closest to the point.

- The complete latitude reading is 42 degrees, 02.1 minutes North.

TECHNIQUE FOR MEASURING LONGITUDE ON A NAUTICAL CHART

Still using the Bell "3", southwest of Hog Island, as our object or target, follow this step-by-step procedure for measuring longitude. Figure 5.4 illustrates this technique.

Step 1. Place the edge of your paraglide plotter along a parallel of latitude or at the top or bottom edge line of the chart. (Note: The top and bottom edge line will not work on a small craft chart. Use a parallel of latitude line only. Don't be confused by any LORAN lattice lines on your chart.)

Step 2. Roll the paraglide plotter to the object (Bell "3") that you are measuring so that the object falls along the edge of your plotter. Using the edge of the plotter as your guide, draw a light pencil line on the nearest meridian of longitude (vertical line) or on the margin scale at the left or right edge of your chart.

Step 3. Using your dividers, measure the distance from the object to the nearest meridian of longitude along the edge of your plotter. In Figure 5.4, I measured toward the right from the object to the right-hand margin on the chart.

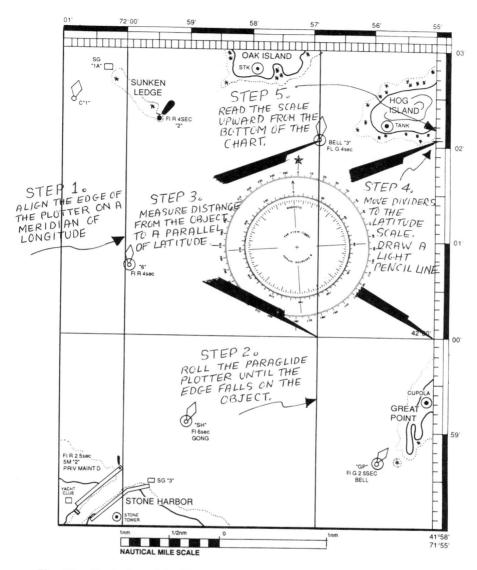

Fig. 5.3 Illustration of the Technique for Measuring Latitude. *(F. J. Larkin)*

Step 4. Without changing the opening of your dividers, move them to the longitude scale along the margin at the top or bottom of the chart. Place one point of the dividers at your measurement reference point (either the meridian or edge of the chart) and lay the other point along the longitude scale line toward the object. In Figure 5.4, I laid the second point of the dividers toward the left. The measurement should be 1.9 minutes. Draw a light pencil mark at this point.

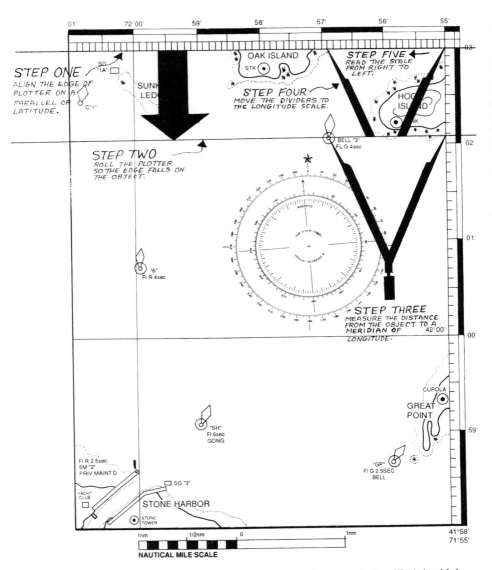

Fig. 5.4   Illustration of the Technique for Measuring Longitude. *(F. J. Larkin)*

Step 5.   Read the longitude scale by starting at the right-hand (east) side of the chart and reading toward the left.

- First find the degrees. In Figure 5.4, the degree reading is 71. It doesn't show on the chart, but because longitude increases from east to west in the area defined by the chart, and the next degree reading is 72, the degree reading at the right-hand edge of the chart must be 71. I am not trying to confuse you here. From a practical sense, you will run into this situation on many charts.

- Next, scan to the left along the longitude scale and stop at the nearest whole minute before your pencil mark. In Figure 5.4, the minute reading is 56'.
- Continue reading left to the pencil mark to find the tenth of a minute or second reading. In Figure 5.4, the pencil mark is at the nine-tenths (9/10) or 0.9 minute (54 seconds) mark.
- The complete longitude reading is: 71 degrees, 56.9 minutes West.

WRITING AND EXPRESSING LATITUDE AND LONGITUDE

In writing or expressing latitude and longitude, latitude is always stated first. Indicate latitude in degrees, minutes, and tenths of minutes. In the northern hemisphere (area above the equator), add the letter "N" for north as a suffix. Add the letter "S" in the southern hemisphere for south. Longitude also can be expressed in degrees, minutes, and tenths of minutes. In the western hemisphere (area west of the prime meridian for 180 degrees), add the letter "W" as a suffix for west. Add the letter "E" as a suffix if you are in the eastern hemisphere for east.

From Figures 5.3 and 5.4, the complete LAT/LON reading for Bell "3" is properly stated as 42 degrees, 02.1 minutes North; 71 degrees, 56 minutes West.

On some nautical charts, a "seconds" scale is used that is divided into seconds rather than tenths of minutes. Be alert to this difference. Read this scale in seconds, remembering that there are 60 seconds to a minute, not 100, which is a very common error in piloting.

THE SAFETY ASPECT OF KNOWING LATITUDE AND LONGITUDE

When you use a Mercator chart's system of latitude and longitude and reference whether you are north or south of the equator and east or west of the prime meridian, you fix your position to one location on the earth's surface. Knowing how to determine your position and how to express it correctly makes you stand out among a few knowledgeable mariners on the water today.

In an emergency, the more accurately you can report your position in a language that is quickly understood by skilled mariners, the quicker you will receive help. You will be able to speak to the Coast Guard in their language, and the Coast Guard will be able to dispatch assistance more readily. In an emergency, a few minutes can often mean the difference between life and death.

PRACTICE PROBLEMS

Compute the latitude and longitude for the following objects on a Piloting Practice Chart (Figure 5.3 or 5.4).

1. What is the latitude of Bell "GP", southwest of Great Point?
2. What is the latitude of C "1", west of Sunken Ledge?
3. What is the longitude of Bell "GP", southwest of Great Point?
4. What are the latitude and longitude of Gong "SH", northeast of Stone Harbor?

ANSWERS

1. 41 degrees, 58.7 minutes North.
2. 42 degrees, 02.5 minutes North.
3. 71 degrees, 55.9 minutes West.
4. 41 minutes, 59.1 minutes North; 71 degrees, 59.1 minutes West.

Reader Study Note

If you haven't completed the practice problems, there's a strong chance that you don't fully understand latitude and longitude yet. This is such an important starting point in your navigation education, please don't skip it. From a boating safety point of view, understanding LAT/LON is critical. For the proper use of electronic navigation systems such as LORAN and DGPS, this knowledge is essential.

Reader Progress Note

Add to your piloting skills the ability to find and express your position on a nautical chart as latitude and longitude. Congratulations! You have just increased your chance for survival in an emergency by a huge margin.

REVIEW QUESTIONS

5.1 The flat or horizontal lines found on a nautical chart are called _____ __ _____.

5.2 Latitude measurements are read from the margin scales on the _____ and _____ hand sides of the nautical chart.

5.3   The _____ lines found on a nautical chart are called meridians of longitude.

5.4   _____ is measured east and west of Greenwich, England.

5.5   One _____ of latitude equals one nautical mile or 6,071.1 feet.

5.6   Since the United States is located _____ of the prime meridian, write the letter "___" as a suffix after an expression of longitude.

5.7   A _____ and _____ measurement pinpoints your location on the surface of the earth.

5.8   Longitude increases _____ in the United States.

5.9   Latitude increases _____ in the United States.

5.10 A degree of longitude is _____ than a degree of latitude.

ANSWERS

5.1   The flat or horizontal lines found on a nautical chart are called PARALLELS OF LATITUDE.

5.2   Latitude measurements are read from the margin scales on the LEFT and RIGHT hand sides of the nautical chart.

5.3   The VERTICAL lines found on a nautical chart are called meridians of longitude.

5.4   LONGITUDE is measured east and west of Greenwich, England.

5.5   One MINUTE of latitude equals one nautical mile or 6,071.1 feet.

5.6   Since the United States is located WEST of the Prime Meridian, write the letter "W" as a suffix after an expression of longitude.

5.7   A LATITUDE and LONGITUDE measurement pinpoints your location on the surface of the earth.

5.8   Longitude increases WESTERLY in the United States.

5.9   Latitude increases NORTHERLY in the United States.

5.10 A degree of longitude is LESS than a degree of latitude.

SIX

How to Plot
a True Course on a
Nautical Chart

SELECTING A PROPER COURSE LINE

Learning to plot a true course on a nautical chart is as simple as learning to draw a line between two points and measuring the course angle of this line with a protractor. Here are a few safety points to consider before you draw your course line.

FIRST: Are there any obstructions along your intended course line?

Check the water depths along your course line against the draft of your vessel. Vessel draft is defined as the measurement from the waterline to the lowest part of your boat (under the water). Remember, your boat draws more water in freshwater than in saltwater. Develop a *margin of error* factor in feet that fits the draft of your boat. I use six feet as my margin of error and I highlight all the areas on the chart that show depths below this level. (My boat draws two feet.) Remember that the water depths shown on nautical charts are averages and are, therefore, subject to variances. In my boating area, the tide can be up to two feet below datum on certain days.

Check for rocks, shoals, and any other obstructions near your course line. Don't plot a course line too near an obstruction. Allow yourself some leeway and a margin for error. When your intended course fails these criteria, plot a different course.

Second: Have you selected the best aids to navigation as waypoints in anticipation of the potential weather that you may experience on your trip?

Lighted aids are best for running at night. Sounding aids are best for reduced visibility operation. Fixed aids are often structures built on rocks, shoals, or piles in shallow water. Approaching close aboard (near) these aids can damage your boat. Prudent mariners avoid operating their vessel in periods of restricted visibility or in heavy seas. For safety's sake, always be prepared for the worst.

Third: Plot to aids at reasonable distances. The larger the interval traveled between aids, the greater your chance for piloting error.

HOW TO MEASURE A COURSE LINE ANGLE WITH A PARAGLIDE PLOTTER

The paraglide plotter is a good navigational instrument to use on a small boat since it rolls easily on a chart without losing the course angle. It is always best to plot your course on a large flat table before you leave the dock. Plotting a course on a bouncing boat when your attention is directed to lookout duties and other boat operation tasks can easily lead to piloting errors.

Paraglide plotters are used along with the meridians of longitude (the vertical lines) on a nautical chart. Be sure that you have selected a meridian and not a LORAN TD line.

Use the following simple procedure for plotting a course with a paraglide plotter:

Step 1. Set the course line.

- Place the edge of the paraglide plotter along your intended course line.
- Check along the course line for obstructions.
- If your course line is clear of obstructions, draw a light course line on the chart using a sharp pencil. I like to use an automatic pencil with a 0.05 HB lead.

Step 2. Establish your general direction.

- Draw a quadrant (see Figure 6.1) on your Piloting Worksheet. You will find a sample Piloting Worksheet in Appendix 7.
- Place an arrow on the quadrant in the direction in which you plan to head.
- Make a mental note of this direction (between 090 and 180 degrees).

Remember that the course scales on your plotter have reciprocal readings. Use the quadrant technique to minimize the possibility of reading your plotter incorrectly. Make it a practice to double check each plotter reading before accepting it.

Figure 6.2 shows Steps 1 and 2. By drawing an arrow on your

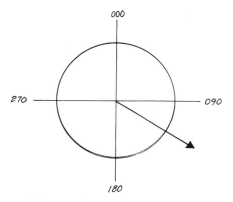

Fig. 6.1   A Quadrant. *(F. J. Larkin)*

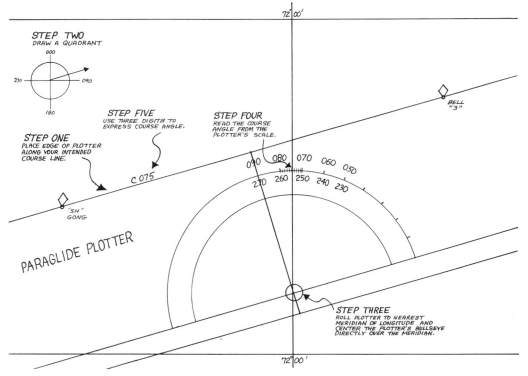

Fig. 6.2   Drawing a True Course Line with a Paraglide Plotter.
(F. J. Larkin)

quadrant in the general direction of your intended course, you have determined that your course will be between 090 and 180 True.

Step 3. Measure the course angle.

- Roll your paraglide plotter to the nearest meridian of longitude and center the plotter's bull's-eye directly over the meridian. Keep a steady downward pressure on your plotter during this procedure so that it doesn't slip and lose the course angle.

- Close one eye and recheck the position of the bulls-eye over the meridian. Figure 6.2 illustrates Step 3.

Step 4. Read your course on the plotter.

- To read your course angle, sight along the meridian of longitude line on the chart from the bull's-eye to where it intersects the course scales on your plotter.

- Double check your quadrant to ensure that you have selected the correct direction reading on the course scale.

- Read your course angle from the plotter. I find that I get more accurate and consistent readings when I close one eye and position myself directly over the plotter when reading a course angle.

Step 5. Write your course.

- Use three digits to express your course angle. For example, a course angle of 9 degrees is written as 009. A course angle of 75 degrees is written as 075.

These five steps are illustrated in Figure 6.2.

HOW TO MEASURE A COURSE LINE ANGLE WITH PARALLEL RULES

Parallel rules are used with the compass rose on a nautical chart. The major difficulty with using parallel rules on a small boat is the potential for slippage when you walk this instrument from your course line to the compass rose. It is always best to plot your course before leaving the dock. As mentioned, plotting a course on a bouncing boat when your attention is distracted by lookout and other duties can easily lead to piloting errors.

Step 1. Set the course line.

- Place the edge of the parallel rules along your intended course line.

- Check along the course line for obstructions.

- If the course line is clear of obstructions, draw a light course line on your chart with a sharp pencil. Figure 6.3 illustrates Step 1.

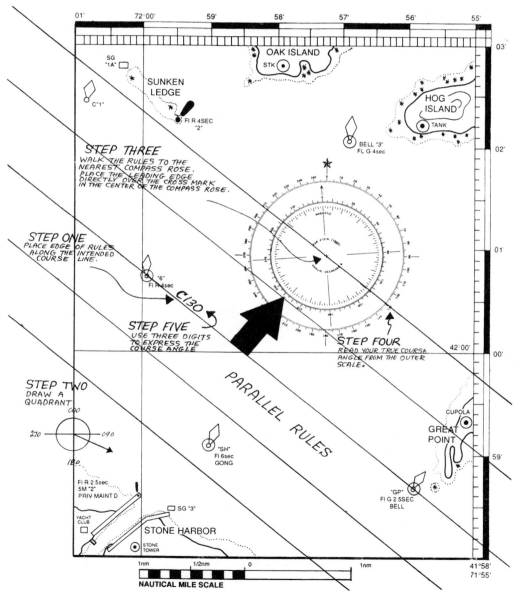

Fig. 6.3 Reading a True Course with Parallel Rules. *(F. J. Larkin)*

Step 2. Establish your general direction.

- Draw a quadrant on your Piloting Worksheet.
- Place an arrow on your quadrant in the direction in which you plan to head.
- Make a mental note of the direction (between 090 and 180 degrees).

As your parallel rules intersect the compass rose, you have the options of reading two course angles in opposite directions. The quadrant technique will help minimize the chance of reading the compass rose backwards. Review Figure 6.3 and note the two course options on the compass rose.

Step 3. Measure the course angle.

- Walk your parallel rules from your course line to the nearest compass rose.
- Place the edge of the rule directly over the cross mark in the center of the compass rose.
- Close one eye and recheck that the edge of the rule is directly over the cross mark.

Step 4. Read your course on the rules.

- Sight along the edge of the rule in the direction that you intend to head. Read your true course angle from the true scale, which is the outer scale on the compass rose.
- Double check the quadrant on your Piloting Worksheet to make certain that you have selected the correct course direction. Many piloting errors are made by selecting the reciprocal or opposite course heading.

Step 5. Write your course.

- Express your course angle with three digits.

Figure 6.3 illustrates this step-by-step procedure.

HOW TO WALK PARALLEL RULES ON A CHART

Step 1. Place the edge of the parallel rules on your intended course line.

Step 2. Press down on one of the rules (call it Rule A) and hold it steady on the chart.

Step 3. Carefully move the other rule (call it Rule B) toward the nearest compass rose.

Step 4. Press down Rule B and hold it steady on the chart.

Step 5. Release the pressure on Rule A and move it to a position alongside (parallel to) Rule B.

Repeat Steps 1 through 5 until the leading edge of your parallel rules is positioned directly over the cross mark at the center of the compass rose. Practice this technique until you can accomplish the movement without the rules slipping and losing the course angle.

LABELING YOUR COURSE ON A NAUTICAL CHART

Only true courses are plotted on a nautical chart. Any other course would be an incorrect angle. It is customary to use true headings in degrees when labeling a course line but the suffix "T" for true is not used. Course headings without suffixes are assumed to be true by experienced navigators. The prefix "C" is written before the three digit course heading to indicate "Course."

Label your course above the course line and toward the point of departure. Always write headings using three digits. A heading of eighty-four degrees is expressed as "C 084." It is not necessary to use the degree sign when labeling a course line (see Figure 6.4).

Some navigators label their course lines with magnetic headings. It is customary to use the suffix "M" when labeling a magnetic heading. A magnetic course heading of two-hundred and seventy-four degrees would be written "C 274M" (see Figure 6.5).

Fig. 6.4 Labeling a Course Line with a True Course. *(F. J. Larkin)*

Fig. 6.5 Labeling a Course Line with a Magnetic Course. *(F. J. Larkin)*

PRACTICE PROBLEMS

These problems will help you develop your skill at measuring course angles. Use a Piloting Practice Chart to plot and label your true courses and a Piloting Worksheet to record your quadrant and other piloting computations. Both these documents are available in Appendix 7.

1. Plan a trip from Gong "SH", northeast of Stone Harbor, to Bell "3", southwest of Hog Island. What is your true course heading? Plot and label your course line.

2. Plan a trip from the Bell "3", southwest of Hog Island, to Lighted Buoy "6", south of Sunken Ledge. What is your true course? Plot and label your course line.

3. Your boat is on a heading of 130 degrees true from Lighted Buoy "6". What aid to navigation can you expect to pass on this heading? Plot and label your true course.

   (Don't become confused. This is just a different twist to the plotting techniques. Simply reverse the plotting process: Step 5 to Step 1. Set the course angle on the plotting tool and move it back to Buoy "6". Then draw your course line from Buoy "6".)

4. A friend has radioed that he is located at 42 degrees, 01.8 minutes North; 72 degrees, 00.5 minutes West. What is the true course to his position from your location at Bell "GP", southwest of Great Point? Plot and label your true course.

   (Another easy twist. First, find your friend's LAT/LON position using the techniques learned in Chapter 5. Plot it and then draw a course line to it from Bell "GP". Then use your plotter to measure the course angle.)

ANSWERS

1. C 024.
2. C 235.
3. Bell "GP" FL G 2.5 sec.
4. C 318.

These answers are plotted for you in Figure 6.6.

Reader Study Note

First understand how to plot a true course. Practice Problems 1 and 2 deal with this issue. Problem 3 is a simple reversal of 1 and 2. You are given the course and asked to plot it from a known point. Problem 4 is

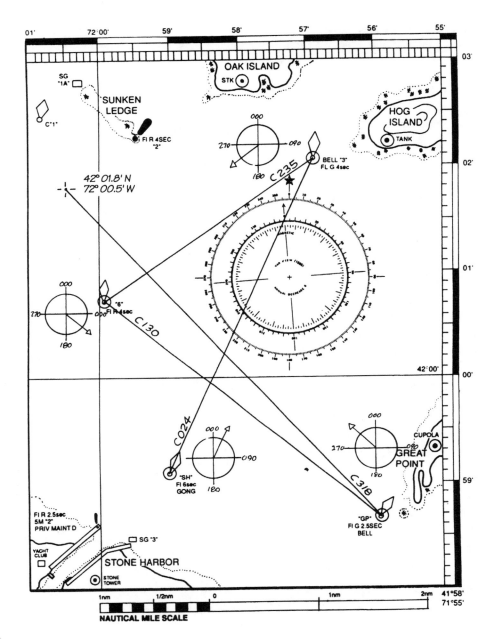

Fig. 6.6   Practice Problems Plotted on a Piloting Practice Chart.
(F. J. Larkin)

the same as 1 and 2 except that you are asked to plot a position using latitude and longitude. These are all typical course plots that you will come across in actual piloting situations.

Reader Progress Note

You now should know how to plot and measure a true course heading on a nautical chart. Remember that you can't use a true course for your boat's compass heading. Converting a true course to a compass course is covered in Chapter 10. True courses are used for plotting on nautical charts only. Also note that you must convert a compass course to true in order to plot it on a nautical chart.

REVIEW QUESTIONS

6.1 Vessel draft is defined as the measurement from the water-line to the _____ part of your boat under the water.

6.2 Before drawing your course line, you should check for _____ along your intended course.

6.3 Lighted aids are best for running at _____.

6.4 _____ aids are best for periods of reduced visibility.

6.5 _____ aids to navigation are often structures built on rocks, shoals, or piles in shallow water.

6.6 Traveling long distances between check points can lead to a greater chance for _____ _____.

6.7 Parallel rules have a tendency to _____ on a small, rocking boat.

6.8 Use of the quadrant technique helps avoid a _____ or _____ course reading error.

6.9 Course angles are expressed with _____ digits and are written with the prefix "___" at the place nearest your starting point on the top of your course line.

6.10 Courses written on a course line without a suffix are considered to be _____ courses.

Answers

6.1 Vessel draft is defined as the measurement from the water-line to the LOWEST part of your boat under the water.

6.2 Before drawing your course line, you should check for OBSTRUCTIONS along your intended course.

6.3 Lighted aids are best for running at NIGHT.

6.4 SOUNDING aids are best for periods of reduced visibility.

6.5 FIXED aids to navigation are often structures built on rocks, shoals, or piles in shallow water.

6.6 Traveling long distances between check points can lead to a greater chance for PILOTING ERRORS.

6.7 Parallel rules have a tendency to SLIP on a small, rocking boat.

6.8 Use of the quadrant technique helps avoid a RECIPROCAL or REVERSED course reading error.

6.9 Course angles are expressed with THREE digits and are written with the prefix "C" at the place nearest your starting point on the top of your course line.

6.10 Courses written on a course line without a suffix are considered to be TRUE courses.

SEVEN

How to Measure
Distance on
a Nautical Chart

In review, you should already know that the latitude scale is located on the right- and left-hand margins of a nautical chart, and that one minute of latitude is equal to one nautical mile (nm). Therefore, only the latitude scale can be used for measuring distance.

Most charts provide a "Nautical Mile Scale," which also can be used for measuring distance on a nautical chart. Remember, the longitude scale is never used because one minute of longitude is less than one nautical mile, except at the equator.

DIVIDERS: YOUR MEASURING TOOL

A good set of dividers is an essential tool for measuring distance. Your dividers should have an adjusting screw to tighten the tension of the arms. A loose divider arm can slip when it is moved and cause a measurement error in piloting. Add a small screwdriver to your navigation kit to use for adjusting the tension of the arms of your dividers.

TECHNIQUE FOR MEASURING A SHORT DISTANCE ON A NAUTICAL CHART

A short distance is one that is less than the width of the opening created when your dividers are expanded to no more than a 60-degree angle. When your dividers are opened more than 60 degrees, the accuracy of your measurement will decrease. Use the measuring technique for long distances, explained in the next section, whenever you need to open the dividers beyond 60 degrees to measure a distance. Follow these simple steps for measuring short distances on a nautical chart:

Step 1. Set one point of your dividers at the starting point on your course line and the other point at the destination point without opening the dividers beyond 60 degrees.

Step 2. Being careful not to disturb the opening, move your dividers to either the latitude scale at the left or right margin or to the nautical mile scale on the chart.

- Place one point of the dividers on a whole mile mark (minute line) and let the other point fall along the scale line into a second or tenth of a minute scale.

Step 3. Read the distance in nautical miles (nm) and tenths of miles. One tenth of a nautical mile equals about 600 feet (about the length of two football fields).

- If the scales on your nautical chart are graded in seconds, remember that one second is equal to 1/60th of a nautical mile or 100 feet.

TECHNIQUE FOR MEASURING A LONG DISTANCE ON A NAUTICAL CHART

A long distance is defined as a distance that cannot be measured within the width of a pair of dividers opened no more than 60 degrees. Follow these simple steps when measuring long distances on a nautical chart:

Step 1. Preset your dividers to a whole mile or a multiple-mile increment. Do not open your dividers more than 60 degrees.

- Write the preset distance that you select on your Piloting Worksheet. Use the nautical mile scale or the latitude scale to preset your dividers.

Step 2. Place one point of your dividers on the starting point of your course line and lay the second point along your course line toward your destination so that it touches the course line.

Step 3. Leaving the second point in place, swing or walk the first point of your preset dividers down your course line toward your destination.

- Continue the swings until you can't make a complete swing without passing your destination point.

- Make it a practice to write the number of swings that you make on your Piloting Worksheet at this time. It is easy to forget this number or use a wrong number and have to remeasure your course line.

Step 4. Without removing the point of your dividers from the last full swing-cycle location on your course line, compress the other arm of your dividers carefully and place its point on your destination place. (Note that the opening of your dividers is now less than the original preset width.)

Step 5. Being careful not to disturb the opening, move your dividers to the latitude scale or the nautical mile scale.

- Maneuver your dividers so that one point is placed at a whole mile mark (minute line) and the other point falls along the scale line within a tenth of a minute or second scale.

- Read the distance in miles and tenths of miles. Note that if your chart has a "second" scale, don't forget that one second is equal to 1/60th of a nautical mile.

Step 6. Compute the total distance by multiplying the number of times that you walked (swung) your dividers by the preset width of the dividers.

- Add the final distance measured in Step 5.

- Do your math on your Piloting Worksheet. For example:

Number of swings or walks	4
Divider opening width	1.0 nm
$4 \times 1.0 =$	4.0 nm
Add Step 5	0.9 nm
Distance of course line is	4.9 nm

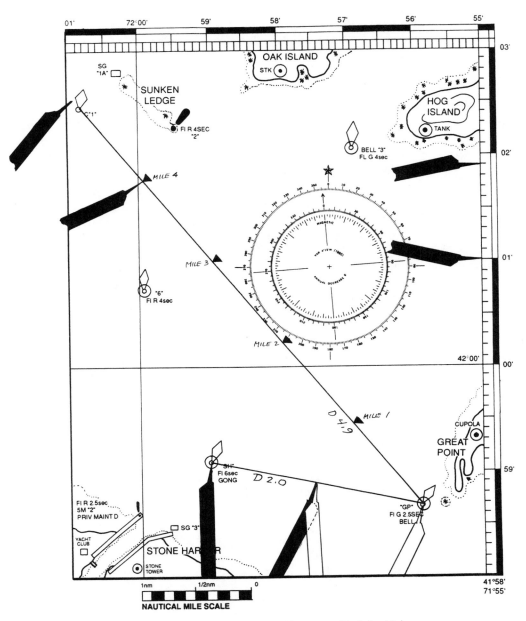

Fig. 7.1 Measuring Distance. *(F. J. Larkin)*

LABELING DISTANCE ON A NAUTICAL CHART

Distance is written under the course line. The smallest increment of distance is 0.1 nautical miles (nm) or approximately 600 feet or 200 yards.

Distance is always calculated in nautical miles. It is not necessary to add a suffix when you write distance because it is assumed to be nautical miles unless labeled differently. The prefix "D" is written before the numbers to indicate distance.

A distance of 4.9 nautical miles is written as "D 4.9." Notice how distance is labeled in Figure 7.1.

EXERCISE: To fully understand these measuring techniques, complete the following exercise. Plan a trip from Gong "SH" to Bell "GP" on a Piloting Practice Chart from Appendix 7.

1. Draw in your course line.
2. Preset your dividers to a one-mile increment (opening) and measure the distance of your course line. You should be able to make two complete walks with your dividers along the course line. Use Figure 7.1 for checking this measurement.
3. Your distance is two nautical miles. Label the distance under the course line.

Now continue your trip from Bell "GP" to Can C "1", west of Sunken Ledge on the Piloting Practice Chart.

1. Draw your course line.
2. Preset your dividers to a one-mile increment and measure the distance of the course line. You should be able to make four complete walks with your dividers along the course line and have a distance of less than a mile remaining (a distance less than the preset opening of your dividers).
3. Next, contract your dividers to measure the distance remaining on your course line. You should get a reading of approximately 9/10th of a mile. Your distance is 4.9 nautical miles. Plot and label the distance under your course line.

Figure 7.1 illustrates this exercise.

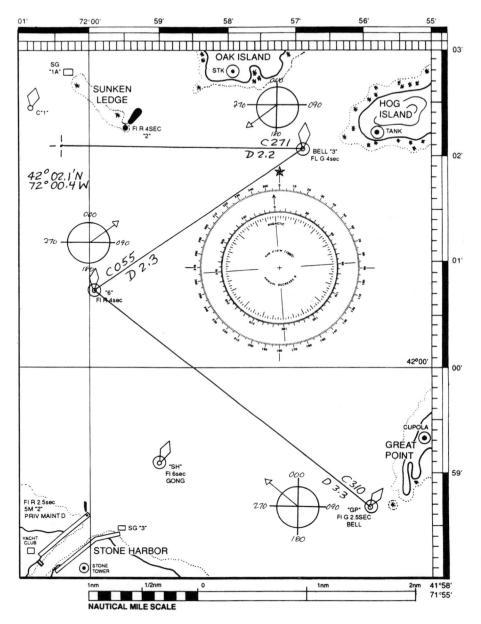

Fig. 7.2 Practice Problems Plotted on a Piloting Practice Chart.
(F. J. Larkin)

PRACTICE PROBLEMS

1. Plan a trip from Bell "GP", off Great Point, to Can "6", south of Sunken Ledge. Plot and label your course. Measure the distance of your course line. Label the distance under your course line.

2. Continue your trip to Lighted Bell "3", southwest of Hog Island. Measure the length of your course line. Plot and label your course.

3. Friends call you on the radio and indicate that they have run out of fuel at 42 degrees, 02.1 minutes North and 72 degrees, 00.4 minutes West. You are still fishing at Bell "3". Plot and label your true course and distance to their location. Solution: Find the LAT/LON position then draw a course line to this point.

Plot these problems on a Piloting Practice Chart which can be found at the back of this book in Appendix 7. If you get stuck, the problems are plotted for you in Figure 7.2. You will learn quicker if you try to plot these problems before you look at the answers.

Reader Study Note

Completing the practice problems is part of the learning experience. Navigation is best learned by doing. It is easy to make simple errors when measuring distance and you will need to master the techniques illustrated in this chapter to minimize these errors in real piloting situations.

Reader Progress Note

In addition to plotting and measuring true courses on a nautical chart, you now should be able to measure and label distance on your course line. Unfortunately, you still can't use these courses on your boat's compass heading. You will learn how to make this conversion in Chapter 10.

REVIEW QUESTIONS

7.1   A good set of dividers has an _____ screw to tighten the _____ of the arms.

7.2   Dividers opened more than 60 degrees can decrease your _____ when measuring distance.

7.3   If the number of walks with your dividers is 20, and the width of the opening of your dividers is 2.0 nm, what is your total distance when the remaining distance of the course line is 1.2 nm?

7.4   What measuring technique would you use to find a distance of 1.8 nautical miles on the Piloting Practice Chart?

7.5   Distance is written _____ the course line.

Answers

7.1   A good set of dividers has an ADJUSTING screw to tighten the TENSION of the arms.

7.2   Dividers opened more than 60 degrees can decrease your ACCURACY when measuring distance.

7.3 $20 \times 2.0 = 40 + 1.2 = 41.2$ nm.

7.4   The technique for measuring a long distance because the dividers would have to be open more than 60 degrees to measure 1.8 nm.

7.5   Distance is written UNDER the course line.

EIGHT

Military Time

Time is defined as the hours and minutes that it takes to travel from your place of departure to a destination point. Military time is commonly used for labeling course lines. A common error in piloting is made when converting time. Here are a few important points to remember:

- Hours have sixty (60) minutes, not 100.
- Minutes have sixty (60) seconds, not 100.
- Time is expressed in minutes in the dead reckoning formula.

In military time, the day starts at one second past midnight. Military time is written as four digits (see Table 8.1).

- The first two digits express the hours of the day (01 through 24).
- The last two digits express the minutes in the hour (01 through 59).

Table 8.1 Military Time

STD	Military	STD	Military
TIME	TIME	TIME	TIME
1 AM	0100	1 PM	1300
2 AM	0200	2 PM	1400
3 AM	0300	3 PM	1500
4 AM	0400	4 PM	1600
5 AM	0500	5 PM	1700
6 AM	0600	6 PM	1800
7 AM	0700	7 PM	1900
8 AM	0800	8 PM	2000
9 AM	0900	9 PM	2100
10 AM	1000	10 PM	2200
11 AM	1100	11 PM	2300
12 AM	1200	12 PM	2400

HOW TO ADD TIME

The secrets for adding time accurately are:

Step 1. Add the minutes first.

Step 2. Convert the minutes over fifty-nine minutes to hours by subtracting increments of 60.

Step 3. Add the hours.

―――――――――

EXAMPLE: Add 45 minutes to 1430 hours:

		hrs.	min.
Add the 45 minutes.		14	30
(30 + 45 = 75 minutes).	+	00	45
	Total	14	75
Convert the excess minutes to hours.	−	00	60
(75 − 60 = 15 min)			15
Add the hours.	+	01	00
(14 + 1 = 15)	Total	15	15

In effect you add 0115 (1 hr, 15 minutes) to 1400 and get 1515 hours.

―――――――――

PRACTICE PROBLEMS

1. Add 24 minutes to 1520 hours.
2. You depart at 0900. Your travel time is 2 hrs and 45 minutes. What is your ETA (estimated time of arrival)?
3. You depart at 1250 and travel for 1 hr and 25 minutes. What is your ETA? (Apply Step 2.)
4. You depart at 2430 and plan to travel 3 hrs and 15 minutes. What is your ETA? (When passing midnight, I do the addition and then subtract 2400 to get the correct early morning time.)

ANSWERS

1.
```
        15 20
      +    24
        15 44
```

2.
```
   DEP    09 00
   TRAV   02 45
   ETA    11 45
```

3.
```
   DEP      12 50
   TRAV   + 01 25
            13 75
          -    60
            13 15
          +01 00
   ETA      14 15
```

4.
```
   DEP      24 30
   TRAV   + 03 15
            27 45
          - 24 00
   ETA      03 45
```

HOW TO SUBTRACT TIME

The secrets for subtracting time are:

Step 1. Subtract the minutes first.

Step 2. When you are subtracting more from less (i.e., 55 from 25) bring a whole hour over to the minute column.

   • Remember that a whole hour is sixty minutes (not 100).

EXAMPLE: Subtract 47 minutes from 1430 hours.

First, bring a whole hour over to the minute column. This leaves the hour column as 13 and the minute column as 90:

$$30 + 60 = 90 \text{ minutes.}$$

Next, subtract 47 from 90:

$$90 - 47 = 43.$$

Write your answer as 1343 hours:

$$
\begin{array}{r}
13\ 90 \\
-\ 00\ 47 \\
\hline
13\ 43
\end{array}
$$

PRACTICE PROBLEMS

1. Subtract 25 minutes from 1030 hours.

2. Your time of travel is 2 hrs and 45 minutes. You want to arrive at 1100. What time should you depart?

3. You plan to depart at 0800 and arrive at 1045. What is your travel time?

4. Your travel time is 4 hrs and 24 mins. You need to arrive at 0130. What is the latest time you can depart? (Watch out for this new twist: 0130 hrs is an early morning time. At midnight, start with 2400 hrs and work backward.)

ANSWERS

$$
\begin{array}{ll}
1. & \begin{array}{r}
10\ 30 \\
-\ 00\ 25 \\
\hline
10\ 05
\end{array}
\end{array}
$$

$$
\begin{array}{lll}
2. & \text{ETA} & 11\ 00 \\
   & \text{TRAV} & -\ 02\ 45 \\
\cline{3-3}
   & \text{DEP} & 08\ 15
\end{array}
$$

3. ETA   10 45
   DEP   − 08 00
   TRAV   02 45

4. First deal with the time back to 2400 hrs:
   TRAV   04 24
             − 01 30
   Time to go   02 54

   Next deal with 2400:

              24 00
   Time to go − 02 54
   DEP   21 06

Reader Study Note

Adding and subtracting time is often confusing to many people. Problem 4 of the subtraction problems stops many novices. Take the time to understand these time calculations. Make up problems of your own to solve until you feel that you are comfortable with time. Time conversions are part of most piloting problems that you must solve to get full enjoyment from your boating experience. Piloting problems should be written out on a Piloting Worksheet (see Appendix 7). This practice gives you a quick reference when you find yourself off your mark and can save you the time of having to redo the entire piloting calculation.

Reader Progress Note

Timing errors are very common in piloting. Using the techniques provided in this chapter, you should be able to convert time with ease. You should be ready to tackle some dead reckoning by now.

NINE

Calculating Your
Dead Reckoning
Position

Many navigation students panic at this point because of their fear of math. Let me relieve your fears. You need only know how to add, subtract, multiply, and divide. Every required piloting computation is explained for you with an easy-to-follow, step-by-step guide to help you understand the dead reckoning (DR) principles.

THE PILOTING WORKSHEET

In Appendix 7, you will find a sample form called a Piloting Worksheet. From this point on, start using this worksheet for all your computations. I suggest that you continue to use this worksheet for plotting all of your boat trips after you complete this book. I use it even after 25 or more years of piloting a boat. On large commercial vessels, similar logs are sometime required by law.

TERMINOLOGY

Before you get to the formula for calculating a dead reckoning (DR) position, you need to become familiar with a few new terms and definitions.

DR Course Line

The DR course line is the line you draw on a nautical chart that your boat is expected to follow. Your course line will always have a course heading, a speed, a distance, and time calculations associated with it.

> CAUTION: *A DR course line makes no allowance for steering errors and for the effects of wind and current on your boat.*

Course Heading

The term *course* refers to the direction in which your boat is supposed to be pointed or your boat's planned direction through the water. It is also called your *heading* or boat's heading.

The course that you steer by the compass on your boat is different than the true course that is plotted on a nautical chart. You will learn to compensate for this difference in Chapter 10.

Distance

Distance is the entire length of your trip or the length of a single leg of a trip that you intend to travel. Distance is always expressed in nautical miles. *Trip leg* is a term that defines one segment of a trip, i.e., the distance from one buoy to another could be a leg of a trip.

Speed

Speed, expressed in knots (nautical miles per hour), is the rate at which your boat travels through the water. Only speed through the water is used to calculate distance in the DR formula. Speed through the water can be different from speed over the ground due to an unfavorable current off the bow of your boat.

Current

Current is defined as a flow of water. Current direction is called *set*. Current speed is called *drift*. Current off (hitting) your boat's bow decreases the speed of your boat. Current off the stern of your boat increases the speed of your boat. Current off the beam (side) of your boat affects both your boat's speed and direction.

Time

Time is defined as the hours and minutes that it takes to travel from your place of departure to a specified destination point. As discussed in Chapter 8, military time is commonly used for labeling time on a course line.

THE DEAD RECKONING FORMULA: 60D = ST

"60 times DISTANCE equals SPEED times TIME."

If you can multiply and divide, you won't have any trouble with this formula. Include a small calculator in your navigation kit to help you with these calculations. Don't forget some spare batteries. Solar calculators don't work very well at night.

The basic principles of the dead reckoning formula are as follows:

1. Whatever you do to one side of the formula, you must do to the other side of the formula.

2. If you know two of the factors in the formula, you can always calculate the value of the third factor.

3. Solve for distance, speed, or time by isolating them to one side of the formula.

Think about how these principles work as you learn how to calculate distance, speed, and time using the DR formula.

HOW TO CALCULATE DISTANCE

Distance is expressed in nautical miles in piloting. You can solve for distance by dividing both sides of the DR formula by 60. This isolates distance (D) to one side of the formula and the value of D to the other side of the equation.

$$60 \times D = S \times T$$

$$\frac{60 \times D}{60} = \frac{S \times T}{60} \quad \text{or} \quad D = \frac{S \times T}{60}$$

or Distance equals Speed × Time divided by 60.

EXAMPLE: If your speed is 10 kts and you travel for 30 minutes, your distance is 5 nautical miles.

$$60 \times D = S \times T$$

$$60 \times D = 10 \times 30 \quad \text{or} \quad D = \frac{10 \times 30}{60} \quad \text{or} \quad D = 5 \, nm.$$

PRACTICE PROBLEMS

1. You have been traveling at 12.5 kts for the past two hours. How far have you traveled?

2. If you travel for 5.5 hours at 18 kts, how much distance will you cover?

3. Your speed is 15 kts. You plan to depart at 0800. Your ETA is 1400. How much distance will you travel? (Don't forget to convert hours to minutes by multiplying by 60.)

Answers to these distance practice problems are found in Figure 9.1.

HOW TO CALCULATE SPEED

Speed is expressed in nautical miles per hour or knots. Solve for speed by dividing both sides of the DR formula by the time. This isolates speed (S) to one side of the formula and the value of S to the other side.

$$60 \times D = S \times T$$

$$\frac{60 \times D}{T} = \frac{S \times T}{T} \quad \text{or} \quad S = \frac{60 \times D}{T}$$

or Speed equals 60 × Distance divided by Time.

PILOTING WORKSHEET

60D=ST   **TVMDC** ADD WEST DOWN

DATE	TRIP
	DISTANCE PROBLEMS

1.
$$S = 12.5 \quad T = 2.0 \text{ HRS} \times 60 = 120 \text{ MINUTES}.$$

$$60 D = S T$$
$$\frac{60 \times D}{60} = \frac{12.5 \times 120}{60} = \underline{25.0 \text{ nm}} \text{ DISTANCE}$$

2.
$$S = 18 \quad T = 5.5 \text{ HRS} \times 60 = 330 \text{ MINUTES}$$

$$60 D = S T$$
$$\frac{60 \times D}{60} = \frac{18 \times 330}{60} = \underline{99 \text{ nm}} \text{ DISTANCE}$$

3.
$$S = 15 \quad \text{DEP } 0800 \quad \text{ETA } 1400$$

$$\begin{array}{l} \text{ETA} \quad 1400 \\ \underline{\text{DEP} \quad 0800} \\ \text{TIME OF TRAVEL } 0600 \end{array} \quad T = 6 \text{ HRS} \times 60 = 360 \text{ MINUTES}.$$

$$60 D = S T$$
$$\frac{60 \times D}{60} = \frac{15 \times 360}{60} = 90 \text{ nm DISTANCE}$$

Fig. 9.1 Piloting Worksheet—Answers for Distance Practice Problems.

EXAMPLE: If your distance is 15 miles and you travel for 90 minutes, your speed is 10 kts (nautical miles per hour).

$$60 \times D \ = \ S \times T$$

$$60 \times 15 \ = \ S \times 90$$

or

$$S \ = \ \frac{60 \times 15}{90} \quad \text{or} \quad S = 10 \text{ kts.}$$

PRACTICE PROBLEMS

1. Departing at 0730, how fast were you going if you traveled 10 nautical miles by 0945?

2. What speed must you use to get to a rendezvous point that is 25 miles down the coast in 3 hours?

3. Departing at 0400, you arrive at a point 20 miles offshore at 0730. What was your speed?

Answers to these problems are found on the Piloting Worksheet shown in Figure 9.2.

Labeling Speed on Your Course Line

Since your speed may vary on each course line or leg of your trip, it is usually not written on the chart. However, speed can be written under your course line toward the starting point of the line if you desire. Use a light pencil that can be easily erased. Define the entry as speed with the prefix "S." There is no need for a suffix with a speed entry because speed is assumed to be knots (nautical miles per hour) unless otherwise labeled (see Figure 9.3).

Many mariners record speed on a separate trip log sheet. A sample Trip Log sheet is included in Appendix 7.

PILOTING WORKSHEET

60D=ST	TVMDC ADD WEST DOWN

DATE	TRIP SPEED PROBLEMS

1. $D = 10.0$ DEP 0730   ETA 0945

    ETA   09 45 $T = 2$ HRS 15 MIN OR $120 + 15 = 135$ MIN.
    − DEP   07 30
TIME OF TRAV. 02 15 $60 D = ST$
$$\frac{60 \times 10}{135} = \frac{S \times \cancel{135}}{\cancel{135}} = \frac{600}{135} \text{ OR } 4.4 \text{ KTS}$$

2. $D = 25.0$ $T = 3$ HRS $\times 60 = 180$ MIN.

    $60 D = ST$
$$\frac{60 \times 25}{180} = \frac{S \times \cancel{180}}{\cancel{180}} = \frac{1500}{180} \text{ OR } 8.3 \text{ KTS}.$$

3. $D = 20.0$ DEP 0400   ETA 0730

    ETA   0730 $T = 3$ HRS 30 MIN
    DEP   0400   OR $180 + 30 = 210$ MIN.
TIME OF TRAV. 03 30

    $60 D = ST$
$$\frac{60 \times 20}{210} = \frac{S \times \cancel{210}}{\cancel{210}} = \frac{120}{21} = 5.7 \text{ KTS}.$$

Fig. 9.2 Piloting Worksheet—Answers for Speed Practice Problems.

C 085
S 10.0

Fig. 9.3 Labeling Speed on a Course Line.
(F. J. Larkin)

HOW TO CALCULATE TIME

Time is expressed in minutes in the dead reckoning formula. Solve for time by dividing both sides of the DR formula by speed. This isolates time (T) to one side of the DR equation and the value of T to the other side of the equation.

$$60 \times D = S \times T$$

$$\frac{60 \times D}{S} = \frac{S \times T}{S} \quad \text{or} \quad T = \frac{60 \times D}{S}$$

or Time equals 60 × Distance divided by Speed.

─────────

EXAMPLE: If your distance is 21 nautical miles and your speed is 12 kts, your time is 105 minutes or 1 hr and 45 mins (0145). Departing at 1300, you would arrive at 1445. Let's look at how it's done.

First determine your time of travel:

$$60 \times D = S \times T$$

$$\frac{60 \times 21}{12} = \frac{12 \times T}{12} \quad \text{or} \quad T = \frac{60 \times 21}{12} \quad \text{or 105 minutes.}$$

Converted, time equals 1 hr, 45 mins:

1300	Time of departure
+ 0145	Time of travel
1445	ETA (estimated time of arrival)

─────────

PRACTICE PROBLEMS

1. How much time will it take to travel 35 miles at 12 kts?

2. You depart at 0900 at a speed of 15 kts on a trip leg of 25 nautical miles. At what time will you arrive at your destination?

3. You want to arrive at your home port at 1330 hrs. Currently, you are moored in a cove that is 34.5 nm down the coast. Your best cruising speed is 12.5 kts. What is the latest time that you can leave the cove to arrive home at 1330 hrs?

Refer to the Piloting Worksheet in Figure 9.4 for the answers to these time problems.

─────────

PILOTING   WORKSHEET

60D=ST   **TVMDC** ADD WEST DOWN

DATE	TRIP *TIME PROBLEMS*

1.   D = 35   S = 12 KTS.

60 D = S T

$5\dfrac{\cancel{60} \times 35}{\cancel{12}} = \dfrac{\cancel{12} \times T}{\cancel{12}}$ = 175 MIN OR 2 HRS 55 MIN.

2.   S = 15 D = 25   DEP 0900

60 D = S T

$4\dfrac{\cancel{60} \times 25}{\cancel{15}} = \dfrac{\cancel{15} \times T}{\cancel{15}}$ = 100 MIN OR 1 HR 40 MIN.

DEP   0900
TRAVEL 0140
ETA   1040

3.   ETA 1330 D = 34.5   S = 12.5

60 D = S T

$\dfrac{60 \times 34.5}{12.5} = \dfrac{\cancel{12.5} \times T}{\cancel{12.5}} = \dfrac{2070}{12.5}$ = 165.6 OR 2 HRS 45.6

ETA   13 30
TRAVEL 02 46
DEP   10 44

Fig. 9.4 Piloting Worksheet—Answers for Time Practice Problems.

How to Label Time at a Fixed Position Along a Course Line

The method for writing time on a course line depends on whether your position is *known* or *calculated*.

Calculated Positions.   Dead reckoning (DR) positions are considered to be projected or calculated positions. Time is written at an angle to the course line at the reckoned position point.

Known Positions.   Your starting point in dead reckoning piloting must always be a known position. Fixes are considered known positions. Buoys are considered equivalent to fixed positions. Time is written horizontally (along the line) at known positions on your DR course line.
     Figure 9.5 shows examples of labeling known and projected time along a course line.

LABELING YOUR DR POSITION

Mark a DR position on your course line with a heavy dot. Draw a semicircle over the dot. Since this is the symbol for a projected or calculated position, write the time at an angle to the course line. Always use four-digit military time. Figure 9.5 shows a labeled DR position.

WHEN YOU SHOULD PLOT YOUR DR POSITION

There are specific times when it is prudent to plot a DR position. A DR position should be plotted:

- Every 30 minutes (at a minimum).
- Each time you change a course heading.
- Each time you change speed.
- Each time you fix your position.
- In confined waters, each time that you pass close aboard an aid to navigation.

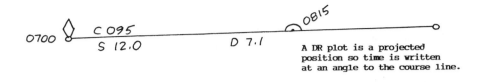

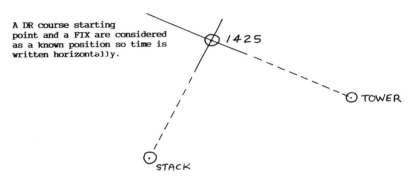

Fig. 9.5   Labeling Time on Calculated and Known Positions.
(F. J. Larkin)

Following these suggestions will keep you aware of your position. The closer you are to hazards, the more frequently you should check your DR position. Factors such as wind and current are constantly acting on your boat and are possibly changing your position.

PRACTICE PROBLEMS

These problems are designed to complete the learning cycle for your dead reckoning calculating techniques. Refer back to the text for the formulas and procedures. Use a Piloting Worksheet and a Piloting Practice Chart for all your calculations and course plots. Write out your 60D = ST calculations. Draw quadrants for each plotted course.

1. You have been traveling at a speed of 12 kts for 45 minutes. How much distance have you traveled?

2. You depart your dock at 0900 and intend to cruise for 9 miles to join some friends. If your speed is 10 kts, what is your ETA (estimated time of arrival) at your friends' position?

3. You want to cruise 25 miles to a harbor at a speed of 18 kts. It is a clear, calm day. To arrive in the harbor by noon, what is the latest time you should depart?

4. At 0900 you depart Bell "GP", off Great Point and head toward Can "1", off Sunken Ledge. With a speed of 5 kts, what is your ETA to the can? Plot and label your course on a Piloting Practice Chart.

5. Arriving at Can "1", you turn immediately and head for Lighted Buoy "6". Your speed is 8 kts for this leg. What is your ETA to Lighted Buoy "6"? Plot and label your course.

6. After fishing for 20 minutes at Lighted Buoy "6", friends call you on the radio and indicate their position is 42 degrees, 01.9 minutes and 71 degrees, 55.3 minutes. Their boat is sinking and they expect to stay afloat for another 10 minutes. There is no other boat around and the top speed of your boat is 15 kts. Can you reach your friends before their boat sinks? What advice would you radio them? Plot and label your course to their position.

7. By 1100, you have successfully rescued your friends and are under way back to your yacht club. One of your friends is hypothermic so you call the harbormaster at Stone Harbor to arrange for an ambulance to meet you at Stone Harbor Yacht Club dock. Estimating that you can make 10 kts in the heavy chop that has just blown up, what ETA to the yacht club dock would you give the harbormaster? Plot and label your course.

The answers to these piloting practice problems are found in Figures 9.6 and 9.7.

Reader Study Note

I like to write the DR formula each time that I make a calculation and always start with 60D = ST. By memorizing this single formula, I can solve for distance, speed, or time by simply moving data around. If you keep the three basic principles in mind, you will not have any problems. This is simple math. Try not to make it complicated for yourself.

Reader Progress Note

You can now compute time, speed, and distance on a true course line and you should be able to calculate your position along a DR course line. Up to this point, you have been working strictly with the nautical chart. Chapter 10 shows you how to convert this work to your boat's compass.

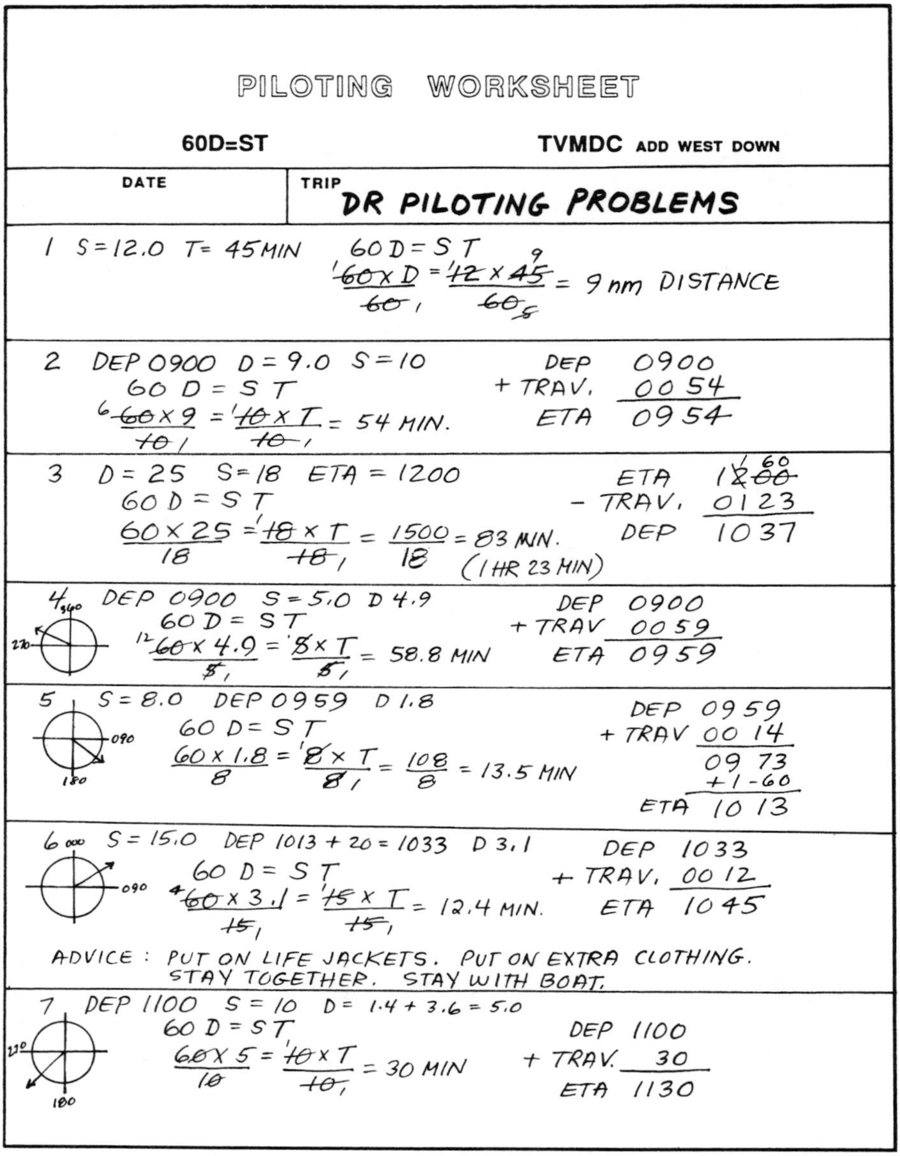

PILOTING WORKSHEET

60D=ST　　　　　**TVMDC** ADD WEST DOWN

DATE	TRIP **DR PILOTING PROBLEMS**

1 $S=12.0$ $T=45MIN$　$60 D = S T$
$\frac{60 \times D}{60} = \frac{12 \times 45}{60} = 9\,nm$ DISTANCE

2 DEP 0900 $D=9.0$ $S=10$
$60 D = S T$
$\frac{60 \times 9}{10} = \frac{10 \times T}{10} = 54$ MIN.

DEP　0900
+ TRAV.　00 54
ETA　0954

3 $D=25$ $S=18$ ETA $=1200$
$60 D = S T$
$\frac{60 \times 25}{18} = \frac{18 \times T}{18} = \frac{1500}{18} = 83$ MIN.
(1 HR 23 MIN)

ETA　1200 60
− TRAV.　0123
DEP　1037

4 DEP 0900 $S=5.0$ D 4.9
$60 D = S T$
$\frac{60 \times 4.9}{5} = \frac{5 \times T}{5} = 58.8$ MIN

DEP　0900
+ TRAV　0059
ETA　0959

5 $S=8.0$ DEP 0959 D 1.8
$60 D = S T$
$\frac{60 \times 1.8}{8} = \frac{8 \times T}{8} = \frac{108}{8} = 13.5$ MIN

DEP 0959
+ TRAV 00 14
09 73
+1 -60
ETA 10 13

6 $S=15.0$ DEP 1013 + 20 = 1033 D 3.1
$60 D = S T$
$\frac{60 \times 3.1}{15} = \frac{15 \times T}{15} = 12.4$ MIN.

DEP　1033
+ TRAV.　00 12
ETA　1045

ADVICE : PUT ON LIFE JACKETS. PUT ON EXTRA CLOTHING. STAY TOGETHER. STAY WITH BOAT.

7 DEP 1100 $S=10$ $D = 1.4 + 3.6 = 5.0$
$60 D = S T$
$\frac{60 \times 5}{10} = \frac{10 \times T}{10} = 30$ MIN

DEP 1100
+ TRAV.　30
ETA 1130

Fig. 9.6　Piloting Worksheet for DR Piloting Practice Problems.

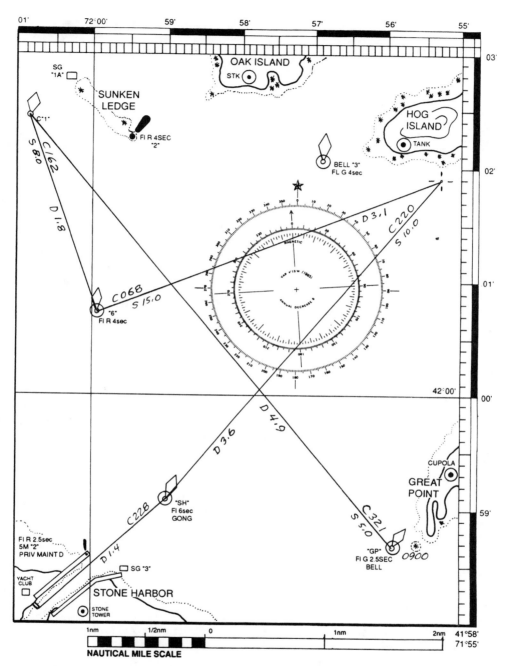

Fig. 9.7   Piloting Practice Chart for DR Piloting Practice Problems.

TEN

Converting True
Courses to
Compass Courses

While true courses work well on a nautical chart, they are useless as a heading for your boat's compass until they are converted to a compass course. The differences between a compass course and a true course are caused by magnetic influences.

One magnetic influence is geographical and is called *variation error*. There are other magnetic influences that are peculiar to your boat. These magnetic influences are called *deviation error*. Both of these magnetic disturbances affect your compass. Therefore, you must learn to understand them and compensate for them in order to pilot your boat accurately and safely.

VARIATION

Variation is a predictable magnetic influence on your compass that is directly related to the position of the magnetic North Pole and the location of your boat on the earth's surface. The needle of your compass is attracted to the magnetic North Pole.

Magnetic north and true north are two distinct locations. The difference (or variation) is the angular measurement between true north and magnetic north from your position on the earth's surface. Because variation is predictable, it is always printed in the center of the compass rose. Flip back to Chapter 1 and review the compass rose in Figure 1.5. When converting courses, always use the compass rose that is closest to your position on a nautical chart.

Variation is expressed in degrees, minutes, and seconds east or west of true north. Note that the compass rose shown in Figure 1.5 has a variation of 4 degrees, 15 minutes West. This means that magnetic north is located 4 degrees, 15 minutes west of true north at this charted position on the earth's surface.

To pilot your boat effectively, you must understand that you can only plot true courses on a nautical chart, that you can only steer a boat using a compass course, and that you must learn to calculate the difference between these two courses.

Annual Increase or Decrease of Variation

The magnetic North Pole is constantly moving. The amount of this movement, or the annual increase or decrease of variation, is shown in the center of the compass rose. You will find that because the magnetic pole is moving, variation must be corrected for the age of the chart by applying this annual change factor.

The annual decrease of variation shown on the compass rose in Figure 1.5 is 8 minutes and the date of the variation is 1985. This means that you should subtract eight minutes of variation for every year since 1985; therefore, in 1987, the variation would be 4 degrees.

In 1990, you would begin to use 3 degrees variation since a total decrease of 45 minutes would have passed during that year due to the rounding up and down process (5 years × 8 minutes = 40 minutes). In 1998 you would use a variation of 2 degrees West.

Note that on a small boat it is often difficult to achieve or maintain single-degree changes to a compass course. Most small-boat compasses are graded in 5- or 10-degree increments. You need to be aware of the annual increase or decrease of variation. However, in the practical setting of a bouncing boat on a choppy sea, the annual increase or decrease of variation becomes a negligent compass course error.

DEVIATION

Magnetic influences found aboard your boat that prevent your compass needle from pointing directly to magnetic north are called *deviation.* Appendixes 1 through 4 explain how to minimize magnetic fields on your boat and how to develop a deviation table.

The difference between your magnetic course (your true course corrected for variation) and your actual compass course is called *deviation error.* In order to compensate for deviation on your boat, you must first measure it and record it in your deviation table.

In a nutshell, computing deviation is accomplished by the following steps:

Step 1. Align your boat on two fixed, charted objects for which you have calculated true bearings from a nautical chart. In Figure 10.1, the tower and the stack have a true bearing of 060 degrees.

Step 2. Calculate your magnetic bearing by applying variation from the nearest compass rose. In Figure 10.1, the variation of 004 degrees West is taken from the nearest compass rose.

Step 3. Record the compass heading of your boat. In Figure 10.1, the compass reads 065 degrees.

Step 4. The difference between the magnetic heading and your compass heading is your deviation.

Compass heading	065
Magnetic heading	064
Deviation	001 W

To develop a full deviation table, take bearings for at least 8 to 12 points of the compass. Plot the findings on a graph and use your deviation table when you convert true and compass courses.

Figure 10.1 illustrates a single step in the deviation table development process. Appendixes 3 and 4 explain a variety of methods for developing your deviation table and provide suggested worksheets and graphs for your use.

THE COURSE CONVERSION FORMULA

MEMORY AID: *"T V M D C, Add West Down."*

I find that the vertical presentation of the course correction formula TVMDC helps me to remember when to add and subtract variation and deviation. Proceed down the formula when you convert a true course to a compass course so that the "Add West Down'" instruction works graphically. Remember that if you "Add West Down," you must "Subtract Easterly Error Down."

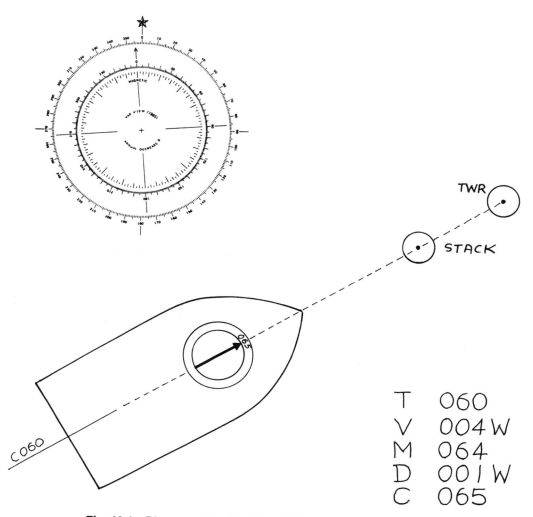

Fig. 10.1   Diagram of the Deviation Table Development Process.
(F. J. Larkin)

EXAMPLE: Convert a true course of 090 degrees to a compass course for use on your boat.

T	True course	090
V	Variation (east or west)	015W
M	Magnetic course	105
D	Deviation (east or west)	005E
C	Compass course	100

Here is how the conversion process works:

- Take the true course from the course that you plot on a nautical chart.
- Read the variation from the compass rose nearest to your plotted course on the nautical chart.
- Calculate the magnetic course by adding westerly to or subtracting easterly variation error from your true course.
- Get the deviation from your boat's deviation table.
- Calculate your compass course by adding westerly to or subtracting easterly deviation error from your magnetic course.

Reread these steps until you fully understand them.

EXAMPLE: Convert a compass course of 270 degrees to a true course for plotting on a nautical chart.

You proceed up the TVMDC formula when you convert from compass to true courses so the "Add West Down" instruction works graphically in reverse. In this case you "Subtract West Up" and "Add East Up."

T	True course	260
V	Variation (east or west)	015W
M	Magnetic course	275
D	Deviation (east or west)	005E
C	Compass course	270

Here is how the conversion process works:

- The compass course is read from your boat's compass.
- Get the deviation from your boat's deviation table.
- Calculate the magnetic course by subtracting westerly from or adding easterly deviation error to the compass course.
- Take the variation from the compass rose nearest to your course line on the nautical chart.
- Calculate the true course by subtracting westerly from or adding easterly variation error to the magnetic course.

COURSE CONVERSION TECHNIQUES

Don't be shy about writing out the TVMDC formula vertically on a Piloting Worksheet when you do piloting problems. The most experienced and accurate navigators follow this practice because it keeps them from making dumb mistakes. In some commercial navigation situations, the use of a worksheet is mandatory. When you do make an error and find yourself off course, the Piloting Worksheet will help you find the problem quicker and help you understand what correction is necessary to get you back on course. Appendix 7 has a sample Piloting Worksheet for your use.

PRACTICE PROBLEMS

	1	2	3	4	5	6
T	___	255	104	025	240	106
V	003W	___	___	010W	005E	___
M	135	250	110	___	___	___
D	005E	___	002E	011E	___	004W
C	___	245	___	___	238	103

ANSWERS

	1	2	3	4	5	6
T	132	255	104	025	240	106
V	003W	005E	006W	010W	005E	007E
M	135	250	110	035	235	099
D	005E	005E	002E	011E	003W	004W
C	130	245	108	024	238	103

Reader Study Note

Remember that you are just correcting two errors. Variation error is always provided in the nearest compass rose. If you operate your boat in a small area, it will pretty much stay the same. If you take my advice in Appendixes 1 through 4, you will minimize your deviation error. It takes a little work to calculate a deviation table, but it really isn't difficult. Follow the step-by-step procedures. Take your time. You'll be glad you did the first time that you get caught in a dense fog!

Reader Progress Note

Not only can you plot your true course on a nautical chart, measure your distance, compute your time, speed, or distance, you can now convert your charted (true) course to a compass course that can be used on your boat. You also should have a basic idea about the creation of a deviation table.

REVIEW QUESTIONS

10.1 _____ influences affect your compass.

10.2 The needle of your compass is _____ to _____ north.

10.3 Because variation is _____, it is printed in the center of the compass rose.

10.4 The magnetic North Pole is constantly _____.

10.5 When converting a true course to a compass course, you must _____ easterly error downward when using the TVMDC formula vertically.

10.6 The annual increase or decrease of the variation is found at the center of the _____ _____.

10.7 True or false:

    a. _____ The magnetic influence called deviation is always found printed on your nautical chart.

    b. _____ The annual increase or decrease of variation is critical to the accuracy of a small boat's compass heading.

    c. _____ The difference between a true course and a magnetic course is called variation error.

    d. _____ The deviation error is the same for all boats.

    e. _____ When converting a compass course to a true course, add easterly deviation.

Answers

10.1   MAGNETIC influences affect your compass.

10.2   The needle of your compass is ATTRACTED to MAGNETIC north.

10.3   Because variation is PREDICTABLE, it is printed in the center of the compass rose.

10.4   The magnetic North Pole is constantly MOVING.

10.5   When converting a true course to a compass course, you must SUBTRACT easterly error downward when using the TVMDC formula vertically.

10.6   The annual increase or decrease of the variation is found at the center of the COMPASS ROSE.

10.7   True or false:

a. FALSE. You must create a deviation table that is unique for your own boat's magnetic problems.

b. FALSE. It is minimal since it is virtually impossible to hold a course within a single degree on a small boat.

c. TRUE.

d. FALSE. The local magnetic influences are different on every boat.

e. TRUE.

ELEVEN

Taking and Plotting Bearings

TERMINOLOGY

Here are a few new terms that you need to become familiar with before you begin to work with bearings.

Heading

A heading is the direction in which the bow of your boat is pointed. Headings are expressed in degrees—000 through 360. The compass course on your boat is a heading. Figure 11.1 illustrates a heading.

A compass heading (course) must always be converted to a true course in order to plot it on a nautical chart. Use the conversion formula TVMDC, which was discussed in Chapter 10, to make this calculation.

Bearing

A bearing is a line of position sighted from your boat to another object. A heading can be a bearing, but a bearing does not have to be a heading. Figure 11.2 illustrates this concept.

Usually, bearings are taken with a hand-held compass or may be taken by aiming the bow of your boat at an object. When using a hand-

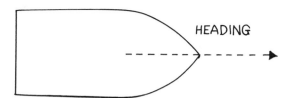

Fig. 11.1   Illustration of a Heading. *(F. J. Larkin)*

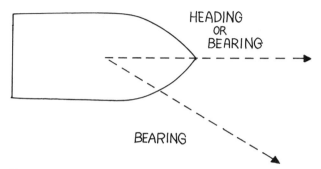

Fig. 11.2   Illustrations of Headings and Bearings. *(F. J. Larkin)*

held compass, it is good practice to determine if there is any magnetic disturbance in the area where you take the bearing. Try to find a spot on your boat that has no magnetic influences. Use this location whenever you take bearings with a hand-held compass. In other words, the direction needle on hand-held compasses can be diverted by stray magnetic problems on your boat just as your boat's compass can be affected.

Line of Position (LOP)

The line that you plot on your nautical chart for your bearing is called a *line of position* or *LOP*. A single LOP tells you that you are located somewhere along the line. Two LOPs for two different objects or targets can give you a position. Your position is said to be located where the two LOPs cross. This is called a *fix*. Figure 11.3 illustrates a LOP. A LOP is labeled with the time when you took the bearing above the plotted line.

A Fix

The intersection of two or more LOPs is called a *fix*. An ideal fix contains bearings that intersect at a 90-degree angle. Three LOPs will define your fix more accurately. An ideal three-bearing fix should have 60-degree angles between the bearings at a minimum. Often the intersecting lines

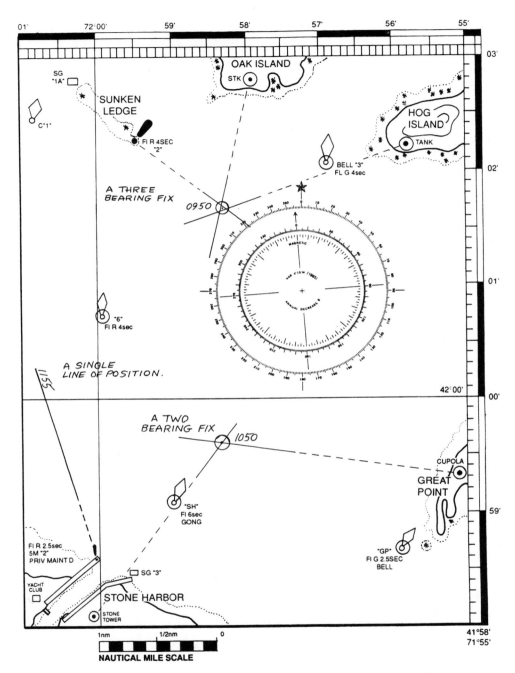

Fig. 11.3 A Line of Position and a Two- and Three-Bearing Fix.
(F. J. Larkin)

of a fix fail to cross at a specific point but form a small triangle. Your position is said to be located in the center of the triangle. Figure 11.3 illustrates a three-bearing fix. A fix is labeled with the time when the LOPs were taken. Since a fix is considered a high-quality position, the time is written horizontally.

Label a fix with a black dot surrounded by a circle, which indicates your position on the chart. This symbol indicates the high quality of the position. The fix shown in Figure 11.3 is labeled properly.

Beam Bearing

A beam bearing is a line sighted from your boat to an object located at a 90-degree angle to your boat's heading. Beam bearings are easy to take and are a quick method for verifying the progress of your boat along a DR course line. Figure 11.4 shows a beam bearing.

Plan for many beam bearing targets along your DR course line as a check on your progress and position. Unlike regular bearings, beam bearings are plotted directly from your DR course line on the chart at a 90-degree angle to the object. This position is considered to be of a higher quality than a DR position. It is called an EP, estimated position. Label an EP obtained by using a bearing and your DR course line with a black dot indicating your position surrounded by a square. Figure 11.5 illustrates the proper labeling of a beam bearing. EP positions are commonly associated with positions that are corrected for current.

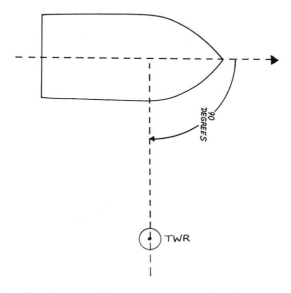

Fig. 11.4   An Illustration of a Beam Bearing. *(F. J. Larkin)*

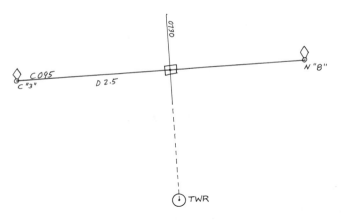

Fig. 11.5   Labeling Bearings. *(F. J. Larkin)*

TAKING BEARINGS

Bearings are taken to fixed and charted objects so that they can be plotted on your chart. If the object or target of your bearing is not printed on the chart, you will not be able to plot an LOP on the chart.

You may use a hand-bearing compass, a pelorus, or your boat's compass for taking bearings. With the exception of beam bearings, bearings are plotted from the charted object. The charted object you select should be a known, surveyed position while your boat's DR course is a mathematical DR calculation. The purpose of taking a bearing is to achieve a higher quality estimate of your boat's position.

Bearings taken with your boat's compass or a hand-bearing compass must be converted to true before they can be plotted on a nautical chart. Use this simple procedure to convert your bearings. Always use a Piloting Worksheet to record your bearing conversion work.

Step 1. Take a bearing from your position to the charted object. Record the angle, for example, 020 degrees.

Step 2. Convert the bearing to true using the TVMDC formula:

T	005
V	015 W
M	020
D	000
C	020

Here is how it works:

- The compass course is the bearing that you read on your compass.

- There may be no deviation because you stood in a

location on your boat where there was no magnetic influence on your hand-bearing compass. In this case, the magnetic course is the same as the compass course. If you use your boat's compass to take the bearing, you would use the deviation from your boat's deviation table. Use the direction from your boat toward the target. Remember the reciprocal deviation could be different.

- Variation is taken from the nearest compass rose (015 W).

- Because you are proceeding up the TVMDC formula (from compass to true), you subtract westerly variation error. The true bearing is 005 degrees.

Step 3. Calculate the reciprocal (opposite) angle of your bearing by adding or subtracting 180 degrees:

$$\begin{array}{ll} 005 & \text{Bearing (true)} \\ +180 & \\ \hline 185 & \text{Reciprocal bearing (true)} \end{array}$$

Step 4. Plot the true reciprocal bearing from the charted object on your nautical chart. Your position is located somewhere along this plotted line or LOP.

LABELING BEARING LOPS

Bearing LOPs are often drawn with a dashed line rather than a solid line. The time when you take the bearing is written in four-digit military time above the bearing's plotted LOP. The true bearing to the object can be written under the line. Bearings are expressed with three digits. The figures in this chapter illustrate the proper labeling of bearings.

RELATIVE BEARINGS

A relative bearing is a line sighted from your boat to another object in relationship to your boat's compass heading. The bearing shown in Figure 11.2 could be a relative bearing.

Relative bearings are taken with an instrument called a *pelorus*. A pelorus is a sighting instrument with a compass card, which, when installed on your boat, is aligned to the keel of the boat with 000 degrees on the compass card aimed at the bow. Correct pelorus bearings to your compass headings.

Use this procedure to convert relative bearings to compass bearings or true bearings. Follow this simple step-by step process:

Step 1. Align your pelorus with the center (keel) line of your boat. Set the compass card on the pelorus with 000 degrees fixed toward the bow of your boat.

Step 2. Take the bearing to a charted object with the pelorus and record it on a Piloting Worksheet. At the same time, record the compass heading of your boat.

Step 3. Convert the compass heading to true using the TVMDC conversion formula. Since your compass heading has a directional relationship to your boat's deviation table, it is crucial to convert it to true before you add the relative bearing. If you don't, you will probably use the wrong deviation in your calculation.

Step 4. Add the relative bearing (pelorus) to the true bearing.

Step 5. Calculate the reciprocal (opposite) bearing by adding or subtracting 180 degrees.

Step 6. Plot the reciprocal bearing from the object. The object should be a fixed-charted position on your chart. You are located somewhere along this LOP.

Figure 11.6 illustrates the following relative bearing problem. Work this problem through to get a solid understanding of the use of relative bearings.

EXAMPLE: Your boat is on a compass course of 085 degrees. At 0845, you take a relative bearing of 030 degrees on the cupola at Great Point on the Piloting Practice Chart (see Figure 11.6). Use a deviation of 005E. Always check the alignment of the compass card on the pelorus before taking a bearing.

Step 1. Convert the compass course to true. Remember that you are going up the TVMDC formula. The true course is 086:

> T   086
> V   004 W
> M   090
> D   005 E
> C   085

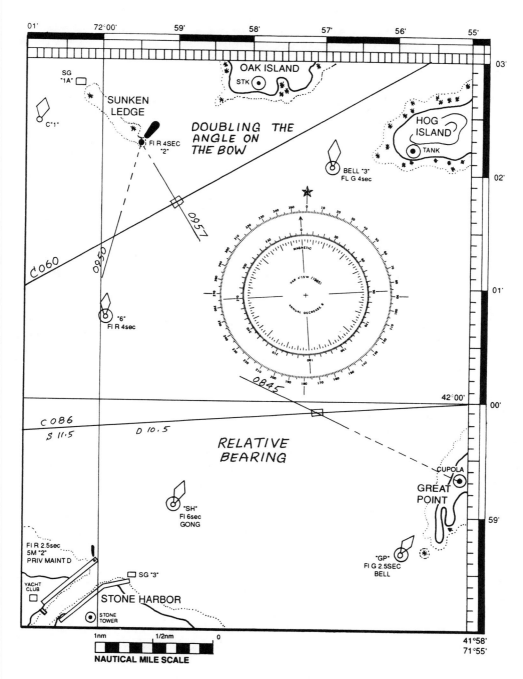

Fig. 11.6 A Relative Bearing and an Illustration of Doubling the Angle on the Bow Plotted on a Piloting Practice Chart.

Step 2.   Add the relative bearing to the true bearing. The answer is 116 degrees relative:

086

+030   Relative

116   R

Step 3.   Because you must plot back from the object, add or subtract 180 degrees to obtain the reciprocal bearing:

116

+180

296

Step 4.   Plot and label a LOP of 296 degrees from the cupola on the Piloting Practice Chart. Figure 11.6 shows this plot.

Your estimated position (EP) is where the relative bearing's LOP intersects your DR course line. Note that if the LOP does not intersect your DR course line, your EP is said to be at the point on your DR course line that is closest to the relative bearing LOP.

DOUBLING THE ANGLE ON THE BOW

Doubling the angle on the bow is a quick, easy technique for determining your distance off a fixed-charted shore object or from an obstruction. The following is an explanation of this important piloting technique using 45- and 90-degree angles. You must have a decent speed curve to use this piloting procedure effectively. Appendix 6 provides instructions and Appendix 7 a worksheet to help you develop a speed curve for your boat.

Step 1.   As you cruise along the coast on your plotted DR course line (i.e., 060 degrees), pick out a fixed-charted object on the shore.

• Take relative bearings to this object until your boat's heading is 45 degrees relative to the object.

• Record the time when you take the 45-degree bearing (i.e., 0950 hrs).

Step 2.   Continue along your planned DR course until the charted object is abeam or 90 degrees relative to your boat's heading. Record the time (i.e., 0957 hrs).

Step 3. Using your DR formula, 60D = ST, calculate the distance run from the time that you were 45 degrees relative until you are abeam of the object.

The distance run is equal to your distance off the object.

0950 – 0957 = 7 minutes. Assume a speed of 5 kts.

$$60 \times D = S \times T$$

$$D = \frac{5 \times 7}{60}$$ or distance = 0.58 or 0.6 nm.

You are 0.6 nm off the object. Figure 11.6 illustrates this example of doubling the angle on the bow. Using your dividers, measure off a 0.6-nm circle from the charted object. The point where this circle's arc intersects your beam bearing LOP is your estimated position.

Note that if you have a wide discrepancy from your DR position, you should question your speed curve unless you can explain the difference with other phenomena such as wind, waves, or current.

PRACTICE PROBLEMS

Use a Piloting Worksheet with these problems. A sample is included in Appendix 7. Plot and label your answers on a Piloting Practice Chart, which is also included in Appendix 7.

1. At 1030, you are traveling on a compass heading of 045 degrees toward the tank on Hog Island. Your deviation is 005E. Plot and label this bearing. What have you learned about your position from this bearing? (*Hint:* Determine the reciprocal true course and plot an LOP back from the tank.)

2. You have taken a bearing of 315 degrees to the light on Sunken Ledge with your hand-held compass. There is no deviation in the location on your boat where you took this bearing. Plot and label your bearing.

3. Problems 1 and 2 have fixed your position. Label this fix for 1030 hrs. What is the latitude and longitude of this position?

4. Departing at 1100, you cruise at a speed of 10 kts from Lighted Buoy "6" toward Bell "GP" off Great Point. At 1110 you are abeam of the stone tower near Stone Harbor.

   a. Calculate and plot your DR position for 1110 hrs. (*Hint:* Use the DR formula and solve for distance. Then, measure off the distance on your DR course line.)

   b. Plot and label your beam bearing (your estimated position for 1110).

   c. What is your actual speed made good to your estimated position?

(*Solution:* Measure the distance to your estimated position where the beam bearing crosses your DR course line. Using the 60D = ST formula, solve for speed.)

Note: The correct label for a beam bearing is a square with a position dot. Because the target of a beam bearing is charted, an estimated position is considered a higher quality position than a DR position.

5. Maintaining your new speed of 9.6 kts, what is your new ETA to the Bell "GP"? Plot and label your new course.

   Note: Because the beam bearing is a higher quality position, measure the remainder of your course from it.

6. What could have caused the difference between your DR position and your estimated position?

The answers to these problems can be found on the Piloting Practice Chart of Figure 11.7 and on the Piloting Worksheet of Figure 11.8.

Reader Study Note

In these problems you have an example of three distinct positioning techniques—a DR position, an estimated position, and a fix. Study these problems carefully until you acquire an appreciation of the accuracy or relative inaccuracy of each technique. Also remember that conditions are constantly affecting your course and position. Prudent mariners continuously check and recheck their positions in order to maintain an accurate course. There are other bearings and other angles that you can use in piloting. I feel that these are the basic and most used ones. Take the time to learn them and you will find that you use them constantly at sea.

Reader Progress Note

You should now have a basic understanding of dead reckoning and be able to plot a course on a nautical chart and convert it for use on your boat's compass.

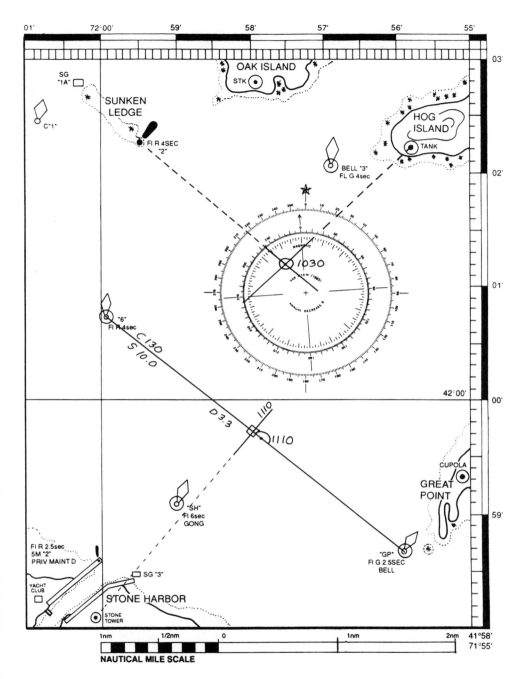

Fig. 11.7 Piloting Practice Chart for Piloting Problems.

PILOTING WORKSHEET

60D=ST   **TVMDC ADD WEST DOWN**

DATE	TRIP
	PROBLEMS FOR CHAPTER 11.

1.
T 046
V 004 W
M 050
D 005 E
C 045

046
+180
226

YOU ARE LOCATED SOMEWHERE ALONG THIS LOP.

2.
T 311
V 004 W
M 315
D
C

311
-180
131

3. 42° 01.2' N
    71° 57.5' W

---

4.   DEP 1100   S=10.0

a. ETA 1110   T = 10 MIN.

$60 D = S \times T$

$\dfrac{60 \times D}{60} = \dfrac{10 \times 10}{60} = \dfrac{100}{60} = 1.7 \, nm.$

c. TIME = 10 MIN   D = 1.6

$60 D = S T$

$\dfrac{60 \times 1.6}{10} = \dfrac{S \times 10}{10} = 9.6 \, KTS \; SMG$

---

5. S = 9.6   DEP 1110   D = 1.6

$60 D = S T$

$\dfrac{60 \times 1.6}{9.6} = \dfrac{9.6 \times T}{9.6} = \dfrac{96}{9.6} = 10 \, MIN.$

DEP   1110
TRAV. 0010
ETA   1120

---

6. ○ AN UNFAVORABLE CURRENT OFF THE BOW.
    ○ WAVE ACTION OFF THE BOW.
    ○ AN ERROR IN YOUR SPEED CURVE.
    ○ MORE GUESTS ABOARD THAN WHEN YOU MADE YOUR
      SPEED CURVE.

Fig. 11.8   Piloting Worksheet for Piloting Practice Problems.

REVIEW QUESTIONS

11.1 The direction in which your boat's bow points is called a
_____.

11.2 True or false: A compass heading can be plotted directly on
a nautical chart. _____

11.3 Bearings are taken to _____ and _____ objects.

11.4 A bearing, plotted on a chart, indicates that your boat is
_____ _____ along the LOP.

11.5 Another name for a bearing is a _____ _____
_____ or _____.

11.6 The intersection of _____ or more _____ or bearings is
called a fix.

11.7 A _____ _____ is a line sighted at a 90-degree angle
from your boat's heading.

11.8 When doubling the angle on the bow, the _____ run
is equal to the _____ from the object.

11.9 A _____ _____ is a line sighted from your
boat to another object in relationship to your boat's
_____ _____.

11.10 Relative bearings are taken with an instrument called a
_____.

11.11 You should have a _____ chart aboard your boat that
is corrected with the latest _____ _____ ___
_____ information.

11.12 A fix is labeled with a position dot and a _____.

11.13 A beam bearing is labeled with a position dot and a
_____.

11.14 A DR position is labeled with a position dot and a
_____.

Answers

11.1 The direction in which your boat's bow points is called a HEADING.

11.2 FALSE. A compass heading must be converted to true before it can be plotted directly on a nautical chart.

11.3 Bearings are taken to FIXED and CHARTED objects.

11.4 A bearing, plotted on a chart, indicates that your boat is LOCATED SOMEWHERE along the LOP.

11.5 Another name for a bearing is a LINE OF POSITION or LOP.

11.6 The intersection of TWO or more LOPS or bearings is called a fix.

11.7 A BEAM BEARING is a line sighted at a 90-degree angle from your boat's heading.

11.8 When doubling the angle on the bow, the DISTANCE run is equal to the DISTANCE from the object.

11.9 A RELATIVE BEARING is a line sighted from your boat to another object in relationship to your boat's COMPASS HEADING.

11.10 Relative bearings are taken with an instrument called a PELORUS.

11.11 You should have a NAUTICAL chart aboard your boat that is corrected with the latest LOCAL NOTICE TO MARINERS information.

11.12 A fix is labeled with a position dot and a CIRCLE.

11.13 A beam bearing is labeled with a position dot and a SQUARE.

11.14 A DR position is labeled with a position dot and a SEMI-CIRCLE.

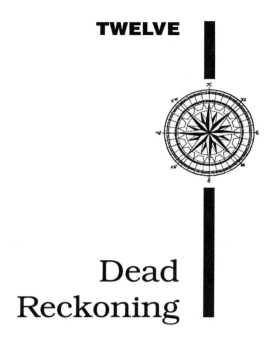

TWELVE

Dead
Reckoning

Hopefully, by now, you understand that dead reckoning is not a perfect science and that many things can influence your boat once you untie it from the dock. Wind, current, weather, visibility, wave action, boating traffic, and many other things will cause you to constantly adjust your trip plan and replot your course. Managing these changes is the key to good piloting.

Piloting is a skill that is refined and developed through practice. Plot and run your courses during daylight hours and in good weather when it is easy to see and correct your mistakes before you put yourself into danger. Try to understand where you go wrong and correct the problem. This will prepare you for running at night or in periods of reduced visibility. I don't encourage you to look for danger. The prudent mariner never takes unnecessary risks. However, you should be ready to handle difficult piloting situations if they should suddenly arise.

Be ready to use everything at your disposal to check and recheck your position. Learn the "doubling the angle on the bow" and the "beam bearing" techniques discussed in Chapter 11. These are great tools for checking your boat's progress. Use your depth sounder to track your position along the bottom.

Always plot a DR course and update it periodically during your trip. Stay aware of your position at all times. Recheck and record your position at least every 30 minutes. Evaluate your progress. Be ready for unexpected periods of restricted visibility. Always be aware of your location and the distance to the nearest harbor. This information may be needed to avoid a sudden summer squall or thunderstorm. During a lightning storm, I have always felt more secure inside a building rather than exposed on the open sea.

If you happen to get caught at sea in restricted visibility, don't panic. Check your last DR position and work forward to your current DR position. If you have some warning, take some bearings quickly. These bearings will help upgrade your position from a DR to an estimated or fixed position and provide you with a more accurate starting point. Deal with one leg at a time. Navigate to lighted or sounding aids to navigation. They will be easier to find. Post lookouts and instruct them on what to look and listen for. Be sure to sound the prescribed fog signals during periods of reduced visibility. The rules of the road publication will provide this information.

Always keep the latest edition of the nautical chart of the area aboard your vessel. Correct this chart weekly with the Local Notice to Mariners. Invest in a *Light List* and a *Coast Pilot*. Become professional about your safety.

Dead reckoning skills are developed through practice. You usually get rusty over the winter or during periods of boating inactivity. Make up your own piloting problems. Plan dream trips. Work their details through by actually plotting them on nautical charts and recording the computations on a Piloting Worksheet. Get yourself some good navigation tools. A good navigation kit should have the following items at a minimum:

- Dividers (with adjusting screw)
- Small screwdriver to adjust the dividers
- Automatic pencil (0.5 mm with HB leads)
- Extra pack of 0.5 HB leads
- Extra pack of erasers for the automatic pencil
- Pink Pearl eraser
- Paraglide plotter
- Ruler
- Small electronic calculator (solar calculators work only during daylight hours)
- Extra batteries for the calculator
- Time, speed, distance calculator
- Special flashlight with a white and red lens (use the red lens to read your chart at night)
- Extra batteries for the flashlight.

As you become more experienced, you will add other items to your navigation kit, but the items on this list will get you started. Here are some other pieces of navigational equipment you may want to acquire:

- A pelorus for taking relative bearings
- A hand-held compass for taking bearings
- A range finder for determining distance off objects
- A lead line for taking soundings as a backup to your depth sounder.

Before you set out, I suggest that you plot the test cruise provided in Chapter 13. Use the Piloting Worksheet to record your calculations. This cruise can be plotted on a Piloting Practice Chart. Both forms are provided in Appendix 7.

In addition, use the Trip Log given in the Appendix 7 to record each leg of your trip. A deviation table is provided for you to use for this practice trip. You will need to develop a unique deviation table for your own boat. This one will not work. Appendixes 3 and 4 deal with creating a deviation table for your boat.

Chapter 13 provides examples that show the plotted trip, the worksheets, and the trip log. If you get stuck on a question, look up the answer. Try to do the piloting work first and then compare it to the figures. This is the quickest way to learn to navigate your boat. Remember! Practice, practice, practice.

THIRTEEN

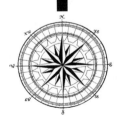

Piloting Exercise:
A Typical Day Cruise

The purpose of this exercise is to build confidence in your piloting skills. Since piloting is a practiced skill, you must "use it or lose it!"

Don't be timid about plotting a course each time you go boating. This practice will help develop your piloting and seamanship skills as you observe your boat's actual performance against your planned DR course line. Practicing in daylight in good weather conditions is a safe method for correcting your errors and increasing your piloting skills without putting yourself in jeopardy.

Finally, when an emergency arises, you will have developed the self-confidence to pilot your boat in fog, rain, or other conditions of restricted visibility. Remember, the prudent mariner never takes foolish chances but is prepared to handle adverse situations if they arise.

Plot all your courses in this exercise on a Piloting Practice Chart. Use a Piloting Worksheet to document your calculations and the Trip Log to record each leg of your trip. These forms are found in Appendix 7. Make copies if you need extras.

The day cruise trip legs are plotted for you in Figures 13.1 and 13.2. Figures 13.3, 13.4, and 13.5 are the Piloting Worksheets that document the calculations for the plotting. Figure 13.6 illustrates a sample Trip Log. These figures appear at the end of the chapter. Table 13.1 is your deviation table.

Work methodically. Plot one trip leg at a time. Relax and enjoy your first cruise.

Table 13.1 Sample Deviation Table

Heading	Magnetic Deviation	Compass Deviation
000	003E	005E
015	003E	003E
030	002E	003E
045	002E	002E
060	001E	002E
075	000	001E
090	000	000
105	001W	000
120	002W	001W
135	003W	002W
150	003W	003W
165	004W	003W
180	004W	004W
195	004W	004W
210	003W	004W
225	003W	003W
240	003W	003W
255	002W	003W
270	001W	002W
285	000	001W
300	001E	000
315	002E	001E
330	003E	002E
345	005E	003E

When proceeding down the TVMDC formula (true to compass), use the magnetic reading as your heading and read your deviation from the magnetic deviation column.

When proceeding up the TVMDC formula (compass to true), use the compass reading as your heading and read your deviation from the compass deviation column.

Leg 1: You plan to take a trip around the area shown on the Piloting Practice Chart, departing at 0900. Your boat is moored at the dock of the Stone Harbor Yacht Club. You plan to motor out of Stone Harbor to Gong "SH". Due to local harbormaster rules, your speed is restricted to 5 kts. Usually there is some morning fog in this area.

a. Plot and label your course to Gong "SH". Update your Trip Log.

b. What is your compass heading to Gong "SH"? (Use the TVMDC formula.) Update your Trip Log.

c. What is your ETA to Gong "SH"? Update your Trip Log. (Use the 60D = ST formula and solve for time.)

Leg 2:   Upon arriving at Gong "SH", you plan to turn toward Bell "GP", off Great Point, increasing your speed to 10 kts. *Note:* Your ETA of Leg 1 is your departure time for Leg 2.

    a. Plot and label your course. Update your Trip Log.

    b. What is your compass heading? Update your Trip Log.

    c. What is your ETA to Bell "SH", off Great Point? Update your Trip Log.

Leg 3:   After fishing for 25 minutes, you decide to head toward Bell "3", near Hog Island. Your new speed is 12 kts.

    a. Plot and label your course. Update your Trip Log.

    b. What is your compass heading? Update your Trip Log.

    c. What is your ETA to Bell "3"? Update your Trip Log. (Remember to add 25 minutes for the time you were fishing.)

At 0958, you are abeam the cupola on Great Point.

    d. Plot and label your beam bearing to the cupola.

    e. Calculate and plot your 0958 DR position. (Note the difference between your beam bearing position and your DR position.)

    f. What is the speed made good to the estimated position at the beam bearing? (You know the time. Measure the distance and solve for speed using the 60D = ST formula.)

    g. What are some reasons for the difference of the beam bearing position and your calculated DR position?

    h. To arrive at Bell "3" at 1012 hrs, as you originally planned, what speed will you need to run? Update your Trip Log. (You can compute the time and measure the new distance from your beam bearing position to the bell. Use the 60D = ST formula and solve for speed.)

At 1010, you turn your boat's bow toward the tank on Hog Island and read a compass bearing of 011 degrees. At the same time you take a hand-held compass bearing of 294 degrees to Light "2", on Sunken Ledge Spit. Because you took the bearing from a location on your boat with no magnetic influence, there is no deviation affecting your hand-held compass.

    i. Plot and label the fix.

    j. What is the latitude and longitude of your fix?

    k. What could account for this position since you were paying strict attention to your steering?

l. Plot and label your 1010 DR position.

m. What speed would you use in order to arrive at Bell "3" at 1030 hrs?

n. What is your new compass course to Bell "3"?

o. Plot and label your new course to Bell "3".

Leg 4:   After fishing at Bell "3" until 1100 hrs, you continue your trip toward Lighted Buoy "6" at a speed of 10 kts.

a. Plot and label your course. Update your Trip Log.

b. What is your compass heading? Update your Trip Log.

c. What is your ETA to Lighted Buoy "6"? Update your Trip Log.

At 1108, your boat's engine dies and Lighted Buoy "6" becomes shrouded in fog. You can see the light off Sunken Ledge Spit, the tank on Hog Island, and the stack on Oak Island. You take three bearings.

The light on Sunken Ledge Spit bears 339 degrees by your boat's compass. Using your hand-held compass, you take a bearing of 068 degrees to the tank on Hog Island and a bearing of 026 degrees to the stack on Oak Island.

d. Plot and label your 1108 DR position.

e. Plot and label your fix.

f. What are the latitude and longitude of this fix?

Leg 5:   The fog is closing in. You finally get your engine restarted and decide to run for home port at 1115.

a. What signals should you sound, if any? [Refer to the *Rules of the Road* for the answer. Every boat owner should keep a copy of the *Rules of the Road* aboard their boat. As stated in the rules, "After January 1, 1983, the operator of each self-propelled vessel 12 meters (39.4 ft.) or more in length shall carry on board and maintain for ready reference a copy of the *Inland Navigation Rules*."]

b. Plot and label your course back to Gong "SH" off Stone Harbor.

c. What is your compass course back to Gong "SH"?

d. Using a speed of 10 kts, what is your ETA to the gong? Update your Trip Log.

e. What can you do to check your boat's position along your course line to the gong?

Gong "SH" becomes obscured by fog. At 1122, you stop your boat in the fog since you cannot find the gong.

    f.   Plot and label your 1122 position.

    g. What steps can you take to find Gong "SH" in the fog?

Leg 6: At 1140, you locate Gong "SH".

    a. Plot and label your course back to the yacht club.

    b. What is your compass course to the yacht club dock?

    c. What is your ETA to the yacht club dock?

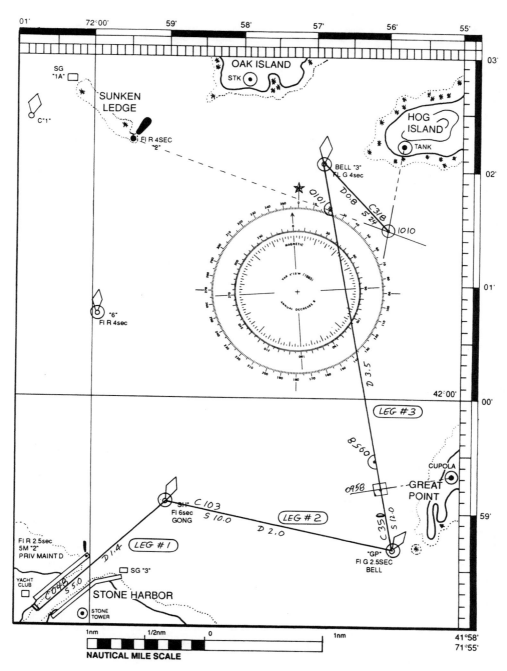

Fig. 13.1 Piloting Practice Chart of Course Plots for Legs 1, 2, and 3 for the Piloting Cruise Exercise.

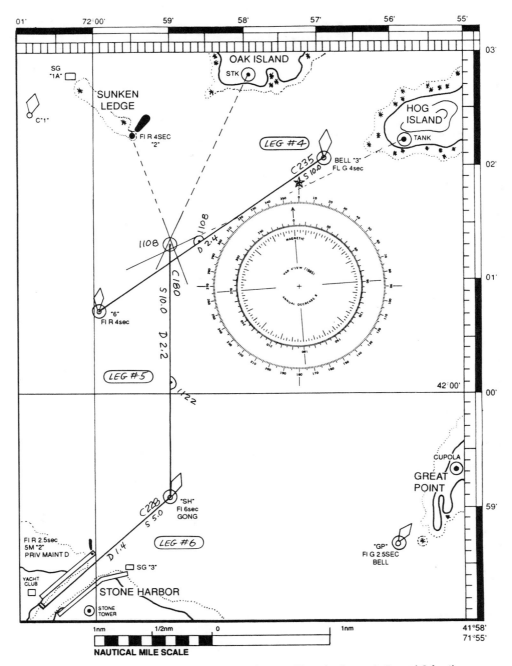

Fig. 13.2 Piloting Practice Chart of Course Plots for Legs 4, 5, and 6 for the Piloting Cruise Exercise.

PILOTING WORKSHEET

60D=ST   **TVMDC** ADD WEST DOWN

DATE	TRIP
	DAY CRUISE — CHAPTER 13

LEG #1 $D = 1.4$ $S = 5.0$ DEP 0900

a. [compass diagram 090]

b.
T   048
V   004 W
M   052
D   002 E
C   050

c. $60 D = ST$

$$^{12}\!\!\frac{60 \times 1.4}{5_1} = \frac{5 \times T}{5_1} = 16.8 \text{ MIN}$$

DEP 0900
TRAV 00 17
ETA 0917

LEG #2 $S = 10.0$ $D = 2.0$ DEP 0917

a. [compass diagram 090 / 180]

b.
T   103
V   004 W
M   107
D   001 W
C   108

c. $60 D = ST$

$$^{6}\!\!\frac{60 \times 2}{10_1} = \frac{10 \times T}{10_1} = 12 \text{ MIN}.$$

DEP 0917
TRAV. 00 12
ETA 0929

LEG #3   DEP $0929 + 0025 = 0954$ $S = 12.0$ $D = 3.5$

a. [compass diagram 270]

b.
T   350
V   004 W
M   354
D   003 E
C   351

c. $60 D = ST$

$$^{5}\!\!\frac{60 \times 3.5}{12_1} = \frac{12 \times T}{12_1} = 17.5 \text{ MIN}$$

DEP 0954
TRAV. 00 18
0972
+ 1-60
ETA 1012

---

e. DEP 0954 ETA 0958 $S = 12.0$

$60 D = ST$

$$^{1}\!\!\frac{60 \times D}{60_1} = \frac{12 \times 4}{60} = 0.8 \text{ nm}.$$

f. $T = 4$ $D = 0.6$

$60 D = ST$

$$^{15}\!\!\frac{60 \times 0.6}{4_1} = \frac{S \times 4}{4} = 9 \text{ KTS}$$

---

g. HEAD WINDS. CURRENT OFF THE BOW. ERROR IN SPEED CURVE. HEAVY SEAS OFF THE BOW. OVERLOADED BOAT.

---

h. $D = 2.9$ DEP 0958 ETA 1012 $T = 14$

$60 D = ST$

$$\frac{60 \times 2.9}{14} = \frac{S \times 14}{14} = \frac{174}{14} = 12.4 \text{ KTS}$$

---

i.
T   010   010
V   004 W   +180
M   014   190
D   003 E
C   011

T   290   290
V   004 W   -180
M   294   110
D
C

j.
$42° 01.5' N$
$71° 56.0' W$

Fig. 13.3 Piloting Worksheet—Page 1 for the Piloting Cruise Exercise.

PAGE 2 OF 3

PILOTING WORKSHEET

60D=ST   **TVMDC** ADD WEST DOWN

DATE	TRIP
	DAY CRUISE – CHAPTER 13

LEG # 3 CONTINUED.

K. WIND OR CURRENT FROM THE PORT SIDE OR WEST

l.   ETA 1010 DEP 0958   S = 12.4 T = 12

$$60 D = S T$$

$$\frac{60 \times D}{60} = \frac{12.4 \times 12}{60} = \frac{12.4}{5} = 2.5 \text{ nm}$$

m.   D = 0.8   DEP 1010 ETA 1030 T = 20

$$60 D = S T$$

$$\frac{3 \; 60 \times 0.8}{20} = \frac{S \times 20}{20} = 2.4 \text{ KTS.}$$

n.   T   318
     V   004 W
     M   322
     D   002 E
     C   320

LEG # 4   PLOTTING IS FOUND ON FIG. 13.2
         DEP 1100   S = 10.0   D = 2.4

a.

b.   T   235   c.   60 D = S T
     V   004 W $\frac{6 \; 60 \times 2.4}{10} = \frac{10 \times T}{10} = 14.4 \text{ MIN}$ DEP 1100
     M   239   TRAV 0014
     D   003 W   ETA 1114
     C   242

d.   S = 10.0 DEP 1100 ETA 1108   T = 8

$$60 D = S T$$

$$\frac{60 \times D}{60} = \frac{10 \times 8}{60} = 1.3 \text{ nm.}$$

e.   SUNKEN LEDGE   OAK IS   HOG IS.

     340   T   340   T   025   T   065
     -180   V   004 W   V   004 W   025   V   004 W   065
     160   M   344   M   029   +180   M   069   +180
            D   005 E   D   003 E   205   D   001 E   245
            C   339   C   026   C   068

Fig. 13.4   Piloting Worksheet—Page 2 for the Piloting Cruise Exercise.

PAGE 3 OF 3

PILOTING WORKSHEET

60D=ST   **TVMDC** ADD WEST DOWN

DATE	TRIP
	DAY CRUISE — CHAPTER 13

LEG # 4 CONTINUED.
   42° 01.3' N
   71° 59.0' W

LEG # 5   DEP 1115

a. SOUND ONE PROLONGED BLAST (4 TO 6 SEC.) EVERY TWO
   MINUTES WHILE UNDERWAY IN RESTRICTED VISIBILITY.

b.
```
     270 ⊕ 090
        180↓
```

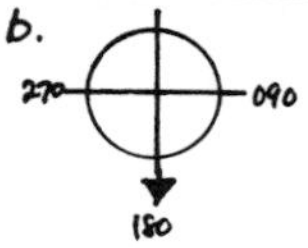

c. T 180
    V 004 W
    M 184
    D 004 W
    C 188

d. S = 10.0   D = 2.2   DEP 1115
    60 D = S T,   TRAV 0013
    $\frac{60 \times 2.2}{10} = \frac{10 \times T}{10} = 13$ MIN   ETA 1128

e. USE A DEPTH SOUNDER TO CHECK DEPTH ALONG COURSE.
   TAKE A BEAM BEARING ON LIGHTED BUOY # 6.

f. S = 10.0   DEP 1115   ETA 1122   T = 7
    60 D = S T
    $\frac{60 \times D}{60} = \frac{10 \times 7}{60} = 1.67$ OR 1.2 nm.

g. LISTEN FOR THE GONG. MAKE WAVES TO ACTUATE GONG.
   COMPLETE THE LENGTH OF YOUR DR COURSE.
   AT END OF DR COURSE, START TO CIRCLE.
   USE DEPTH SOUNDER TO TRACK DEPTH CONTOUR LINES.

LEG # 6.   DEP 1140   D = 1.4   S = 5.0

a.
```
   270 ⊕
      180
```

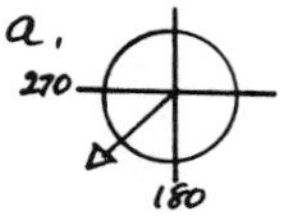

b. T 228
    V 004 W
    M 232
    D 003 W
    C 235

c. 60 D = S T
    $\frac{60 \times 1.4}{5} = \frac{5 \times T}{5} = 16.8$

    DEP 1140
    TRAV 00 17
    ETA 1157

Fig. 13.5 Piloting Worksheet—Page 3 for the Piloting Cruise Exercise.

TRIP LOG

Leg/WPT	To	DIST NM	SPEED/RPM	COMP Heading	TIME (min)	Planned DEP	Planned ETA	Actual DEP	Actual ETA
Date:	Boat: IDYLE TIME					Page / of /			
Start	STONE HBR Y.C. DOCK								
1	GONG "SH"	1.4	5.0	050	17.0	0900	0917		0917
Notes									
2	BELL "GP" GREAT POINT	2.0	10.0	108	12.0	0917	0929		0929
Notes	FISHED FOR 25 m.								
3	BELL "3" HOG ISLAND	3.5	12.0	351	17.5	0954	1012		0958
Notes	0958, ABEAM CUPOLA ON GREAT POINT								
	BELL "3" HOG ISLAND	2.9	12.4	351	14.0	0958	1012		
Notes	1010 FIX 42° 015' N 71° 056.0' W								
	BELL "3" HOG ISLAND	0.8	2.4	320	20.0	1010	1030		1030
Notes									
4	LT BUOY #6	2.4	10.0	242	14.4	1100	1114		1108
Notes	FISHED UNTIL 1100 1108 ENGINE DIED, RESTARTED AT 1115.								
5	GONG "SH" STONE HBR	2.2	10.0	188	13.0	1115	1128		1140
Notes	1122 STOP DUE TO FOG 1140 FIND GONG SH.								
6	STONE HBR Y. CLUB	1.4	5.0	235	17.0	1140	1157		1157
Notes									
Notes									
Notes									
Notes									

Fig. 13.6 Trip Log for Piloting Cruise Exercise.

FOURTEEN

Electronic Navigation Systems

LORAN-C

LORAN, an acronym for LOng RAnge Navigation, is an electronic aid to navigation system that is transmitted from land-based radio transmitters. This means that you must equip your boat with a LORAN signal receiver in order to use the system.

How LORAN-C Works

A LORAN-C chain uses three to five transmitting stations separated by several hundred miles. One station is designated as the *master* within a chain while others are designated as *secondary stations.* Figure 14.1 shows a typical LORAN-C chain where M is the master station, and X, Y, and Z represent secondary stations.

The master station is always the first to send a signal by transmitting a series of pulses. The secondary stations then transmit an 8-pulse signal in turn at precisely timed intervals. This master/secondary pulse cycle repeats itself continuously. The length of each cycle is measured in microseconds and is called a *group repetition interval* (GRI). Your on-board LORAN-C receiver measures the slight difference in time that it takes for these pulsed signals to reach it from the master and secondary stations. This *time difference* (TD) is used by your LORAN set to calculate the latitude and longitude position of your boat.

How Your Position Is Determined

Your boat's position is calculated by your LORAN set by measuring the TDs from two LORAN secondary stations (Figure 14.2). Usually, you tell the LORAN your position when you start up your set. Most newer sets have an automatic correction feature that compensates for any propagation error in your area. Read your set's manual and use this feature for more accurate results.

The latitude and longitude computation on some LORAN receivers is based on an all-seawater propagation path for the master and secondary signals. Newer sets are programmed for local anomalies. This means that land masses between your boat and the signal towers have not been factored into the formula. This may lead to error when signals involve appreciable overland propagation paths. These errors can put you at risk especially in inland water areas such as entering a harbor when you may want to rely heavily on the LORAN data.

CAUTION: *The latitude and longitude computation on some LORAN receivers is based on an all-seawater propagation path. This means it doesn't account for the effect on the signal from land masses between your boat and the transmitter. This may lead to error when the LORAN-C signals involve appreciable overland propagation paths. These errors can put you at risk in areas requiring precise positioning if the proper correctors (ASF) are not applied. If your LORAN receiver uses coordinate converters, check the manufacturer's operating manual to determine if and how corrections are to be applied to compensate for the error generated by the overland paths.*

The Accuracy of LORAN-C

Accuracy for LORAN is defined with the terms *absolute* and *repeatable*. *Absolute accuracy* is a measure of the ability of your LORAN receiver to deliver accurate position information. The absolute accuracy of LORAN is 0.25 nautical miles with a confidence ratio of 95%. This means that 5% of the time the error is greater. However, if your set has an automatic correction feature and you can provide an accurate position to it when you turn it on, your error decreases dramatically. If you don't have this feature, you should be careful when using the data and operating in inshore areas.

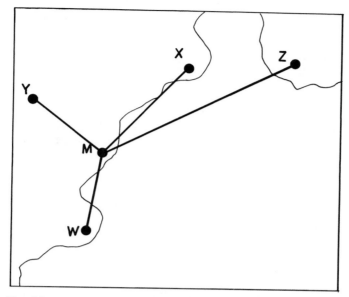

Fig. 14.1 Diagram of a Typical LORAN-C Chain. *(F. J. Larkin)*

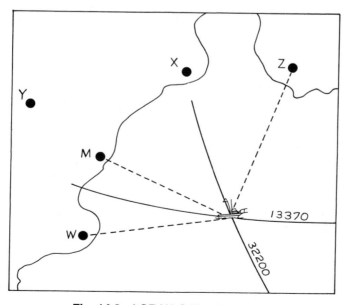

Fig. 14.2 LORAN-C Fix. *(F. J. Larkin)*

Repeatable accuracy is the measure of the ability of your LORAN receiver to return to a position where actual LORAN readings were previously taken. LORAN has very high-quality repeatable accuracy. Ask any lobsterman. Here are a few tips for taking position readings with your LORAN:

- Stop and let your LORAN catch up before you select a position reading. Your set needs time to complete the necessary calculations. When the numbers stop moving, press the event key to record the position. Your LORAN will bring you back to this position with high accuracy.

- Record positions or waypoints on your trip out so you can use them on the way back in case of bad weather.

- Use the *Light List* to get the latitude and longitude of buoys. This will give you waypoint information when entering a new harbor or area.

LORAN Installation Tips

Antenna Location.   The best spot for a LORAN antenna is as high as possible and away from all stays, metal masts, and other antennas. If your LORAN antenna must compete with other antennas, you may position it at a lower location but keep it away from metal objects. Do not share the LORAN antenna with any other equipment. Use only the antenna recommended by the manufacturer of your LORAN equipment.

Grounding Your LORAN Equipment.   Equal in importance to antenna placement is the grounding of your LORAN receiver and antenna coupler. Install a ground plate on your boat's hull and run a separate ground line to your set.

Receiver Placement.   Your LORAN receiver is a valuable aid to navigation so you will want to locate it near your chart table or navigation station. On small boats, you may want to mount it near the helm or steering station. Protect your receiver from heat, dampness, salt spray, and vibration. Read your manual carefully. Many sets are water resistant, which is quite different from waterproof. Do not mount your set in direct sunlight since you may not be able to read the screen. Before final installation, check that the LORAN does not interfere with your compass.

GLOBAL POSITIONING SYSTEM

The Global Positioning System (GPS) is a highly accurate, worldwide navigation and positioning system that can be used 24 hours a day. Designed at the impetus of the Department of Defense primarily for military use, GPS is available to a variety of users worldwide, including recreational boaters and fishing and shipping fleets.

The system is based on a constellation of satellites that, when completed, will consist of 21 satellites and 3 working spares orbiting the earth twice each day in six orbital planes. Each satellite is in a fixed orbit approximately 10,900 nautical miles above the earth, and inclined at 55 degrees from the equator.

Cautions

The Global Positioning System is operated by the U.S. government, which is solely responsible for the accuracy and maintenance of GPS. Certain conditions can make the system less accurate, such as changes in orbit or health of the satellite.

Accuracy can also be affected by poor satellite geometry. Accuracy warnings will appear on the screen of your GPS receiver. When this occurs, use the data with extreme caution.

The Global Positioning System is still developmental. The government can make changes to the system which could affect the performance of GPS receivers. Such a change could require a modification to your set. Most GPS manufacturers will provide the buyer with the opportunity to upgrade GPS receivers and/or their software. Usually the return of the registration/warranty card received with the set at purchase is sufficient to protect you. Consult your GPS dealer about this important service when you are buying your unit. Don't assume that you are protected. Be sure that it is in writing.

Data Transmission

Each satellite continuously transmits two types of orbit data:

- *Almanac data:* Contains data on the health and approximate location of every satellite in the system.
- *Ephemeris data:* Contains data on the precise orbital parameters of each satellite.

Your GPS receiver can gather almanac data from any available satellite. Using information from the almanac, your receiver determines which set of satellites will give the best geometries for a position fix.

The GPS satellites also transmit two codes:

- *Encrypted code (P-code):* This code is the more accurate and is reserved for military use.

- *Course acquisition code (C/A code):* This code is available to all users. It is used to determine the precise range of the user from each satellite, and it serves as the first step in calculating a position fix with GPS. C/A code is generated 1,000 times per second.

All transmissions from the satellites are in real time.

How a Position Fix Is Obtained

Navigation with GPS and a well-designed GPS receiver is very simple for the user (see Figure 14.3). The receiver uses the data collected from three to four satellites to solve a fundamental geometric equation and then presents it in navigation displays.

1. The GPS unit determines which satellites to use to obtain the position fix. Then, the receiver obtains ephemeris data from those satellites.

   - Three satellites are used in two-dimensional positioning.

   - Four satellites are used in three-dimensional positioning to determine altitude.

2. Your GPS receiver accesses the transmission time and signal quality from each satellite. Each satellite is 10,900 miles away so there is a measurable delay from the time when the code is transmitted until it is received at your boat. Your receiver multiplies the difference in the transmission time by the speed of light (186,000 miles per second) to arrive at an estimate of the satellite's distance from the receiver (range). It uses the 60D = ST formula.

3. Your GPS receiver calculates (by triangulation) and displays your position fix. Although accuracy varies slightly with satellite constellation geometry, a position fix accuracy of 25 meters or better is typical with C/A-code receivers.

Interference

GPS uses a high-frequency radio signal (1575.42 MHz) that operates in a wave environment where there is little interfering radiation. Also, GPS uses spread-spectrum technology to protect its navigation signals. The

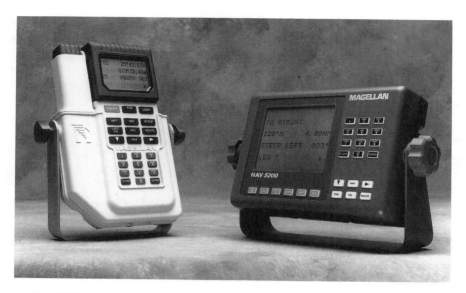

Fig. 14.3   Magellan 5-Channel NAV 5000 and NAV 5200 GPS Receivers.
(Source: Magellan Corporation)

GPS signal is therefore extremely resistant to conditions that disturb other electronic navigation systems.

In general, weather conditions, on-board electronics, passing boats and ships, on-shore electronic installations, on-board engine ignitions, and portable radio receivers do not affect the GPS signal.

Monitoring and Controlling GPS

GPS is operated by the U.S. Air Force from a master control station in Colorado. The facility is equipped for satellite monitoring, telemetry, tracking, command and control, data uploading, and navigation message generation.

Monitor stations and ground antennas located throughout the world passively track the GPS satellites and relay data to the master control station. Exact satellite position and signal-data accuracy can be constantly updated and maintained. Minor discrepancies between where the satellite "thinks" it is and where the monitor station "knows" it is can also be adjusted. When any satellite emits erroneous data or is otherwise not operational, a ground station marks it "unhealthy." The affected satellite broadcasts its status to your GPS receiver, which is programmed to ignore an unhealthy satellite and use the next best satellite to obtain a fix.

The master control station in Colorado can selectively degrade satellite data. This degradation, or *selective availability* (SA), can cause positioning errors of 100 meters. The Local Notice to Mariners publishes data on the accuracy of GPS.

Startup of Your GPS Receiver

A GPS receiver responds more quickly when used within 300 miles (482.7 km) of the initialized position of its last fix. To initialize, you must know your location within 300 miles. You should also know your altitude as accurately as possible. Note that, at sea level, normal tidal fluctuations do not affect this measurement. If you are using an external antenna, enter the antenna's altitude (height) above sea level.

Orienting Your Antenna

To obtain a position fix or collect an almanac from a satellite, your GPS unit must be held or placed in direct view of the satellite overhead. Hold manual GPS receivers upright or rotate the antenna up. If your signal appears to be blocked, sometimes moving a few feet in any direction will let you receive the signal. This is especially true in an area of dense or overhanging vegetation or structures.

A GPS unit generally will not receive signals if its view of the satellites is blocked by objects or people, or if you attempt to use your unit indoors or in a cabin without an external antenna.

Collecting an Almanac

The almanac is a schedule maintained by all satellites that is updated as required to reflect current conditions by GPS operators. Almanac information can be collected from any satellite. This means that before you obtain a position fix, your GPS receiver already knows which satellites are scheduled to be in view (given your last position or initialized position) and where in the sky to look for them. GPS units, while in current operation, maintain a current almanac.

When a unit has not been used recently (generally nine months or more), its almanac may be out of date. This unit can still obtain a position fix but it will first collect a new almanac. It takes about 12 minutes to collect a complete almanac once a satellite signal is located.

Collecting an almanac can be a heavy drain on the batteries of a portable unit. You may want to connect your unit to external power while collecting an almanac.

If your GPS receiver loses its memory, it must be reinitialized and a new almanac must be collected. This can happen if a delay occurs while you are changing a battery pack. Check your owner's manual for the programmed time interval that protects the memory in your GPS set when batteries are changed.

Continuous Operation

When a GPS receiver is in continuous operation, it updates its position fix approximately every second. As satellites set (pass over the horizon) or their signals become blocked, and as other satellites rise (appear over the horizon), the receiver occasionally changes which satellites it is using. This does not affect the updating of the position fix.

Problem Messages

A GPS receiver is usually preprogrammed with a series of messages that appear on the screen when a situation arises that may affect the quality of the position. Here are a few typical messages:

ALMANAC VERIFY: The entire almanac was not collected. The unit is in the process of identifying the missing data and collecting it. Do not turn your set off while this is in process.

NOW IN 2D: This message appears briefly when the set is turned on and when the unit switches from three- to two-dimensional reception. *Note:* Due to the limitation of crystal clocks used in GPS receivers for economy, the ordinary GPS receiver doesn't achieve the accuracy needed to synchronize the codes with the satellites. A method was developed to check and compensate for the crystal clock's timing error by using an additional satellite fix. A timing error of 1/1000th of a second could mean a surface error of 186 nautical miles. This clock bias computation takes place many times a second.

NOW IN 3D: This message appears briefly when the set is turned on and when the unit switches from two- to three-dimensional operation.

OLD DATA: This message appears when:
- Satellites have set (passed over the horizon).
- Satellite(s) signals have been blocked.
- There are not enough satellites to update a position fix.

SIGNAL QUALITY: Signal grades can be interpreted as:

> 7 - 9   Strong
> 4 - 6   Good
> 0 - 3   Weak, may lose lock.

The weak message appears when:

- The signal quality (SQ) of one or more satellites is 3 or lower.
- The lock on the satellite signal is not strong and may not be maintainable.

GEOMETRIC QUALITY: Signal grades can be interpreted as:

> 7 - 9   Strong
> 4 - 6   Good
> 0 - 3   Unreliable, do not use.

The unreliable message appears when:

- The accuracy of the fix is uncertain. Do not use this fix for navigational purposes.
- The satellites are too close to each other. The closer the satellites are to each other, the less accurate the fix capability of your receiver.

Search and Acquisition Errors

Under the following conditions, your GPS receiver may be unable to obtain a position fix:

1. Initialization was not done correctly. Here are some possible problems:
   - The initial position entered may not be incorrect by more than 300 miles.
   - Your GPS receiver was moved more than 300 miles from its last position fix or initial position.

2. There is a poor signal environment.
   - The signal quality of one or more satellites is 3 or less.

3. An insufficient number of satellites is available.
   - Some units check their almanac before beginning to search for satellites. Your receiver may not turn on if the almanac

indicates that not enough satellites are within view to establish a position fix.

4. The unit searches constantly. If the unit has an almanac and is unable to locate satellites, it searches continually until a satellite is found. Your GPS set may not be able to locate a satellite for the following reasons:

   • The antenna is not positioned correctly.

   • The satellite signals are blocked from view by buildings, mountains, etc.

   • There are signal reflections that can be corrected by moving your set's antenna.

   • There are satellite outages.

   • Satellites are set to "OFF" in Sat Status.

Choosing a Datum

All charts are produced using a system that includes the scale, type of projection, and a chart datum. Hundreds of map datums are in use throughout the world, but only a few are in widespread use today. You must set your GPS receiver to use the same datum as your charts and equipment. A position in one datum can differ by 300 meters or more from one calculated using another datum.

Before setting the datum, check the datum used on your charts and the manuals for your electronic navigation equipment. The National Oceanic and Atmospheric Administration (NOAA) is currently changing its charts to NAD 83. For most purposes, this is the same as WGS 84. Most older NOAA charts in use currently are referenced to NAD 27 or NAD 83 datums.

GPS Position Accuracy

The accuracy potential of GPS is fantastic if you are not moving. Claims of 1 centimeter are believable with a highly specialized receiver mounted on a stable tripod in an open field and enhanced with a technique called *differential GPS* (DGPS). However, many factors can significantly affect how precisely GPS can fix your position on a chart.

Motion. One factor is motion. If you mount the highly specialized surveyor's GPS equipment on a moving boat, the accuracy will drop to 15 to 18 meters using the higher accuracy P-code, or to 20 to 30 meters using the C/A-code. This wouldn't be bad accuracy if it were left in place. The Department of Defense has announced its intentions to purposely throw off the satellite clock accuracy. Called *selective availability,* this technique will further degrade C/A-code accuracy to 100 meters. Accuracy of 100 meters means that your GPS receiver would not be usable to a prudent mariner in coastal waters. SA wipes out the super accuracy that is so appealing to the GPS system.

Predictable Accuracy. This is the ability of the GPS receiver to correctly locate your actual latitude and longitude on the earth's surface. As indicated above, GPS has a very accurate predictable accuracy—2 to 30 meters without the introduction of SA error when the C/A-code accuracy degrades to 100 meters. In comparison, in coverage areas LORAN-C predictable or "absolute" accuracy varies from 100 meters out to 400 meters.

Repeatable Accuracy. Often LORAN-C is used for relocating a favorite fishing spot or for zeroing in on a lobster pot. This type of accuracy is called *repeatability* and is much more accurate than absolute accuracy.

GPS has no repeatability accuracy due to the dynamic arrangement of the satellites. If you took a GPS reading over a sunken boat and returned the next day to relocate it, an entirely different combination of satellites would be used by your GPS receiver on the second day. By comparison, LORAN-C locks onto the exact same signals every time yielding a repeatability of 50 to 100 feet. However, with the advance of differential GPS stations, the GPS receiver will attain the capability of 3- to 5-meter precision.

Differential GPS

Differential GPS is a technique for calculating out any inaccuracies that may be introduced by the U.S. government's use of SA. As mentioned, the yielded accuracy with DGPS is to a 3- to 5-meter precision. A ground-based receiving station located in a carefully surveyed location would compute the GPS position. Any error between the actual location and the GPS calculated location would produce an adjustment that could be transmitted to other GPS receivers. This technique effectively bypasses any errors, including SA.

The U.S. Coast Guard has tested this concept with good results using existing marine low-frequency beacon stations. DGPS would be effective in a region of 125 to 300 miles away from the DGPS land station. Accuracy decreases with distance from the station. The Coast Guard is currently positioning aids to navigation in selected areas using DGPS. At the moment, DGPS station installations are limited. However, before you buy a GPS set, be sure that it is compatible with DGPS use and that

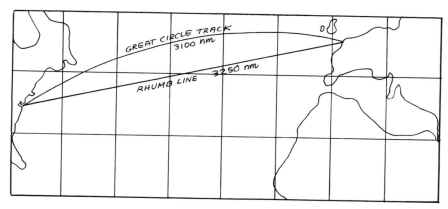

Fig. 14.4 Great Circle Bearing to Rhumb Line.

the manufacturer is planning a DGPS addendum to its line that will allow you to use DGPS with your GPS receiver. I believe that DGPS will be the future for GPS users in coastal navigation situations.

SCREENS AND READOUTS OF ELECTRONIC NAVIGATION EQUIPMENT

Since you should now know basic navigation techniques, the use of electronic navigational equipment will enhance your piloting experience and pleasure in boating. The following is a commentary on the capabilities that are commonly available on both LORAN-C and GPS sets. Make up your own mind and select those features that best fit your boating navigational needs.

> CAUTION: *Most electronic navigation systems plot and read out bearings that are termed great circle bearings. Great circle bearings generally cannot be accurately plotted on a regular Mercator projection chart. The dead reckoning plotting described in this book produces a rhumb line that can be plotted on a Mercator projection. A rhumb line is a straight line on a Mercator projection chart while a great circle bearing is actually a curved line. Figure 14.4 illustrates the differences between a great circle bearing and a rhumb line bearing. From a practical point of view, for the small craft vessel operator transiting on short legs in coastal navigation, the bearing error is minimal. However, be aware that it exists and take the precautions to continuously check and recheck your position, always using more than one method to validate your position.*

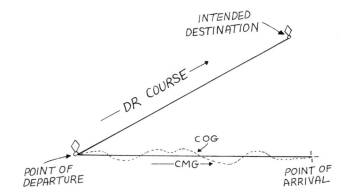

Fig. 14.5   Illustration of Navigation Terminology. *(F. J. Larkin)*

Electronic Navigation System Features

Here is a brief explanation of some of the features found on electronic navigation systems.

Waypoints (WPT).   This is a position that you pre-enter into your electronic navigation system. The initials "WPT" are used for waypoint.

Waypoint Storage.   This is the capability of an electronic navigation system to store the TDs or latitude and longitude of a number of waypoints. The capability to store more than 100 waypoints is common in newer sets.

Waypoint Routing.   This feature allows you to chain a series of preprogrammed waypoints so that you can travel along a number of legs in a route on your trip so you don't need to enter waypoints one at a time as you progress to your planned destination. When you pass one waypoint, the navigation system will automatically direct you to the next waypoint. This is a highly desirable feature to look for when you purchase a LORAN or GPS system.

Distance To Go (DTG).   This is usually the distance in nautical miles to go in order to reach the next waypoint that you have selected on your electronic navigation system. Be sure that you get a knot reading. I have seen some sets that show miles per hour. As you know, a nautical chart uses nautical miles.

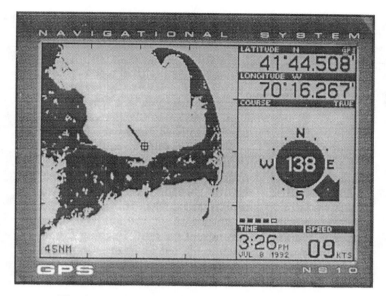

Fig. 14.6 Plotter Data Screen with Chart Feature.

Course Over Ground (COG). This is the actual path of your boat in relationship to the earth's surface. Course over ground is often shown on a plotter screen. Figures 14.6 and 14.9, shown later in this chapter, illustrate a plot of course over ground on a display screen. The initials "COG" are used.

Speed Over Ground (SOG). This is your boat's actual speed in relationship to the earth's surface along your course over ground (COG). The initials "SOG" are used for speed over ground.

Average Speed. This is the average speed that you are making from one waypoint to another.

True Bearing (TBRG). This is the true (great circle) bearing from your latest position to your next waypoint (WPT). The initials "TBRG" are used for true bearing.

Magnetic Bearing (MBRG). This is a true (great circle) bearing that is corrected for variation by the electronic navigation system. The bearing is from your latest position as determined by the electronic navigation system to the next waypoint that you have selected. Electronic navigation systems do not correct for deviation. On some older systems you may have to pre-enter the variation. The initials "MBRG" are used for magnetic bearing.

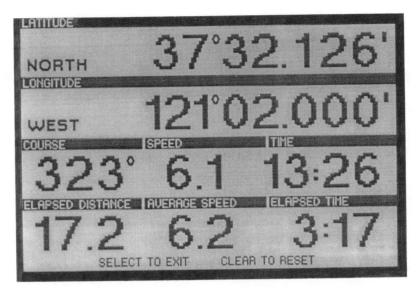

Fig. 14.7 A Position Screen.

Cross Track Error (XTE). This is the distance that you are off course to the right or left of the bearing to the next waypoint. There are many new techniques that are being used to display cross track error. Some sets show a bearing correction and direction left or right of the course line to the waypoint. Other sets simply show the distance in nautical miles that you are off the course line. The initials "XTE" are used for cross track error.

Elapsed Time. This is the time that has been expended from the starting waypoint of the route leg on which you are transiting.

Time To Waypoint. The system uses your current speed and the DTG, distance to go, to compute the time to your next waypoint.

Electronic Navigation System Data Display Screens

A brief explanation follows of some of the electronic navigation system data displays that are currently available. Obviously, these data arrays are constantly changing as manufacturers develop additional features for their products. A variety of examples are provided along with a brief explanation of the particular data presented on the screen.

Satellite Status Information Screen (GPS Only). This display provides data about the satellites the system is currently tracking. Some of the data supplied are:

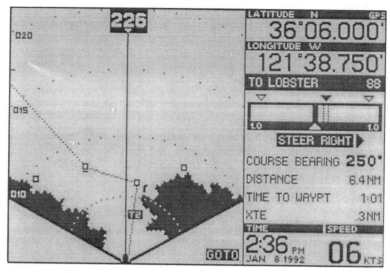

Fig. 14.8   A Dimensional Steer-to-Screen Display.

- The numbers of the satellites that are currently being tracked by the set.
- The elevation of the satellite.
- The azimuth to the satellite.
- The signal-to-noise ratio.
- How many and which satellites are currently in view.

Split Screen Data Screen: Sonar/GPS.   Many of the newest electronic navigation systems combine a series of features on their display screen. Sonar or depth is very common. Some sets provide fish finders and water temperature readings on their screen with sonar and LORAN-C data.

Plotter Display.   Usually you are able to watch your boat's progress on this display. This technique was used in the televising of the last America's Cup races. Some plotters simply show the meridians and parallels on the screen, while others present a graphic representation of a chart. Both Figures 14.6 and 14.8 show a chart in their display.
Other features that appear in the plotter display are:

- Latitude and longitude of your current position.
- DTG, distance to go to the next waypoint.
- True bearing to the next waypoint.
- SOG, speed over ground.

- COG, course over ground.
- Waypoint (WPT) number to which you are heading.
- Time and date. Some sets show elapsed time.

Position Screen. This screen will show your position in latitude and longitude. Most LORAN-C sets and some GPS sets will also display TDs. Figures 14.7 and 14.10 are examples of position displays. Some other features included in position screens are:

- The course that you have been traveling. This will be your COG, course over ground.
- Your speed. This will be your SOG, speed over ground.
- Your bearing required to reach the next waypoint. The initials "BRG" for bearing are most often used. Remember that these will be great circle bearings.

Dimensional Steer-to-Screen Display. This display feature graphically shows your boat's current position with a pointer to indicate when you are off course. Other data such as DTG, SOG, and WPT number are often bundled in this display. You may also find magnetic bearing (MBRG) and true bearing (TBRG) readings included. Most new sets correct for variation automatically.

Navigation Screen. This is usually a display and system that can interface with other systems on the boat, such as radar, sonar, water temperature, etc. Some sets offer the capability of interfacing with automatic steering systems. As these electronic navigation systems develop, it appears that their profuse capabilities will only be limited by the imagination of the manufacturer.

Figure 14.5 illustrates the difference between intended track (TR), course made good (CMG), and course over ground (COG).

In Figure 14.6, the cross mark target on the display is the waypoint. The dark line leading to the waypoint is your course over ground (COG). Note that this display shows the chart for the Cape Cod, Massachusetts, area.

Other data provided by the screen:

- Longitude and latitude of your latest position.
- Your true course (great circle bearing).
- A compass display of your true course.
- The date and time.
- Your speed over ground (SOG).

The screen of Figure 14.7 presents data to help you navigate. It appears that a waypoint is not involved with the data shown on this example:

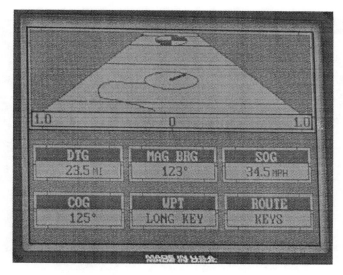

Fig. 14.9 A Dimensional Steer-to-Screen Display.

- The latitude and longitude of your latest position.
- Your course. (You will have to read the system manual to determine whether it is a true or magnetic course.)
- Speed. Most likely speed over ground but check the manual to be positive.
- Time.
- Elapsed time.
- Elapsed distance.
- Average speed.

The plotter display of Figure 14.8 presents the navigational data to help you steer your boat. It appears to be presenting a waypoint route. The display shows a chart and the heading bearing of your boat. It is not clear whether it is true or magnetic. You would need to check the system's manual to find out. It also presents cross track error information that tells you how much to correct your course to the waypoint and in which direction to steer. Other data presented by this screen include:

- The latitude and longitude of your latest position.
- The number and name of your next waypoint (TO LOBSTER 88).
- The course bearing (great circle) to Waypoint 88. (Again you must determine whether it is magnetic or true by consulting the system's manual.)

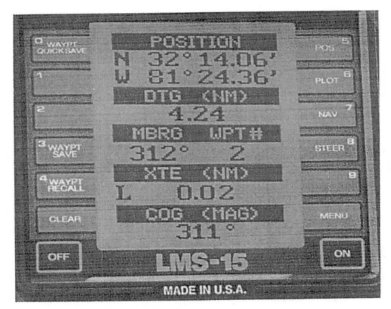

Fig. 14.10 A Position Screen.

- Distance. I assume that this is DTG to Waypoint 88. (Check the system's manual to be positive.)
- Time to waypoint.
- Cross track error (XTE). This feature is presented in a graphic format as well as in nautical miles.
- Date and time.
- Speed. Most likely SOG, but check your manual to be sure.

Figure 14.9 is another version of the types of steer-to-screen displays that are available. Note that this system does not incorporate a chart. It does provide a cross track error display, but it doesn't provide directions to steer or the amount of correction needed. There is a display of COG on the screen. The target appears to be a visual of your waypoint's position on the screen. The other data presented by this screen include:

- DTG, distance to go.
- MAG BRG, magnetic bearing (great circle bearing).
- SOG, speed over ground.
- COG, course over ground.
- WPT, waypoint (LONG KEY).
- Route (KEYS).

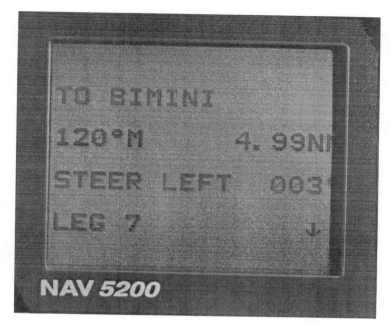

Fig. 14.11   A Steer-to-Data Screen.

Figure 14.10 shows a simple position screen that prints the following essential data:

- Latitude and longitude of your latest position.
- DTG, distance to go.
- MBRG, magnetic bearing.
- WPT#, waypoint number.
- XTE, cross track error. XTE is presented in nautical miles with a direction of "L" for left.
- COG (MAG), magnetic course over ground (great circle bearing).

Figure 14.11 presents a much simplified but effective version of the steering screen that shows the following data:

- TO BIMINI, name of waypoint.
- 120° M, magnetic course to waypoint.
- 4.99NM, distance to go to waypoint.
- STEER LEFT 003°, cross track error with steering direction and number of degrees to correct.
- LEG 7, number of the leg in the route that you are transiting.

HOW TO USE ELECTRONIC NAVIGATIONAL SYSTEMS

Trip Planning

When you plan a trip, determine the LAT/LON of all of the checkpoints along the way. Set up these positions in your LORAN or GPS as waypoints. Usually you need to establish the series of waypoints in numerical order. (The first checkpoint is waypoint 1, the second is waypoint 2, etc.)

The first waypoint is your starting position. List these waypoints on your Trip Log.

A series of waypoints is called a *route.* You will be able to enter the route in your LORAN or GPS (From ___ To ___). Your set will guide you to each waypoint along the way to your destination, providing you with heading directions and time-to-go data.

To get back home, simply reverse the direction of the route. Some sets have a "home" capability that reverses the route automatically.

Finding a Destination Point

In this case, you want to go to a position offshore. Look up the LAT/LON on your chart. Enter the LAT/LON into your receiver as a waypoint. Press the GO TO button and your set will provide a heading and time-to-go information.

On long tacks offshore, use your LORAN to tell you when to change course. Lay your boat on a comfortable course. Convert your compass heading to true. Plot it on a chart. Measure the LAT/LON of the position where you want to turn. Enter the LAT/LON into your receiver as a waypoint. Press the GO TO button to the waypoint and your set will provide a heading and time-to-go information and will beep when it is time to tack.

FIFTEEN

The Height of the Tide at Any Time

I estimate that there may be five situations when you need to know the exact depth of the water; 99 percent of the time, the depth printed on the chart is sufficient for the average boater. The question asked most often by the boater is "When is high tide?" Unfortunately, most new boaters don't realize that the depths marked on their charts refer to the low water mark and that their greatest concern should be for the time of lowest water. Here is a list of the five situations.

First, you will want to know the times of high or low water. This is the simplest solution because all you have to do is read Table 1 in the *Tide Tables* and then adjust the time to your local time. The tide tables are not adjusted for daylight saving time.

Tide data from Table 1 is often printed in your daily newspaper. Most newspapers correct the times to local time. Also, many local marinas and bait stores offer free tide calendars, which provide this basic information. Many of these tide tables are corrected to local time.

Second, you may need to know the height of the tide at a specific point in time.

Third, you may want to know the depth of the water at various points of time over an extended period. Setting up a tide graph will supply you with this information. The use of the tide graph is explained later in this chapter.

Fourth, you may want to determine the height (distance) from the waterline to the span of a bridge for a specific point in time. This simple calculation is made after you determine the height of the tide. It is also explained later in this chapter.

Fifth, you may want to know the time when you have a certain clearance of depth over an obstruction such as a shoal or bar.

CAUTION: *Remember that shoals and bars are always subject to change and shifting depths. Also understand that certain weather conditions can change the predicted depth of a tide significantly. As I have stated before, navigation appears to be a perfect science that is trying to predict events in an imperfect environment. Never trust any depth without verifying your predictions by more than one navigational technique.*

TERMINOLOGY

Before you do the depth and height calculations, you need to understand a few new terms.

Tide Tables

The term *tide tables* usually refers to Table 1 in the *Tide Tables*, which gives daily predictions of the times and heights of high and low water for a reference station. The actual *Tide Tables*, however, is a book that contains all three tables for predicting tide times and heights.

Reference Station

A reference station is a fixed tide station for which independent daily predictions of high and low tides are given in the *Tide Tables*. Reference stations appear in Table 1 of the *Tide Tables*.

Substation

A substation is a fixed location for which tide predictions are determined by applying correction data to predictions for a reference station. Substations appear in Table 2 of the *Tide Tables*.

Range of Tide

The range of tide is the vertical difference in feet or meters of the depth of the water from the point of high water to the point of low water or vice versa.

Duration of Tide

The duration of tide is the predicted time interval in hours and minutes from the time of high water to the time of low water or vice versa.

THE TIDE TABLES

Before you become completely confused about tides, familiarize yourself with Tables 1, 2, and 3 of the *Tide Tables*. Sample pages from each are reproduced as figures in this chapter. As you read about each table, refer to its corresponding figure until you have a firm picture in your mind about the information provided by each table.

A brief description follows of the three tables that are used in calculating the height of the tide.

Table 1: Table of Daily Tide Predictions

Table 1 (see Figure 15.1) contains the predictions of the time and height of high and low water for every day of the year for reference stations. The predictions in Table 1 change yearly. You will have to buy a new *Tide Tables* each year to get the latest time and height predictions. Nevertheless, there are other sources for these data. Here are a few samples:

- Daily newspaper
- *Eldridge Tide and Pilot* book
- Local bait stores and marina calendars.

The reference stations used in the *Tide Tables* for the East Coast of the United States are:

Argentia, Newfoundland
Pictou, Nova Scotia
Harrington Harbour, Quebec
Quebec, Quebec
Halifax, Nova Scotia
St. John, New Brunswick
Eastport, ME

Boston, MA
Newport, RI
New London, CT
Bridgeport, CT
Willets Point, NJ
New York (The Battery), NY
Albany, NY

BOSTON, MASS.

Times and Heights of High and Low Waters

JANUARY

Day	Time (h m)	Height ft	Height m	Day	Time (h m)	Height ft	Height m
1 Su	0537	8.9	2.7	16 M	0556	10.3	3.1
	1154	1.7	0.5		1223	0.2	0.1
	1805	8.0	2.4		1838	8.7	2.7
2 M	0006	1.9	0.6	17 Tu	0035	0.9	0.3
	0627	9.0	2.7		0657	10.3	3.1
	1249	1.5	0.5		1328	0.2	0.1
	1902	7.9	2.4		1942	8.6	2.6
3 Tu	0057	1.9	0.6	18 W	0135	1.1	0.3
	0716	9.2	2.8		0758	10.3	3.1
	1344	1.2	0.4		1430	0.0	0.0
	1954	8.0	2.4		2045	8.6	2.6
4 W	0148	1.8	0.5	19 Th	0235	1.1	0.3
	0805	9.5	2.9		0856	10.4	3.2
	1435	0.8	0.2		1528	-0.1	0.0
	2045	8.2	2.5		2142	8.7	2.7
5 Th	0237	1.5	0.5	20 F	0328	1.0	0.3
	0853	9.9	3.0		0949	10.4	3.2
	1522	0.3	0.1		1617	-0.2	-0.1
	2135	8.5	2.6		2231	8.9	2.7
6 F	0325	1.2	0.4	21 Sa	0417	0.9	0.3
	0939	10.4	3.2		1036	10.5	3.2
	1609	-0.2	-0.1		1703	-0.3	-0.1
	2221	8.9	2.7		2317	9.0	2.7
7 Sa	0413	0.8	0.2	22 Su	0503	0.8	0.2
	1026	10.8	3.3		1121	10.5	3.2
	1654	-0.6	-0.2		1744	-0.3	-0.1
	2307	9.2	2.8		2358	9.1	2.8
8 Su	0500	0.4	0.1	23 M	0549	0.7	0.2
	1112	11.1	3.4		1203	10.3	3.1
	1740	-1.0	-0.3		1822	-0.2	-0.1
	2353	9.6	2.9				
9 M	0549	0.1	0.0	24 Tu	0036	9.2	2.8
	1200	11.3	3.4		0631	0.7	0.2
	1826	-1.2	-0.4		1242	10.1	3.1
					1901	0.0	0.0
10 Tu	0039	9.9	3.0	25 W	0113	9.2	2.8
	0637	-0.2	-0.1		0712	0.8	0.2
	1249	11.3	3.4		1324	9.8	3.0
	1912	-1.3	-0.4		1938	0.3	0.1
11 W	0126	10.2	3.1	26 Th	0151	9.2	2.8
	0727	-0.3	-0.1		0754	0.9	0.3
	1338	11.1	3.4		1404	9.4	2.9
	1958	-1.2	-0.4		2018	0.6	0.2
12 Th	0215	10.4	3.2	27 F	0231	9.2	2.8
	0822	-0.3	-0.1		0839	1.1	0.3
	1431	10.7	3.3		1448	9.0	2.7
	2049	-0.9	-0.3		2057	1.0	0.3
13 F	0307	10.5	3.2	28 Sa	0313	9.1	2.8
	0918	-0.2	-0.1		0924	1.3	0.4
	1527	10.2	3.1		1534	8.5	2.6
	2141	-0.4	-0.1		2140	1.3	0.4
14 Sa	0401	10.5	3.2	29 Su	0356	9.0	2.7
	1017	0.0	0.0		1014	1.4	0.4
	1628	9.6	2.9		1625	8.1	2.5
	2237	0.1	0.0		2227	1.7	0.5
15 Su	0457	10.4	3.2	30 M	0445	8.9	2.7
	1119	0.1	0.0		1108	1.6	0.5
	1730	9.1	2.8		1718	7.8	2.4
	2335	0.6	0.2		2318	2.0	0.6
				31 Tu	0537	8.9	2.7
					1205	1.5	0.5
					1816	7.7	2.3

FEBRUARY

Day	Time (h m)	Height ft	Height m	Day	Time (h m)	Height ft	Height m
1 W	0014	2.0	0.6	16 Th	0118	1.5	0.5
	0630	9.1	2.8		0745	9.7	3.0
	1302	1.3	0.4		1419	0.5	0.2
	1915	7.7	2.3		2037	8.3	2.5
2 Th	0109	1.9	0.6	17 F	0221	1.4	0.4
	0726	9.4	2.9		0846	9.8	3.0
	1358	0.9	0.3		1515	0.4	0.1
	2011	8.0	2.4		2131	8.6	2.6
3 F	0205	1.6	0.5	18 Sa	0317	1.2	0.4
	0821	9.9	3.0		0938	10.0	3.0
	1451	0.3	0.1		1603	0.2	0.1
	2106	8.5	2.6		2219	8.8	2.7
4 Sa	0258	1.1	0.3	19 Su	0405	1.0	0.3
	0914	10.4	3.2		1024	10.1	3.1
	1542	-0.3	-0.1		1643	0.1	0.0
	2154	9.0	2.7		2257	9.1	2.8
5 Su	0351	0.4	0.1	20 M	0448	0.7	0.2
	1005	11.0	3.4		1106	10.1	3.1
	1630	-0.9	-0.3		1720	0.1	0.0
	2242	9.7	3.0		2334	9.3	2.8
6 M	0440	-0.2	-0.1	21 Tu	0529	0.5	0.2
	1052	11.4	3.5		1143	10.1	3.1
	1716	-1.4	-0.4		1756	0.1	0.0
	2329	10.3	3.1				
7 Tu	0529	-0.7	-0.2	22 W	0008	9.5	2.9
	1142	11.6	3.5		0608	0.4	0.1
	1802	-1.6	-0.5		1220	9.9	3.0
					1829	0.2	0.1
8 W	0015	10.8	3.3	23 Th	0042	9.6	2.9
	0619	-1.1	-0.3		0645	0.4	0.1
	1231	11.6	3.5		1257	9.7	3.0
	1848	-1.7	-0.5		1904	0.4	0.1
9 Th	0101	11.1	3.4	24 F	0117	9.6	2.9
	0710	-1.2	-0.4		0725	0.5	0.2
	1322	11.3	3.4		1335	9.4	2.9
	1935	-1.4	-0.4		1941	0.7	0.2
10 F	0149	11.2	3.4	25 Sa	0153	9.5	2.9
	0802	-1.1	-0.3		0806	0.7	0.2
	1415	10.8	3.3		1415	9.0	2.7
	2023	-0.9	-0.3		2018	1.0	0.3
11 Sa	0239	11.1	3.4	26 Su	0231	9.4	2.9
	0857	-0.8	-0.2		0848	0.9	0.3
	1510	10.1	3.1		1458	8.6	2.6
	2116	-0.3	-0.1		2100	1.4	0.4
12 Su	0332	10.8	3.3	27 M	0311	9.2	2.8
	0956	-0.4	-0.1		0935	1.1	0.3
	1608	9.4	2.9		1545	8.1	2.5
	2211	0.4	0.1		2145	1.7	0.5
13 M	0430	10.4	3.2	28 Tu	0358	9.1	2.8
	1057	0.1	0.0		1027	1.4	0.4
	1712	8.7	2.7		1639	7.8	2.4
	2310	1.0	0.3		2237	2.0	0.6
14 Tu	0533	10.0	3.0				
	1204	0.4	0.1				
	1821	8.3	2.5				
15 W	0014	1.4	0.4				
	0638	9.8	3.0				
	1313	0.6	0.2				
	1932	8.2	2.5				

MARCH

Day	Time (h m)	Height ft	Height m	Day	Time (h m)	Height ft	Height m
1 W	0453	9.0	2.7	16 Th	0619	9.4	2.9
	1123	1.4	0.4		1253	1.0	0.3
	1736	7.7	2.3		1913	8.2	2.5
	2335	2.1	0.6				
2 Th	0549	9.1	2.8	17 F	0102	1.8	0.5
	1223	1.3	0.4		0728	9.3	2.8
	1838	7.8	2.4		1400	0.9	0.3
					2017	8.4	2.6
3 F	0035	1.9	0.6	18 Sa	0206	1.6	0.5
	0651	9.4	2.9		0827	9.4	2.9
	1323	0.9	0.3		1453	0.8	0.2
	1938	8.2	2.5		2109	8.7	2.7
4 Sa	0135	1.5	0.5	19 Su	0259	1.3	0.4
	0750	9.9	3.0		0920	9.6	2.9
	1421	0.3	0.1		1538	0.7	0.2
	2035	8.8	2.7		2153	9.0	2.7
5 Su	0233	0.8	0.2	20 M	0346	1.0	0.3
	0849	10.5	3.2		1003	9.7	3.0
	1512	-0.4	-0.1		1615	0.5	0.2
	2126	9.6	2.9		2231	9.3	2.8
6 M	0328	0.0	0.0	21 Tu	0427	0.7	0.2
	0941	11.0	3.4		1044	9.8	3.0
	1603	-1.0	-0.3		1650	0.5	0.2
	2215	10.3	3.1		2303	9.6	2.9
7 Tu	0420	-0.8	-0.2	22 W	0506	0.4	0.1
	1033	11.5	3.5		1120	9.8	3.0
	1649	-1.4	-0.4		1724	0.5	0.2
	2303	11.1	3.4		2335	9.8	3.0
8 W	0510	-1.4	-0.4	23 Th	0543	0.3	0.1
	1122	11.7	3.6		1155	9.7	3.0
	1736	-1.7	-0.5		1757	0.6	0.2
	2348	11.6	3.5				
9 Th	0600	-1.8	-0.5	24 F	0009	9.9	3.0
	1213	11.6	3.5		0620	0.2	0.1
	1823	-1.6	-0.5		1231	9.5	2.9
					1832	0.7	0.2
10 F	0034	11.8	3.6	25 Sa	0042	9.9	3.0
	0650	-1.9	-0.6		0658	0.3	0.1
	1304	11.2	3.4		1309	9.2	2.8
	1909	-1.2	-0.4		1909	1.0	0.3
11 Sa	0123	11.8	3.6	26 Su	0117	9.8	3.0
	0742	-1.6	-0.5		0737	0.4	0.1
	1356	10.6	3.2		1346	8.9	2.7
	1959	-0.7	-0.2		1946	1.2	0.4
12 Su	0212	11.5	3.5	27 M	0155	9.7	3.0
	0836	-1.1	-0.3		0819	0.6	0.2
	1451	9.9	3.0		1428	8.6	2.6
	2051	0.0	0.0		2028	1.5	0.5
13 M	0308	10.9	3.3	28 Tu	0237	9.5	2.9
	0934	-0.4	-0.1		0903	0.9	0.3
	1549	9.2	2.8		1516	8.3	2.5
	2147	0.8	0.2		2114	1.8	0.5
14 Tu	0406	10.3	3.1	29 W	0324	9.3	2.8
	1035	0.2	0.1		0956	1.1	0.3
	1654	8.6	2.6		1608	8.0	2.4
	2249	1.4	0.4		2206	2.0	0.6
15 W	0512	9.8	3.0	30 Th	0419	9.3	2.8
	1143	0.7	0.2		1051	1.2	0.4
	1804	8.2	2.5		1706	8.0	2.4
	2354	1.7	0.5		2305	2.0	0.6
				31 F	0519	9.3	2.8
					1152	1.0	0.3
					1806	8.2	2.5

Time meridian 75° W.   0000 is midnight.   1200 is noon.
Heights are referred to mean lower low water which is the chart datum of soundings.

Fig. 15.1   Table 1: Table of Daily Tide Predictions.
(Source: The Tide Tables)

Sandy Hook, NJ	Savannah, GA
Breakwater Harbor, DE	Mayport, FL
Reedy Point, DE	Miami Harbor Entrance, FL
Philadelphia, PA	Key West, FL
Baltimore, MD	St. Petersburg, FL
Washington, DC	St. Marks River Entrance, FL
Hampton Roads, VA	Pensacola, FL
Wilmington, NC	Mobile, AL
Charleston, SC	Galveston, TX
Savannah River Entrance, GA	Tampico Harbor, Mexico

Figure 15.1 shows a sample page from Table 1. Take a moment to review this figure so that you fully understand how to read this table and know what the data mean.

Table 2: Tidal Differences and Other Constants

Table 2 (see Figure 15.2) lists substations that are associated with specific reference stations. This table shows the position (LAT/LON) of the substation along with the time and height differences of high and low tide from the predictions of their associated reference stations shown in Table 1. Table 2 remains fairly constant year to year. You can't use data from Table 2 without the appropriate base data from Table 1.

> CAUTION: *The time and height differences listed in Table 2 are average differences calculated from comparisons of simultaneous tide observations at the reference stations and the substation. Because Table 2 figures are constant, they do not make provision for the daily variances of the actual tide at a substation's location.*

The predictions at the substations are not as accurate as the predictions at the reference stations. Table 2 should only be used to approximate the times and heights of high and low water at the substations. This means that you should expect to have some error or difference from your calculated depth to the actual depth at the location. Act accordingly. Figure 15.2 shows a sample of the substations associated with the various reference stations near Labrador.

TABLE 2. — TIDAL DIFFERENCES AND OTHER CONSTANTS

NO.	PLACE	POSITION		DIFFERENCES				RANGES		Mean Tide Level
		Lat.	Long.	Time		Height		Mean	Spring	
				High water	Low water	High water	Low water			
		° ' N	° ' W	h. m.	h. m.	ft	ft	ft	ft	ft
	BAFFIN BAY, etc., West Side Time meridian, local			on HALIFAX, p.20						
101	Fort Conger, Discovery Harbor...........	81 44	64 44	+3 48	+3 25	-1.4	-1.3	4.3	5.9	3.0
103	Cape Lawrence........................	80 21	69 15	+3 46	+3 40	-0.2	-1.3	5.5	7.2	3.6
105	Payer Harbour, Cape Sabine..............	78 43	74 25	+3 36	+3 30	+1.7	-0.9	7.0	9.4	4.7
107	Cape Adair............................	71 33	71 30	+3 06	+3 06	+0.4	-1.2	6.0	7.8	3.9
109	Cape Hewett...........................	70 16	67 47	+2 56	+2 56	+0.6	-0.5	5.5	7.2	4.4
	DAVIS STRAIT, West Side Time meridian, 60°W			on PICTOU, p.8						
111	Cape Hooper, Baffin Island.............	68 23	66 45	-5 52	-5 41	*0.47	*0.43	1.6	1.9	1.8
113	Kivitoo, Baffin Island.................	67 56	64 56	-5 17	-5 10	*0.51	*0.43	1.8	2.4	1.9
				on SAINT JOHN, N. B., p.24						
115	Cape Dyer, Baffin Island...............	66 34	61 40	-6 19	-6 21	*0.31	*0.45	5.8	7.3	4.7
117	Clearwater Fiord, Cumberland Sound......	66 36	67 20	-5 36	-5 38	-5.5	-0.6	15.9	20.6	11.4
119	Frobisher Bay.........................	63 29	68 02	-4 13	-4 15	+5.5	+3.3	23.0	29.8	18.8
	HUDSON STRAIT and BAY									
121	Pikyulik Island, Payne River...........	60 00	69 55	-2 15	-1 54	+3.7	+3.2	21.3	26.8	17.9
	Time meridian, 75°W									
123	Sorry Harbor, Resolution Island........	61 37	64 44	-5 30	-5 30	-8.3	-0.9	13.4	17.6	9.8
125	Lower Savage Islands...................	61 46	65 51	-4 46	-4 55	-1.2	+2.0	17.6	25.4	14.8
127	Ashe Inlet, Big Island.................	62 33	70 35	-3 46	-3 43	+4.2	+2.2	22.8	30.9	17.6
129	Schooner Harbour, Baffin Island........	64 24	77 52	-0 49	-0 44	-6.2	+0.4	14.2	18.9	11.5
131	Winter Island, Foxe Basin..............	66 11	83 10	+1 02	+1 10	-12.1	-0.8	9.5	12.4	8.0
	Time meridian, 90°W									
133	Coral Harbour, Southampton Island.......	64 08	83 10	-0 25	+0 04	-14.4	-1.5	7.9	10.3	6.5
135	Chesterfield Inlet....................	63 20	90 42	-8 17	-8 20	-12.4	-0.8	9.2	11.8	7.8
137	Churchill............................	58 47	94 12	-4 25	-4 36	-11.5	-1.4	10.7	13.4	7.9
				on QUEBEC, p.16						
139	Port Nelson, Nelson River entrance......	57 05	92 36	+3 56	+4 35	-3.1	-0.9	11.5	12.9	6.4
	Time meridian, 75°W									
141	Moosonee, James Bay....................	51 17	80 38	+9 29	+9 32	*0.48	*1.81	4.5	5.4	5.2
143	Moose Factory, James Bay...............	51 16	80 35	+9 33	+10 37	*0.42	*1.56	4.0	5.4	4.5
145	Charlton Island, James Bay.............	51 57	79 16	+8 00	+6 38	*0.39	*1.06	4.3	5.3	3.9
				on SAINT JOHN, N. B., p.24						
147	Digges Harbour.......................	62 30	77 42	-2 11	-2 05	*0.39	*0.62	7.1	9.3	6.1
149	Port de Boucherville, Nottingham Island.	63 12	77 28	-2 07	-2 02	-11.6	-1.2	10.4	14.0	8.0
151	Wakeham Bay..........................	61 43	71 57	-3 52	-3 55	-0.4	+2.2	18.2	27.0	15.3
153	Stupart Bay..........................	61 35	71 32	-4 10	-4 17	0.0	+2.4	18.4	27 2	15.6
155	Diana Bay............................	60 52	70 04	-4 00	-4 03	+2.8	+3.1	20.5	26.8	17.4
157	Hopes Advance Bay, Ungava Bay..........	59 21	69 38	-3 59	-4 00	*1.44	*2.20	27.0	34.4	22.3
159	Leaf Bay, Ungava Bay..................	58 55	69 00	-4 00	-4 00	*1.49	*2.25	28.0	36.0	23.0
161	Leaf Lake, Ungava Bay.................	58 45	69 40	-3 00	-3 00	(*1.54+5.8)		32.0	40.0	28.0
163	Koksoak River entrance................	58 32	68 11	-3 50	-3 53	*1.47	*2.00	28.5	36.4	22.3
165	Port Burwell, Ungava Bay..............	60 25	64 52	-4 13	-4 13	-6.5	-0.9	15.2	19.9	10.7
	LABRADOR Time meridian, 52°30'W									
167	Button Islands.......................	60 37	64 44	-2 38	-2 38	-9.5	-0.3	11.6	15.4	9.5
169	Williams Harbour.....................	60 00	64 19	-3 07	-3 27	*0.32	*0.30	6.8	8.2	4.6
				on HALIFAX, p.20						
171	Eclipse Harbour......................	59 48	64 09	+0 25	+0 02	-2.4	-1.0	3.0	3.7	2.6
173	Kangalaksiorvik Fiord.................	59 23	63 47	+1 00	+0 42	-2.6	-1.5	3.3	4.1	2.2
175	Nachvak Bay..........................	59 03	63 35	+0 04	-0 20	-1.5	-1.1	4.0	5.0	3.0
177	Port Manvers.........................	56 57	61 25	-0 55	-0 55	-2.3	-1.2	3.3	4.2	2.6
179	Hebron, Hebron Fjord..................	58 12	62 38	-0 49	-1 05	-1.4	-0.9	3.9	4.7	3.2
181	Nain.................................	56 33	61 41	-0 32	-0 54	+0.3	-0.5	5.2	6.5	4.2
183	Hopedale Harbour.....................	55 27	60 13	-0 46	-1 09	-0.4	-0.3	4.3	5.6	4.0
185	Webeck Harbour.......................	54 54	58 02	-1 07	-1 38	-1.3	-0.8	3.9	5.0	3.3
	Hamilton Inlet and Lake Melville									
187	Indian Harbour....................	54 27	57 12	-0 37	-1 33	-1.0	-0.4	4.3	5.7	3.4
189	Ticoralak Island..................	54 17	58 12	-0 35	-0 55	-0.9	-0.5	4.0	4.9	3.7
191	Rigolet...........................	54 11	58 25	-0 02	-0 17	-1.9	-1.0	3.5	4.5	2.8
193	Goose Bay.........................	53 21	60 24	+4 22	+4 24	(*0.27+0.4)		1.2	1.7	1.6

Fig. 15.2   Table 2: Tidal Differences and Other Constants.
(Source: The Tide Tables)

Table 3: Height of Tide at Any Time

Table 3 provides a means to correct the height of tide based on the duration of the tide, the time from the nearest high or low water, and the range of tide. Figure 15.3 shows the complete Table 3. Follow these steps to use this table:

- Enter Table 3 at the top section of the table at the time nearest to the duration of tide (6h 50m).

- Follow across to the column that is closest to the time from nearest high or low tide (2h 15m).

- Staying in this column, follow down to where the column intersects with the row closest to the range of the tide (9.1). Read the correction to height (2.2 ft).

- If the tide is rising, add the correction to the depth reading. (Depth 8.5 ft + 2.2 = 10.7 ft). If the tide is falling, subtract the correction from the depth reading. (Depth 8.5 ft – 2.2 = 6.3 ft).

The *Tide Tables* provides a full explanation on the use of these three tables. Due to the dynamic nature of tide, it is often better to use graphs to depict the change in the depth of water over the duration of a tide. Computer programs are available that perform this task for you. Many large vessels follow a standard practice of printing out and posting height of tide curves each day. Two simple manual graphing techniques are provided in this chapter.

TIDE GRAPH: "ONE-QUARTER/ONE-TENTH RULE"

This is an another simple method for determining the height of tide at any time. Use this tide graph technique when you want to know the depth of the water at various times on the same day or during a tide cycle. This technique is also called the one-quarter/one-tenth rule.

Note that you must develop a curve graphic for each substation where you may be operating during the day.

TABLE 3.—HEIGHT OF TIDE AT ANY TIME

Time from the nearest high water or low water

Duration of rise or fall (h.m.)	h.m.	h.m.	h.m.	h.m.	h.m.	h.m.	h.m.	h.m.	h.m.	h.m.	h.m.	h.m.	h.m.	h.m.	h.m.
4 00	0 08	0 16	0 24	0 32	0 40	0 48	0 56	1 04	1 12	1 20	1 28	1 36	1 44	1 52	2 00
4 20	0 09	0 17	0 26	0 35	0 43	0 52	1 01	1 09	1 18	1 27	1 35	1 44	1 53	2 01	2 10
4 40	0 09	0 19	0 28	0 37	0 47	0 56	1 05	1 15	1 24	1 33	1 43	1 52	2 01	2 11	2 20
5 00	0 10	0 20	0 30	0 40	0 50	1 00	1 10	1 20	1 30	1 40	1 50	2 00	2 10	2 20	2 30
5 20	0 11	0 21	0 32	0 43	0 53	1 04	1 15	1 25	1 36	1 47	1 57	2 08	2 19	2 29	2 40
5 40	0 11	0 23	0 34	0 45	0 57	1 08	1 19	1 31	1 42	1 53	2 05	2 16	2 27	2 39	2 50
6 00	0 12	0 24	0 36	0 48	1 00	1 12	1 24	1 36	1 48	2 00	2 12	2 24	2 36	2 48	3 00
6 20	0 13	0 25	0 38	0 51	1 03	1 16	1 29	1 41	1 54	2 07	2 19	2 32	2 45	2 57	3 10
6 40	0 13	0 27	0 40	0 53	1 07	1 20	1 33	1 47	2 00	2 13	2 27	2 40	2 53	3 07	3 20
7 00	0 14	0 28	0 42	0 56	1 10	1 24	1 38	1 52	2 06	2 20	2 34	2 48	3 02	3 16	3 30
7 20	0 15	0 29	0 44	0 59	1 13	1 28	1 43	1 57	2 12	2 27	2 41	2 56	3 11	3 25	3 40
7 40	0 15	0 31	0 46	1 01	1 17	1 32	1 47	2 03	2 18	2 33	2 49	3'04	3 19	3 35	3 50
8 00	0 16	0 32	0 48	1 04	1 20	1 36	1 52	2 08	2 24	2 40	2 56	3 12	3 28	3 44	4 00
8 20	0 17	0 33	0 50	1 07	1 23	1 40	1 57	2 13	2 30	2 47	3 03	3 20	3 37	3 53	4 10
8 40	0 17	0 35	0 52	1 09	1 27	1 44	2 01	2 19	2 36	2 53	3 11	3 28	3 45	4 03	4 20
9 00	0 18	0 36	0 54	1 12	1 30	1 48	2 06	2 24	2 42	3 00	3 18	3 36	3 54	4 12	4 30
9 20	0 19	0 37	0 56	1 15	1 33	1 52	2 11	2 29	2 48	3 07	3 25	3 44	4 03	4 21	4 40
9 40	0 19	0 39	0 58	1 17	1 37	1 56	2 15	2 35	2 54	3 13	3 33	3 52	4 11	4 31	4 50
10 00	0 20	0 40	1 00	1 20	1 40	2 00	2 20	2 40	3 00	3 20	3 40	4 00	4 20	4 40	5 00
10 20	0 21	0 41	1 02	1 23	1 43	2 04	2 25	2 45	3 06	3 27	3 47	4 08	4 29	4 49	5 10
10 40	0 21	0 43	1 04	1 25	1 47	2 08	2 29	2 51	3 12	3 33	3 55	4 16	4 37	4 59	5 20

Correction to height

Range of tide (Ft.)	Ft.	Ft.	Ft.	Ft.	Ft.	Ft.	Ft.	Ft.	Ft.	Ft.	Ft.	Ft.	Ft.	Ft.	Ft.
0.5	0.0	0.0	0.0	0.0	0.0	0.0	0.1	0.1	0.1	0.1	0.1	0.2	0.2	0.2	0.2
1.0	0.0	0.0	0.0	0.0	0.1	0.1	0.1	0.2	0.2	0.2	0.3	0.3	0.4	0.4	0.5
1.5	0.0	0.0	0.0	0.1	0.1	0.1	0.2	0.2	0.3	0.4	0.4	0.5	0.6	0.7	0.8
2.0	0.0	0.0	0.0	0.1	0.1	0.2	0.3	0.3	0.4	0.5	0.6	0.7	0.8	0.9	1.0
2.5	0.0	0.0	0.1	0.1	0.2	0.2	0.3	0.4	0.5	0.6	0.7	0.9	1.0	1.1	1.2
3.0	0.0	0.0	0.1	0.1	0.2	0.3	0.4	0.5	0.6	0.8	0.9	1.0	1.2	1.3	1.5
3.5	0.0	0.0	0.1	0.2	0.2	0.3	0.4	0.6	0.7	0.9	1.0	1.2	1.4	1.6	1.8
4.0	0.0	0.0	0.1	0.2	0.3	0.4	0.5	0.7	0.8	1.0	1.2	1.4	1.6	1.8	2.0
4.5	0.0	0.0	0.1	0.2	0.3	0.4	0.6	0.7	0.9	1.1	1.3	1.6	1.8	2.0	2.2
5.0	0.0	0.1	0.1	0.2	0.3	0.5	0.6	0.8	1.0	1.2	1.5	1.7	2.0	2.2	2.5
5.5	0.0	0.1	0.1	0.2	0.4	0.5	0.7	0.9	1.1	1.4	1.6	1.9	2.2	2.5	2.8
6.0	0.0	0.1	0.1	0.3	0.4	0.6	0.8	1.0	1.2	1.5	1.8	2.1	2.4	2.7	3.0
6.5	0.0	0.1	0.2	0.3	0.4	0.6	0.8	1.1	1.3	1.6	1.9	2.2	2.6	2.9	3.2
7.0	0.0	0.1	0.2	0.3	0.5	0.7	0.9	1.2	1.4	1.8	2.1	2.4	2.8	3.1	3.5
7.5	0.0	0.1	0.2	0.3	0.5	0.7	1.0	1.2	1.5	1.9	2.2	2.6	3.0	3.4	3.8
8.0	0.0	0.1	0.2	0.3	0.5	0.8	1.0	1.3	1.6	2.0	2.4	2.8	3.2	3.6	4.0
8.5	0.0	0.1	0.2	0.4	0.6	0.8	1.1	1.4	1.8	2.1	2.5	2.9	3.4	3.8	4.2
9.0	0.0	0.1	0.2	0.4	0.6	0.9	1.2	1.5	1.9	2.2	2.7	3.1	3.6	4.0	4.5
9.5	0.0	0.1	0.2	0.4	0.6	0.9	1.2	1.6	2.0	2.4	2.8	3.3	3.8	4.3	4.8
10.0	0.0	0.1	0.2	0.4	0.7	1.0	1.3	1.7	2.1	2.5	3.0	3.5	4.0	4.5	5.0
10.5	0.0	0.1	0.3	0.5	0.7	1.0	1.3	1.7	2.2	2.6	3.1	3.6	4.2	4.7	5.2
11.0	0.0	0.1	0.3	0.5	0.7	1.1	1.4	1.8	2.3	2.8	3.3	3.8	4.4	4.9	5.5
11.5	0.0	0.1	0.3	0.5	0.8	1.1	1.5	1.9	2.4	2.9	3.4	4.0	4.6	5.1	5.8
12.0	0.0	0.1	0.3	0.5	0.8	1.1	1.5	2.0	2.5	3.0	3.6	4.1	4.8	5.4	6.0
12.5	0.0	0.1	0.3	0.5	0.8	1.2	1.6	2.1	2.6	3.1	3.7	4.3	5.0	5.6	6.2
13.0	0.0	0.1	0.3	0.6	0.9	1.2	1.7	2.2	2.7	3.2	3.9	4.5	5.1	5.8	6.5
13.5	0.0	0.1	0.3	0.6	0.9	1.3	1.7	2.2	2.8	3.4	4.0	4.7	5.3	6.0	6.8
14.0	0.0	0.2	0.3	0.6	0.9	1.3	1.8	2.3	2.9	3.5	4.2	4.8	5.5	6.3	7.0
14.5	0.0	0.2	0.4	0.6	1.0	1.4	1.9	2.4	3.0	3.6	4.3	5.0	5.7	6.5	7.2
15.0	0.0	0.2	0.4	0.6	1.0	1.4	1.9	2.5	3.1	3.8	4.4	5.2	5.9	6.7	7.5
15.5	0.0	0.2	0.4	0.7	1.0	1.5	2.0	2.6	3.2	3.9	4.6	5.4	6.1	6.9	7.8
16.0	0.0	0.2	0.4	0.7	1.1	1.5	2.1	2.6	3.3	4.0	4.7	5.5	6.3	7.2	8.0
16.5	0.0	0.2	0.4	0.7	1.1	1.6	2.1	2.7	3.4	4.1	4.9	5.7	6.5	7.4	8.2
17.0	0.0	0.2	0.4	0.7	1.1	1.6	2.2	2.8	3.5	4.2	5.0	5.9	6.7	7.6	8.5
17.5	0.0	0.2	0.4	0.8	1.2	1.7	2.2	2.9	3.6	4.4	5.2	6.0	6.9	7.8	8.8
18.0	0.0	0.2	0.4	0.8	1.2	1.7	2.3	3.0	3.7	4.5	5.3	6.2	7.1	8.1	9.0
18.5	0.1	0.2	0.5	0.8	1.2	1.8	2.4	3.1	3.8	4.6	5.5	6.4	7.3	8.3	9.2
19.0	0.1	0.2	0.5	0.8	1.3	1.8	2.4	3.1	3.9	4.8	5.6	6.6	7.5	8.5	9.5
19.5	0.1	0.2	0.5	0.8	1.3	1.9	2.5	3.2	4.0	4.9	5.8	6.7	7.7	8.7	9.8
20.0	0.1	0.2	0.5	0.9	1.3	1.9	2.6	3.3	4.1	5.0	5.9	6.9	7.9	9.0	10.0

Fig. 15.3 Table 3: Height of Tide at Any Time. *(Source: The Tide Tables)*

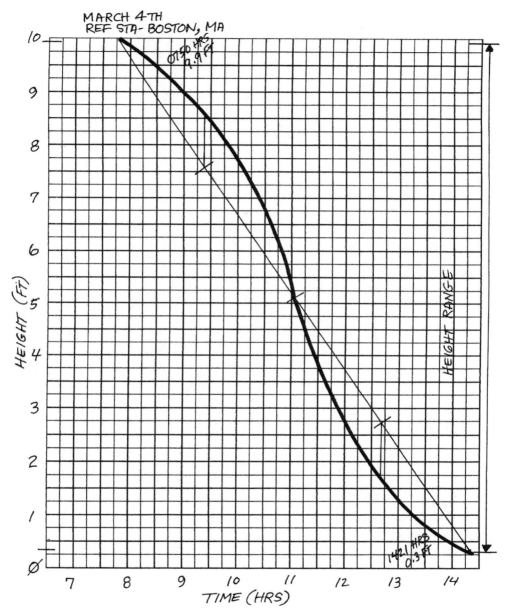

MARCH 4TH
REF STA- BOSTON, MA

0750 HRS
9.9 FT

1421 HRS
0.3 FT

HEIGHT RANGE

HEIGHT (FT)

TIME (HRS)

Fig. 15.4   Tide Graph Illustrating the One-Quarter/One-Tenth Rule. *(F. J. Larkin)*

MARCH		
DAY	TIME h m	HEIGHT ft
4	0135	1.5
SA	0750	9.9
	1421	0.3
	2035	8.8

Fig.15.5   Sample Data from Table 1 for the Tide Graph.

Setting Up the Tide Graph

Make a copy of the Tide Graph form from Appendix 7 whenever you set up a tide graph. Here are a few simple steps to follow to help you make a tide graph.

Step 1.   Label the vertical scale (left-hand side of the graph) with the height of tide gradients. These are the height figures from Table 1. You may need to start with a negative number depending on the tidal predictions for the day. Start your labeling in the lower left-hand corner and increase the height upwards. In our example, the height of low tide is 0.3 feet and high tide is 9.9 feet. Start your labeling at zero and increase up the scale to ten feet (refer to Figure 15.4).

Step 2.   Label the horizontal scale (bottom of the graph) in hours. Start at the lower left-hand corner and proceed toward the right along the bottom of the graph. Example: Use the times and heights of high and low water for Saturday, March 4, from Figure 15.5.

In our example, we will be operating between 0800 and 1400. Always correct the *Tide Tables* for daylight saving time. Since the month in the example is March, daylight saving time is not in effect so we can read the time directly from Table 1.

Label the vertical scale of the tide graph from 0.0 feet to 10.0 feet. Label the horizontal scale from 0700 to 1400 hours. Figure 15.4 shows a labeled tide graph.

Plotting the Height of Tide Curve

Now that the graph is set up, you can begin to plot the tidal data. Follow these simple steps to complete this part of the graph.

Step 1.   On the tide graph, plot the height and time of the high and low water in the order of their occurrence for the day you have selected. These plotted points become the starting and ending points of your tide curve. Example: The high tide plot will be on the vertical 0750 hour line at the 9.9-ft horizontal line. The low tide plot will be on the 1421 vertical line and the 0.3-ft horizontal line. These points are plotted in Figure 15.4.

Step 2.   Draw a straight line connecting the high point and the low point. You may need to plot successive high and low water lines depending on the time of day that you expect to be under way. Figure 15.4 shows this plotted line.

Step 3.   Divide your plotted line into four equal parts. The halfway point on this line is the intersecting point for your curve.

Step 4.   At the margin of your graph, measure the distance between the high and low water marks that you just plotted. This length is your height range or range of tide.

- At the upmost quarter mark on your line, draw a vertical line upward. This vertical line should be equal to one-tenth of the height range.

- At the lower quarter mark on your line, draw a vertical line downward. This vertical line should be equal to one-tenth of the height range. Figure 15.4 shows an example of these vertical lines.

Step 5.   On the plotted line, draw a smooth curve starting at the plotted high water point, tangent to the high-water quarter vertical line point, through the center point, tangent to the low-water quarter vertical line point, ending at the plotted low water point. Round the curve well.

This curve approximates the actual tide curve. The heights of tides for any time of the day can be readily scaled from this type of curve. Add or subtract the height of tide to or from the depth of water printed on your nautical chart.

EXAMPLE: Using the tide graph plotted in Figure 15.4, find the height of tide for 1130 hrs. The depth of the water printed on your chart is 5 feet at 1130 hrs. The tide graph shows the height of tide for 1130 to be 3.75 feet or 3' 8". Added to the charted depth of 5 feet, your estimated depth would be 8' 8".

> CAUTION: *The one-quarter/one-tenth rule is based on the assumption that the rise and fall of tide conforms to simple cosine curves. The heights obtained will always be approximate. The roughness of the approximation will vary as the tide curve differs from the cosine curve.*

PRACTICE PROBLEMS

Use the tide graph in Figure 15.4 to solve these problems.

1. What is your estimated depth at 0930 if your charted depth is stated as 2.5 feet?

2. The charted depth is 9.3 ft. What is the estimated depth at 12 noon?

3. The charted depth is 5 ft. The MHW datum is 9.5 ft for this area. The vertical height of the bridge is 12 ft. At what time would your estimated clearance under the bridge be 15 ft?

4. The charted depth of a shoal is 2 feet. You need a minimum of 6 ft to clear the shoal with a 3-ft safety margin. What is the latest time that you should plan to cross over this shoal?

ANSWERS

1. Simply measure your estimated depth for 0930 and add it to the charted depth.

Estimated depth from graph	8.4 ft
Charted depth	+2.5 ft
Estimated depth at your position	10.9 ft

2. Find the estimated depth from the graph for 1200 hrs and add it to the charted depth.

Estimated depth from graph	2.7 ft
Charted depth	+9.3 ft
Estimated depth at your position	12.0 ft

3. You need 15 ft. The vertical clearance for the bridge is 12 ft. Subtracting 12 from 15 shows that you need an additional 3 ft. The height of tide at high water is 9.9 ft, which is 0.4 ft above the MHW datum. Subtract 3.4 ft from the high water height and find the time on the graph for that depth.

Clearance required	15.0 ft
Vertical clearance of bridge	− 12.0 ft
Additional clearance required	3.0 ft
Height of tide at high water	9.9 ft
MHW datum for place	9.5 ft
Difference over MHW datum	0.4 ft
Additional clearance required	+ 3.0 ft
Total clearance required	3.4 ft
Height of tide at high water	9.9 ft
Total clearance required	− 3.4 ft
Depth to enter graph	6.5 ft
Time when vertical clearance is 15 ft	1036 hrs

4. You need to enter the graph at the 4-ft point on the vertical scale and read the time from the horizontal scale.

Minimum depth required	6 ft
Charted depth	2 ft
Additional clearance required	4 ft
Graphed time at 4 ft	1124 hrs

THE RULE OF TWELVES

The rule of twelves is a simplified method for predicting the height of the tide at any time. This technique involves dividing the range of tide into twelve equal parts and applying the rule. The resulting data may be graphed if you need multiple height predictions during a tidal cycle. Follow these simple steps to complete the rule of twelves tidal predictions.

Step 1.   Determine the range of tide. The range of tide is the difference between the high and low height predictions on a specific day for a particular tide cycle. As an example, use the data found in Figure 15.5. Because the date is March 4, you don't have to correct for daylight saving time. Use the range of tide between 1421 and 2035 hrs.

Depth at 2035 hrs	8.8 ft
Depth at 1421 hrs	− 0.3 ft
Range of tide	9.1 ft

Step 2. Divide the range of tide by twelve: 9.1 ft divided by 12 equals 0.76 ft.

Step 3. Apply the rule of twelves.

END OR START OF HIGH TIDE	RULE OF TWELVES	TIDE CHANGE IN FEET	DEPTH PREDICTION
Start			0.30 ft
First Hour	1/12	0.76 ft	1.05 ft
Second Hour	2/12	1.52 ft	2.57 ft
Third Hour	3/12	2.27 ft	4.84 ft
Fourth Hour	3/12	2.27 ft	7.11 ft
Fifth Hour	2/12	1.52 ft	8.63 ft
Sixth Hour	1/12	0.76 ft	9.39 ft

Going from low to high water, add the tide change. Going from high to low, subtract the tide change.

Step 4. When you need to predict the height of tide for various times during a tidal cycle, plot your data on a tide graph. The vertical scale is height of tide and the horizontal scale is time. Figure 15.6 shows the data plotted for the example calculated in Step 3. Notice how, when the curve is rounded, it looks like the tide curve that was developed using the one-quarter/one-tenth rule.

> CAUTION: *The rule of twelves is based on the assumption that the rise and fall of tide conforms to simple cosine curves. The heights obtained will always be approximate. The roughness of the approximation will vary as the tide curve differs from the cosine curve.*

PRACTICE PROBLEMS

Use the tide graph in Figure 15.6 to solve these problems.

1. What is the estimated depth at 4:30 PM if the charted depth is 3.5 ft?

2. The charted depth is 5 ft. You need 10 ft to cross a shoal. What is the earliest estimated time that you can make this crossing?

3. At what time will the depth be 7.5 feet above the charted depth?

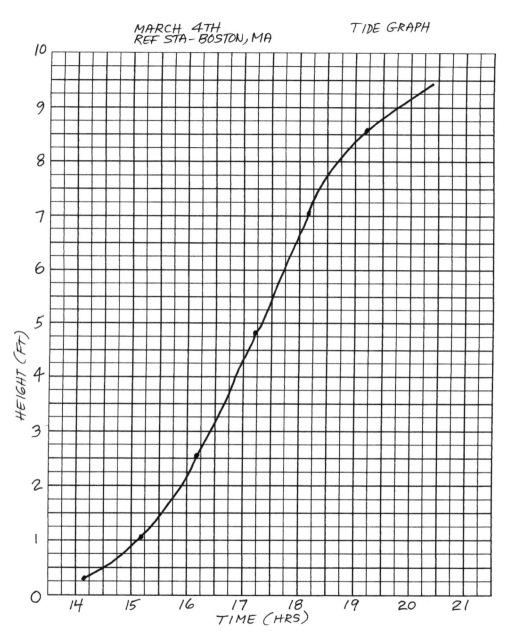

Fig. 15.6 Tide Graph Illustrating the Rule of Twelves. *(F. J. Larkin)*

ANSWERS

1. Convert 4:30 PM to military time or 1630 hrs. Enter the graph at 1630 and read out the feet or 3.1 ft.

Charted depth	3.5 ft
Graph depth	+3.1 ft
Estimated depth	6.6 ft

2. You have 5 ft and need 5 more. Enter the graph at 5 ft and read out the hours: 17.3 or 1718 hours or 5:18 PM.

3. Enter the graph at 7.5 feet and read out the hours: 18.3 or 1818 hours or 6:18 PM.

HEIGHT AVAILABLE UNDER A BRIDGE

Now that you know how to find the depth of water at any time, it is a simple matter to determine the depth under a bridge at any time. There are a few facts that you need to know that will help you understand this calculation:

- Bridge heights are measured from MHW, mean high water, upward to the lowest part of the span over the navigation channel.

- The tidal information block on each nautical chart shows the height of MHW, mean high water.

Here are a few simple steps that will help complete this height calculation.

Step 1. Look up the mean high water datum from the tidal information block on your nautical chart. There may be more than one MHW datum listed so use the one closest to your position. Enter the MHW datum on your worksheet. Figure 15.7 shows the tidal information block from a Boston Harbor chart. The place nearest to Neponset is Charlestown, which has a MHW datum of 9.5 ft.

Step 2. Copy the projected height of tide for the point in time that you will be passing under the bridge. Use either of the graphing methods explained in this chapter. Using Figure 15.6, assume you plan to pass under the bridge at

BOSTON INNER HARBOR

Mercator Projection
Scale 1:10,000 at Lat. 42°22′
North American 1927 Datum

SOUNDINGS IN FEET
AT MEAN LOW WATER

TIDAL INFORMATION

Place	Height referred to datum of soundings (MLW)			
	Mean High Water	Mean Tide Level	Mean Low Water	Extreme Low Water
	feet	feet	feet	feet
Charlestown	9.5	4.7	0.0	−3.5

(1279)

Fig. 15.7 Sample Tidal Information Block. *(Source: NOAA nautical chart)*

1730 hours or 5:30 PM. The projected depth is 5.5 ft at that time for that day.

Step 3. Determine the additional clearance provided by the tide by subtracting the projected height of tide from the nearest MHW datum. Post the result on your worksheet. In our example, the mean high water datum is 9.5 feet.

MHW datum for nearest place	9.5 ft
Projected Height of Tide	− 5.5 ft
Additional clearance	4.0 ft

Step 4. Enter the vertical clearance listed for the bridge. These data will be found on your chart. The Bascule Bridge in the Neponset area has a vertical clearance of 12 ft.

Step 5. To compute the available height under the bridge, add the additional clearance figure to the vertical clearance listed for the bridge. For our example:

Vertical clearance of bridge	12.0 ft
Additional clearance	+ 4.0 ft
Available height under the bridge	16.0 ft

The available height under the bridge at 1730 hours on March 4th is 16.0 ft.

SUMMARY

What do you now know? You can correct a depth for the time of the tide and can figure the height clearance under a bridge for a specific time. However, never forget that these are *estimated* depths and heights and that you should use multiple methods to verify all data in navigation. Nothing stays the same on the sea. Weather changes the depth of the water—both high and low. Shoals are generated where they never were before. Become very suspicious and double-check everything. Above all, use common sense. If it doesn't feel right, don't go there.

SIXTEEN

Compensating Your Course for Current and Other Factors

Unfortunately, the only time that you can use a DR heading and speed prediction is on a day when there is no wind, and the current is slack, the water depth is over 18 feet, and the weight of your boat is exactly the same as when you ran your speed curve. After many attempts at predicting an exact ETA without great success, I have isolated five elements that affect the accuracy of a DR calculation:

1. The accuracy of your DR speed prediction.
2. The presence of current along your DR course line.
3. Weight differences from your boat's baseline weight.
4. Water depth under 18 feet.
5. The presence of wind along your DR course line.

Every navigator needs to deal with DR predictions and current problems. Owners of heavy displacement vessels may find that changes in boat weight and wind velocity have minimal impact on their ETA predictions due to the large size of their boats. However, boat owners of small planing boats will soon discover that any weight change and wind will have a great effect on their navigation speed predictions.

Without any understanding of the five elements, you could be led to think that your piloting errors are due to something that you failed to understand about the DR formula, $60 \times D = S \times T$. Not so! The following five examples illustrate a complete piloting prediction and will help you understand why a DR speed prediction does not work on its own.

The DR Prediction

To illustrate the situation, suppose you are on a leg of a trip that is 2.8 nm long, on a heading of 090 degrees, and at a speed of 12.3 knots. If you started this leg at 0900, what is your ETA?

$60 \times 2.8 = 12.3 \times T$ or 13.659 minutes or 13 m 40 s. Your ETA is 09:13:40.

Mathematical errors are the biggest problem with this first element. Get yourself a good calculator or install the formula on your computer. I use a computer to check all my navigation data when I plan a trip.

The Current Problem

Assume 0.500 kts of current is striking your boat directly on the stern. Your speed prediction must change since current at the stern will make your boat go faster. Starting this leg at the same time as the preceding example, you will find a 32-second change in your ETA due to the current.

12.3 kts + 0.500 kts = 12.800 kts

$60 \times 2.8 = 12.800 \times T$ or 13.125 minutes or 13 m 8 s.

Your DR ETA of 09:13:40 changes to 09:13:08. If you hadn't corrected for this element, you would be 32 seconds or about 100 yards off on this leg of your trip. This could be disastrous in the fog or on a night run.

A Weighty Issue

Now presume you had been running for 5 hrs before you began this leg of your trip. Your boat is 25 feet in length, your fuel consumption is 12.5 gallons per hour, and the boat has a base weight of 4,350 lbs. The effect of this lengthy run and the resultant loss of weight due to fuel consumption would be an increase of 0.501 knots in your predicted speed because a lighter boat will go faster.

5 hr × 12.5 gal/hr = 62.5 gals × 5.667 lbs/gal = 354 lbs/4,350
     = 0.081/2 = 0.040 × 12.3 kts = 0.501 kts

You add the weight correction in this example since it lightens the boat and a lighter boat goes faster.

(Drift correction + 0.500 kts) + (Weight correction + 0.501 kts) + (Planned speed 12.300 kts) = 13.301 kts

60 × 2.8 = 13.301 × T or 12.631 minutes or 12 m 38 s

Assuming that the DR and current elements are the same, your ETA is now estimated to be 09:12:38. This is a 30-second difference from your current-corrected time. The weight change correction is similar to the current correction in this example—a difference often missed by the average skipper, but very important to a Predicted Logging enthusiast.

Water Depth

Water depths of under 18 feet impact the speed of your boat by approximately 0.125 knots for every foot of depth change. The effect is different for displacement and planing boats. Let's suppose that you have a planing boat and you are transiting an area that has a water depth of 15.8 feet on this leg. The effect on predicted speed would be 0.275 knots. Since planing boats speed up in shallow water, the 0.275 would be added to your predicted speed.

15.8 ft – 18.0 ft = 2.2 ft × 0.125 kts = 0.275 kts

13.300 kts + 0.275 kts = 13.575 kts

60 × 2.8 = 13.575 × T or 12.376 minutes or 12 m 23 s

Your new ETA is 09:12:23. Each of the first four elements have caused you to reach your ETA sooner. There is a 1 minute 17 second difference from your original DR-generated ETA. That time difference would put you almost six football fields (588 yards) off your mark.

The Effect of Wind

Wind has a distinct influence on the speed of small, light boats. Presume that a 16-knot wind is blowing directly on your boat's stern. This wind velocity causes your boat to drift downwind at a rate of 1.2 knots. Assuming that the DR, current, depth, and weight are the same as calculated above, your predicted speed would be changed since your boat speed would be increased by the wind at the stern.

$$13.575 \text{ kts} + 1.200 \text{ kts} = 14.775 \text{ kts}$$

$$60 \times 2.8 = 14.775 \times T \text{ or } 11.371 \text{ minutes or } 11 \text{ m } 22 \text{ s}$$

Your ETA now is 09:11:22. Because your boat is moving faster, you get there sooner.

Normally, you won't be able to predict the effect of the wind in advance. You will experience it while under way. A technique for predicting the effect of the wind is explained later in this chapter.

Let's take a summary look at the total effect of the five elements:

PLANNED SPEED 12.300	CHANGE	PREDICTED SPEED	ETA	EFFECT
DR calculation	0.000	12.300	09:13:40	None
Effect of drift	+0.500	12.800	09:13:08	Off the stern. ETA is 32 s sooner. Boat SOA increases.
Effect of weight	+0.501	13.301	09:12:38	Boat weight decreases. ETA is 30 s sooner. Boat SOA increases.
Effect of depth	+0.275	13.575	09:12:23	Shoal increases speed. ETA is 15 s sooner. Boat SOA increases.
Effect of wind	+1.200	14.775	09:11:22	Off the stern. ETA is 61 s sooner. Boat SOA increases.
Speed of advance	+2.476 kts	14.775	09:11:22	ETA is 2m 18 s sooner.

The point you need to understand is that your ETA prediction is often a moving target. Don't be distressed that the DR-generated ETA isn't the complete answer. Certainly, it may appear sufficient on a clear, calm day. However, it won't be accurate enough for running in fog, in rain, or at nighttime. It is important to make it a practice of calculating each element and performing test runs in clear weather. This practice is the only way to improve your navigational skills and learn how your boat operates. Only then will you be able to handle fog and night running. When you run at night, select slow speeds. It is very difficult to see floating logs or lobster trap buoys. Also at night, avoid all white light to preserve your night sight.

If, in the fifth example, the wind shifted to the bow rather than the stern, this would be a good instance of an incident when the five elements almost balance themselves out due chiefly to the wind.

However, if you had not corrected for the wind, you would be 61 seconds off your ETA. When you use the DR calculation exclusively, and you arrive at your ETA close to your predicted time, you can be sure that you have experienced compensating speed adjustments from any or all of the other four elements. I hope this gives you enough incentive to learn and understand the other four elements. You should have already mastered the DR procedure in Chapter 9.

CORRECTING YOUR COURSE FOR CURRENT

Current can have a major effect on your ability to hold a course and arrive at a planned destination at a specified time. I have found over the years that most of the current that you will experience will be less than 1 knot. I have also found that the traditional current vector technique does not work well with these slow currents but is effective with currents over 1 knot. Both systems are explained for you.

To understand current, become familiar with this new terminology:

Intended track: This is the planned heading for your boat after you have compensated for current, wind, or seas. When calculated correctly, your boat's heading will be the intended track but it, actually, should crab along the DR line that you plotted on your chart assuming that none of the other four elements is present.

Track: Track is the direction of your planned (intended) track line. Track is abbreviated TR.

Speed of advance: Speed of advance is the planned (intended) rate of travel along your planned (intended) track line after you have compensated your planned speed for the other outside elements. The abbreviation for speed of advance is SOA.

Course made good: This is the net direction of the actual path of your boat. The abbreviation is CMG. Ideally, you want your DR line and your CMG to be equal. The reason for the additional term is that often they are different due to any of the five elements.

Speed made good: This is the actual rate of travel along the track. The abbreviation is SMG. Again, it should be the same as your SOA. This skill of understanding your boat's characteristics is to make SMG and SOA equal.

Set: Set is the direction of the current or the direction to which the current is flowing. Set is expressed in degrees. This term is used for water flow only, not wind. Note that wind direction is expressed in the direction from which the wind is blowing.

Drift: Drift is the speed of the current. Drift is usually stated in knots and must always be corrected for the calendar date by a factor when using tidal current charts. This factor is related to the predicted drift for each day of the year. It is usually different for ebbs and floods.

WHERE DO YOU FIND INFORMATION ABOUT TIDES AND CURRENTS?

Obviously, you can't predict current without specific information about the speed and drift that is present in an area that you are transiting. Go back and review Chapter 2. Specifically, look over tide tables, tidal current tables, tidal current charts, and tidal current diagrams. Depending on the geographical area where you do your boating, different publications are better than others. Also review nautical publications such as Eldridge and Reeds, which may be more appropriate for your area. Each of these publications has a section that explains the use of their current charts and tables. Visit a good marine book store and ask for specific advice about your boating area.

Always keep in mind that navigation is an imperfect science that is affected by natural elements. Don't expect your calculated results to be perfect. Things constantly change on the water. The proficient navigator learns how to recognize when changes happen under way and corrects for them. This knowledge takes time to attain but it's worth the effort.

THE EFFECTS OF CURRENT

Current is the horizontal movement of water and it can affect your boat's speed and course from any angle. This effect can be separated into three conditions:

1.   **Current striking your boat directly on the bow.**
2.   **Current striking your boat directly on the stern.**
3.   **Current coming from any other direction.**

The first two conditions can be explained easily with the following simple rules:

Rule 1.   When the current is striking your boat directly on the bow, there is no effect on the direction or heading of your boat. However, your forward progress will be slowed by the drift of the current.

To compute your SOA (speed of advance), subtract the drift (speed of the current) from your planned boat speed. For example, your planned boat speed is 10 knots (by your speed curve). The drift of the current on your bow is 1.5 knots. Your SOA is 8.5 knots (10 kts – 1.5 kts = 8.5 knots).

Rule 2. When the current is striking directly on the stern of your boat, there is no effect on its direction or heading. However, the forward progress of your boat will be faster.

To compute your SOA, add the drift to your planned boat speed. For example, your planned boat speed is 10 knots (by your speed curve). The current off your stern has a drift of 1.5 knots. Your SOA is 11.5 knots (10 kts + 1.5 kts = 11.5 kts).

The third condition needs more explanation.

Current Striking Your Boat from Any Other Direction

Unfortunately, the situation where current is striking your boat's hull from a direction other than the bow and stern is the most common. This correction is accomplished by using either current vectors or simple tables:

- Tables are efficient to use with currents under 1 knot.
- Current vectors or tables can be used for currents over 1 knot.
- Canals or guts that have high-velocity currents can be very dangerous if you have a slow boat. It is prudent to plan your transit through these areas around times of slack water in order to avoid losing control of your boat and endangering yourself and crew.

Current Vectors. A current vector is simply a triangle where one side represents the set and drift, one side represents your DR course, and the third side depicts the track of your boat. When any two sides of the triangle are known, the third side can be calculated or measured. I find that it is easier to draw a current vector by using speed as the controlling element.

Figure 16.1 graphically depicts the parts of a current diagram. Assume your true course is 090 degrees, your planned speed is 9 knots, the set of the current is 030 degrees, and the drift of the current is 2 knots. This current problem can be easily solved by drawing a current vector using speed in knots. Select a fixed interval to represent a knot. I use the millimeter scale on a ruler and plot on graph paper. Assume true north is at the top of the page. Draw a vector as large as possible and your angle and speed measurements will be more accurate.

Step 1. Plot the direction of your DR course line (090 degrees). Label the starting point "A" and the ending point "D." The length of the line is not important as long as it is longer

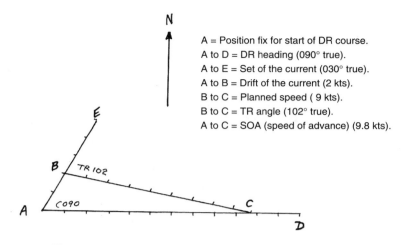

Fig. 16.1   A Vector Diagram. *(F. J. Larkin)*

than your planned speed multiplied by your selected knot interval. (That is, planned speed is 9 kts and the selected knot interval is 1 inch. The length of line A—D would be longer than 9 inches.)

Step 2.   Plot the set and drift of the current. From point A, draw a line at 030 degrees. The length is not important as long as it is longer than the selected knot interval times the drift. Label the ending point "E." The line A—E is a projection of the set (direction) of the current.

Step 3.   From point A, measure off the set of the current toward point E. The set is 2 knots so the distance would be equal to two of your selected knot intervals. Label this new point "B." The line A—B is a representation of the set and drift of the current.

Step 4.   From point B, measure off the planned speed of the boat so that it intersects the A–D line. The planned speed is 9 knots so the length of the line would be equal to nine of your selected knot intervals. Label this new point "C." Draw a line from point B to point C. Line B–C represents your intended track.

Step 5.   To find the angle of your track (TR), use a plotter and measure the angle of the B–C line. (102 degrees.)

Step 6.   To find your SOA, measure the A–C line using the selected knot interval. (9.8 knots.)

Note: This current solution assumes that you know the set and drift of the current in advance. Figure 16.1 illustrates this current vector solution.

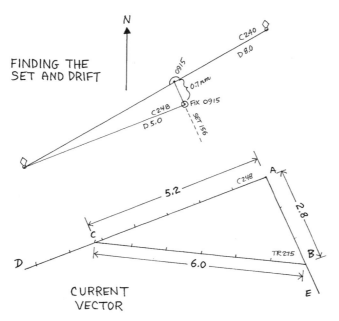

Fig. 16.2   A Course Plot and Vector Diagram. *(F. J. Larkin)*

THE BEFORE AND AFTER CURRENT PROBLEM

Dealing with current is a little like "Pay me now, or pay me later." There are two ways to correct for current, *planning ahead* or *correcting afterwards.* Planning ahead was just explained.

In a "correcting afterwards" circumstance, you may want to determine the current in an area that has no current prediction, or you may discover that you are off course after a period of travel and suspect that the error is due to current. The unfortunate thing is that the effect of all of the elements will be bundled in your solution and you may not be able to attribute your solution to any single element.

A simple problem is used to explain the piloting procedure. Your DR course is 240 degrees and your planned distance is 8.0 nm. Initially, the planned speed is 12 knots and your departure time is 0900. After traveling for 15 minutes, you discover that you are off your DR course line. By taking a fix, you determine your 0915 position.

To solve this piloting problem, first, determine the set and drift of the current and, second, plot a new course to your destination point. Now we can find the Set and Drift:

Step 1.   Calculate and plot your DR course to your destination point.

$$60 \times 8.0 \text{ nm} = 12.0 \text{ kts} \times T \text{ or } 40 \text{ m; ETA is } 0900 + 0040$$
$$= 09 \text{ h } 40 \text{ m.}$$

Step 2.　Calculate and plot your 0915 DR position. This is a simple DR formula ($60D = ST$) solution for distance. Time and speed are known.

$$60 \times D = 12.0 \text{ kts} \times 15 \text{ m} = 3 \text{ nm}$$

Measure 3 nm down from the departure point and label your DR position.

Step 3.　Plot your 0915 fix. You can use a LORAN fix, a GPS fix, a fix obtained by plotting two or three bearings, or, if you pass close aboard an aid to navigation, you can use it as a fix. These alternatives are all considered valid position fixes.

Step 4.　Measure the distance from your 0915 fix to your 0915 DR position plot. (0.7 nm.)

Step 5.　Calculate the drift of the current. You know the time. You measured the distance in Step 4. Use the DR formula and solve for speed.

$$60 \times 0.7 \text{ nm} = S \times 15 \text{ m} = 2.8 \text{ kts}$$

Step 6.　Using a plotter, measure the set of the current. (Set equals 156 degrees.) Figure 16.2 shows this plotted course and fix.

Correcting Your Course to Your Destination Point

Now that you have discovered your error and have calculated the set and drift of the current, you can develop a current vector for the remainder of your trip. Your new starting point is your 0915 fix since it is a higher grade position than your 0915 DR position. Draw a current vector employing the new data using the following steps. Use 6 kts as your new planned speed. Be aware that, in reality, a current may not remain constant over the entire leg of a trip. Train yourself to be alert for changes in current set and drift.

Step 1.　Measure and plot the direction of your new DR course line (248 degrees). Use your 0915 fix as the starting position because it is considered a higher level position than a DR position. Label the starting point "A" and the ending point "D." When using a vector to solve a current problem, you can draw it directly on the chart or use graph paper. The principles are the same. However, it is much neater to use graph paper. Keep the writing on your charts to a minimum, especially items that are constantly changing.

Step 2.   Plot the set of the current. From point A, draw a line at 156 degrees. Label the ending point "E."

Step 3.   Plot the drift of the current. From point A, measure off the set of the current toward point E. Set is 2.8 knots so the distance would be equal to 2.8 of your selected knot intervals. Label this new point "B." The line A–B now represents the set and drift of the current.

Step 4.   Draw a line from point B so that it intersects the A–D line at the length of your planned speed (measured with your selected space interval). Your new planned speed is 6 knots so the length would be equal to six of your selected knot intervals. Label this new point "C."

Step 5.   Find the track (TR). Use a plotter and measure the angle of the B–C line (275 degrees).

Step 6.   Find your speed of advance. Measure the A–C line using the selected knot interval (5.2 kts).

Calculating the New ETA to Your Destination Point

With the knowledge of the set and drift that originally pushed you off course, you can now calculate a new ETA.

Step 1.   Measure the distance from the 0915 fix to your destination point (5.0 nm).

Step 2.   Calculate your ETA. You know the new distance (5.0 nm) and have a new SOA (5.1 knots). Use the DR formula to compute your time.

$$60 \times 5.0 \text{ nm} = 5.1. \text{ kts} \times T = 58.82 \text{ m or } 58 \text{ m } 49 \text{ s}$$

Your new ETA is 09:15:00 + 00:58:49 or 10:13:49.

Step 3.   Correct your new TR of 274 degrees for variation and deviation using TVMDC before running this course with your boat's compass.

T	274
V	016 W (from the nearest compass rose)
M	290
D	004 E (from your boat's deviation table)
C	286

You would steer your boat on a compass heading of 286. The boat would crab along your DR line toward your destination being pushed on the port bow by the 2.8-kt current. Note that just because a current affected the first half of a leg, it may not continue throughout the entire leg. However, it is a best estimate. You should always be alert for changes.

Estimated Positions

Positions calculated using current vectors and tables are called *estimated positions* (EPs). They are considered more accurate than DR positions but less accurate than fixes. Use the symbol of a position dot surrounded by a square when labeling estimated positions (Figure 16.3).

Fig. 16.3   Estimated Position. *(F. J. Larkin)*

USING TABLES TO CORRECT FOR CURRENT

Because most of the current drift that you will encounter will be less than a knot, you will find that tables are more convenient to use for correcting your predicted speed and heading. You will also find that predicted speed corrections are more important than corrections for headings, especially on small boats. Trying to steer a heading correction of 1 or 2 degrees is at best impossible on a small boat.

Two tables are provided:

Table 1—Course Corrections for Current

Table 2—Speed Corrections for Current

To illustrate the use of these tables, assume the following conditions: The drift of the current is 0.600 kts. The DR heading is 090 degrees. The set of the current is 030 degrees. The planned boat speed is 12.3 kts.

How to Use Table 1—Course Corrections for Current

To use Table 1, you need to know two facts:

1.   The angle between your DR heading and the set of the current.
2.   The ratio of drift to planned boat speed.

Follow these simple steps to determine your heading correction.

Step 1.   Find the angle between your boat's heading and the set of the current. Subtract one from the other. If the answer is greater than 180, subtract 180.

Heading = 090;   set = 030;   030 – 090 = 060

Step 2.   Find the ratio of drift to planned boat speed. Divide your planned boat speed into the drift.

Planned boat speed = 12.300 kts;   drift = 0.600 kts;   0.600 kts / 12.300 kts = 0.049

Step 3.   Using the angle and ratio, find the course correction from Table 1 (Figures 16.4a and b).

Angle = 060;   ratio = 0.05;   course correction from Table 1 = 002 degrees

Step 4.   Add the heading correction to your DR heading when the current is striking your boat's starboard side. You always steer into the direction of the current.

Planned heading = 090 + 002 = 092 degrees
(This is the case for the example.)

Or subtract the heading correction from your DR heading when the current is striking your boat's port side:

Planned heading = 090 – 002 = 088 degrees

You will find that trying to correct a heading change of 002 on a small boat is a very difficult task unless the weather is calm and there are not a lot of boats around making waves.

How to Use Table 2—Correcting Speed for Current

I think you will find that this is the table you will use most often. While heading corrections are minimal on a small boat over short distances,

Table One	Heading Corrections Due to Current									Page 1

		Ratio of Speed to Drift								
Angle	Angle	0.01	0.02	0.03	0.04	0.05	0.06	0.07	0.08	0.09	0.10
000	180	0	0	0	0	0	0	0	0	0	0
001	179	0	0	0	0	0	0	0	0	0	0
002	178	0	0	0	0	0	0	0	0	0	0
003	177	0	0	0	0	0	0	0	0	0	0
004	176	0	0	0	0	0	0	0	0	0	0
005	175	0	0	0	0	0	0	0	0	0	0
006	174	0	0	0	0	0	0	0	0	0	0
007	173	0	0	0	0	0	0	0	0	0	0
008	172	0	0	0	0	0	0	0	0	0	1
009	171	0	0	0	0	0	0	0	0	1	1
010	170	0	0	0	0	0	0	0	1	1	1
011	169	0	0	0	0	0	0	0	1	1	1
012	168	0	0	0	0	0	0	1	1	1	1
013	167	0	0	0	0	0	1	1	1	1	1
014	166	0	0	0	0	0	1	1	1	1	1
015	165	0	0	0	0	0	1	1	1	1	1
016	164	0	0	0	0	1	1	1	1	1	1
017	163	0	0	0	0	1	1	1	1	1	1
018	162	0	0	0	0	1	1	1	1	1	1
019	161	0	0	0	1	1	1	1	1	1	1
020	160	0	0	0	1	1	1	1	1	1	1
021	159	0	0	0	1	1	1	1	1	1	1
022	158	0	0	0	1	1	1	1	1	1	1
023	157	0	0	0	1	1	1	1	1	1	2
024	156	0	0	0	1	1	1	1	1	1	2
025	155	0	0	0	1	1	1	1	1	1	2
026	154	0	0	1	1	1	1	1	1	2	2
027	153	0	0	1	1	1	1	1	1	2	2
028	152	0	0	1	1	1	1	1	1	2	2
029	151	0	0	1	1	1	1	1	2	2	2
030	150	0	0	1	1	1	1	1	2	2	2
031	149	0	0	1	1	1	1	1	2	2	2
032	148	0	0	1	1	1	1	1	2	2	2
033	147	0	0	1	1	1	1	2	2	2	2
034	146	0	0	1	1	1	1	2	2	2	2
035	145	0	0	1	1	1	1	2	2	2	2
036	144	0	0	1	1	1	1	2	2	2	2
037	143	0	0	1	1	1	1	2	2	2	2
038	142	0	1	1	1	1	2	2	2	2	3
039	141	0	1	1	1	1	2	2	2	2	3
040	140	0	1	1	1	1	2	2	2	2	3
041	139	0	1	1	1	1	2	2	2	2	3
042	138	0	1	1	1	1	2	2	2	3	3
043	137	0	1	1	1	1	2	2	2	3	3
044	136	0	1	1	1	1	2	2	2	3	3
045	135	0	1	1	1	1	2	2	2	3	3
046	134	0	1	1	1	1	2	2	2	3	3
047	133	0	1	1	1	1	2	2	3	3	3
048	132	0	1	1	1	1	2	2	3	3	3
049	131	0	1	1	1	1	2	2	3	3	3
050	130	0	1	1	1	1	2	2	3	3	3

Fig. 16.4a Table 1—Course Corrections for Current, Page 1

Table One	Heading Corrections Due to Current									Page 2

Angle	Angle	Ratio of Speed to Drift									
		0.01	0.02	0.03	0.04	0.05	0.06	0.07	0.08	0.09	0.10
051	129	0	1	1	1	2	2	2	3	3	3
052	128	0	1	1	1	2	2	2	3	3	3
053	127	0	1	1	1	2	2	2	3	3	4
054	126	0	1	1	1	2	2	3	3	3	4
055	125	0	1	1	1	2	2	3	3	3	4
056	124	0	1	1	1	2	2	3	3	3	4
057	123	0	1	1	2	2	2	3	3	3	4
058	122	0	1	1	2	2	2	3	3	3	4
059	121	0	1	1	2	2	2	3	3	4	4
060	120	0	1	1	2	2	2	3	3	4	4
061	119	0	1	1	2	2	2	3	3	4	4
062	118	0	1	1	2	2	2	3	3	4	4
063	117	0	1	1	2	2	3	3	3	4	4
064	116	0	1	1	2	2	3	3	3	4	4
065	115	0	1	1	2	2	3	3	3	4	4
066	114	0	1	1	2	2	3	3	4	4	4
067	113	0	1	1	2	2	3	3	4	4	4
068	112	0	1	1	2	2	3	3	4	4	5
069	111	0	1	1	2	2	3	3	4	4	5
070	110	0	1	1	2	2	3	3	4	4	5
071	109	0	1	1	2	2	3	3	4	4	5
072	108	0	1	1	2	2	3	3	4	4	5
073	107	0	1	1	2	2	3	3	4	4	5
074	106	0	1	1	2	2	3	3	4	4	5
075	105	0	1	2	2	2	3	3	4	4	5
076	104	1	1	2	2	3	3	4	4	5	5
077	103	1	1	2	2	3	3	4	4	5	5
078	102	1	1	2	2	3	3	4	4	5	5
079	101	1	1	2	2	3	3	4	4	5	5
080	100	1	1	2	2	3	3	4	4	5	5
081	099	1	1	2	2	3	3	4	4	5	5
082	098	1	1	2	2	3	3	4	4	5	5
083	097	1	1	2	2	3	3	4	4	5	6
084	096	1	1	2	2	3	3	4	4	5	6
085	095	1	1	2	2	3	3	4	4	5	6
086	094	1	1	2	2	3	3	4	5	5	6
087	093	1	1	2	2	3	3	4	5	5	6
088	092	1	1	2	2	3	4	4	5	5	6
089	091	1	1	2	2	3	4	4	5	5	6
090	090	1	1	2	2	3	4	4	5	5	6

Fig. 16.4b   Table 1—Course Corrections for Current, Page 2

Table Two   Correcting Drift

Use this table for the weaker currents—1.0 knots or less.
When the angle is less than 90 degrees, current is on the bow.
When the angle is more than 90 degrees, current is off the stern.

ANGLE	ANGLE	CORR %	ANGLE	ANGLE	CORR %
000	180	1.000	046	134	0.489
001	179	0.989	047	133	0.478
002	178	0.978	048	132	0.467
003	177	0.967	049	131	0.456
004	176	0.956	050	130	0.445
005	175	0.944	051	129	0.433
006	174	0.933	052	128	0.422
007	173	0.922	053	127	0.411
008	172	0.911	054	126	0.400
009	171	0.900	055	125	0.389
010	170	0.889	056	124	0.378
011	169	0.878	057	123	0.367
012	168	0.867	058	122	0.356
013	167	0.856	059	121	0.345
014	166	0.844	060	120	0.333
015	165	0.833	061	119	0.322
016	164	0.822	062	118	0.311
017	163	0.811	063	117	0.300
018	162	0.800	064	116	0.289
019	161	0.789	065	115	0.278
020	160	0.778	066	114	0.267
021	159	0.767	067	113	0.256
022	158	0.756	068	112	0.245
023	157	0.744	069	111	0.233
024	156	0.733	070	110	0.222
025	155	0.722	071	109	0.211
026	154	0.711	072	108	0.200
027	153	0.700	073	107	0.189
028	152	0.689	074	106	0.178
029	151	0.678	075	105	0.167
030	150	0.667	076	104	0.156
031	149	0.656	077	103	0.145
032	148	0.644	078	102	0.133
033	147	0.633	079	101	0.122
034	146	0.622	080	100	0.111
035	145	0.611	081	099	0.100
036	144	0.600	082	098	0.089
037	143	0.589	083	097	0.078
038	142	0.578	084	096	0.067
039	141	0.567	085	095	0.056
040	140	0.556	086	094	0.045
041	139	0.544	087	093	0.033
042	138	0.533	088	092	0.022
043	137	0.522	089	091	0.011
044	136	0.511	090	090	0.000
045	135	0.500			

Fig. 16.5   Table Two—Speed Corrections for Current.

corrections to your predicted speed for drift are more meaningful for accurate piloting.

In order to use Table 2, you only need to know one fact: the angle between your DR heading and the set of the current.

Follow these simple steps to determine your heading correction:

Step 1.   Find the angle between your boat's heading and the set of the current. Subtract one from the other. If the answer is greater than 180, subtract 180.

Heading = 090;   set = 030;   030 − 090 = 060

Step 2.   Referencing the angle (060), find the speed correction factor from Table 2 (0.333).

Step 3.   Multiply the drift of the current by the speed correction factor from Table 2 (Figure 16.5).

Drift of 0.600 × 0.333 = 0.200 kts

Step 4.   If the current is striking the forward half of your boat, subtract the result from your predicted speed. Current from this direction will be slowing your boat.

Predicted speed = 12.3 kts − 0.200 kts = 12.1 kts SOA

(Remember, if you are using tidal current charts, you must also factor the drift for the calendar date.) Or, if the current is striking the aft (rear) half of your boat, add the result to your predicted speed. Current from this direction is increasing the speed of your boat as is the case in our example.

Predicted speed = 12.3 kts + 0.200 kts = 12.500 kts SOA

Note: If you are using tidal current charts, remember to factor your drift before using Table 2.

As an aid to graphically viewing how the current is striking your boat, draw a diagram similar to Figure 16.6. It is easy to see that the current is striking the port quarter with this diagram.

CORRECTING PREDICTED SPEED FOR WEIGHT CHANGE

The weight of your boat at the time when you ran your speed curve is called the base weight of your boat. Your speed curve is only valid at this base weight. Changes in a boat's base weight cause changes in the speed of the boat. Loss of base weight increases the speed of your boat

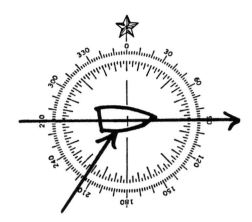

Fig. 16.6 Current Diagram. *(F. J. Larkin)*

while additions of weight slow your boat. Weight changes are most evident on smaller boats. To use an existing speed curve when your boat's base weight has changed, you must learn to correct your predicted speed for the change. Here are the rules of thumb:

- The percentage change in boat speed is equal to approximately one-half of the percentage change in the weight of the boat.
- The loss of weight increases the speed of a boat.
- The addition of weight decreases the speed of a boat.

For example, a weight decrease of 425 pounds (75 gallons of gasoline) produces a 10% weight change in a boat weighting 4,250 pounds. Half of 10% equals 5%, which will be the increase in boat speed due to this weight loss. If your predicted speed was 12.3 knots, the speed increase would be 0.615 knots (i.e., 12.3 kts × 0.05 = 0.615 kts).

In this situation, you would need to correct your predicted speed upward by 0.615 kts to 12.915 kts due to this 425-lb loss of weight (12.300 kts + 0.615 kts = 12.915 kts). Your only other alternative is to rerun your speed curve at the new boat weight.

Computation of Fuel Consumption Rate

The most common weight loss on a boat is due to the consumption of fuel while underway. Here is a simple procedure for calculating this correction.

Step 1. Establish your boat's base weight with full fuel tanks (e.g., 4,350 lbs).

Step 2.   Make a long run with your boat over a measured course at your normal running speed. This run should be at least 25 to 50 nautical miles in length (e.g., 50 miles).

Step 3.   Refill your fuel tanks noting the gallons purchased (e.g., 25 gallons).

Step 4.   Compute your nautical miles per gallon (e.g., 2 NMPG). Divide the nautical miles run into the gallons purchased:

50 miles/25 gallons = 2 NMPG

Step 5.   Compute your fuel consumption rate by dividing the nautical miles per gallon (2 NMPG) into your planned speed (i.e., 12.3 kts):

12.3 kts/2 NMPG = 6.15 gallons per hour

Computation of Fuel Consumption Weight Loss and Predicted Speed Correction

When you need very accurate speed predictions, always compute weight lost due to fuel consumption. This procedure works for any addition or loss of weight such as when you add extra guests or remove equipment from your boat. The secret to accurate piloting is to maintain your boat's weight as close as possible to its weight when you ran your speed curve—your boat's base weight.

Step 1.   Determine your time under way:

Depart time = 09:00:00

Current time = 10:52:12

Travel = 01:52:12 or 1.87 hours

Step 2.   Calculate your fuel consumption by multiplying the time under way by your fuel consumption rate.

Fuel consumption rate of 6.15 × 1.87 hr = 11.5 gallons used

Step 3.   Figure the weight of the fuel lost by multiplying the gallons used by 5.667 lbs per gallon (weight of a gallon of gasoline).

11.5 gals × 5.667 lbs/gal = 65.2 lbs

Step 4.   Determine the percentage of weight lost by dividing the weight lost by the base weight of your boat.

65.2 lbs/4,350 lbs = 0.015%

Divide the percentage by 2.

0.015/2 = 0.0075%

Step 5.   Compute the predicted speed change by multiplying the percentage of weight lost by the predicted speed.

Predicted speed of 12.3 kts × 0.0075 = 0.092 kts

Step 6.   Develop the corrected speed prediction. If the weight is decreased, add the predicted speed change to the predicted speed.

12.300 kts + 0.092 kts = 12.392 kts

If the weight is increased, subtract the predicted speed change from the predicted speed.

To make the weight problem more realistic, suppose you add two additional guests weighing a total of 410 pounds to the 65.2-pound weight loss due to fuel consumption (410 lbs added, minus 65.2 lbs lost equals a 344.8-pound increase). The percentage of weight gained would be 7.93% and the predicted speed would change to 11.813 knots because the increased weight will slow your boat. Assume your boat's base weight is 4,350 lbs.

344.8 lbs/4,350 lbs = 0.0793/2 = 0.0396% × 12.300 kts = 0.487 kts – 12.300 kts = 11.813 kts

You can see from these weight calculations that the impact on predicted speed on small boats can be significant. To become a serious navigator, pay attention to these suggestions:

- Develop an awareness for things that affect the weight of your boat.

- Run tests to verify the relationship between changes in boat weight and the actual speed of your boat.

- Using your speed curve and the formula, produce a table that shows the relationship between RPMs and weight changes. Start with 100-lb changes.

Things to Consider When Establishing Your Boat's Base Weight

		SAMPLE WEIGHTS
Fixed weight factors:		
Hull weight. Your dealer should provide this figure.	3,750	
Engine(s) weight. Your dealer should provide this figure.	525	
Batteries. Ask any marine store.	50	**4,325**
Variable weight items:		
Capacity/weight of fuel tanks (125 gallon – gas @ 5.667 lbs/gal).	709	
Capacity/weight of water tanks (20 gallon @ 8.3 lbs/gal).	167	
Capacity/weight of holding tanks (10 gallon @ 8.3 lbs/gal).	83	**959**
(Gas weighs 5.667 lbs per gallon; diesel weighs 7.2 lbs per gallon; water weighs 8.3 lbs per gallon.)		
Weight of gear:		
Spare engine oil.	20	
Anchor and chain.	45	
Anchor rode.	25	
Lines.	25	
Cushions.	45	
Bed blankets and sheets.	15	
Boat cover/canvas.	40	**215**
Other equipment:		
Electronic equipment.	15	
First aid kit.	10	
Tool kit.	13	
PFDs.	15	
Manuals.	12	
Fishing gear.	30	
Refreshment cooler.	15	
Ice and drinks.	15	
Food.	10	**135**
Captain, crew, and guests:		
Skipper.	250	
Mate.	150	
Guests (1) (or ballast).	125	**525**
Total		**6,159**

You can easily load your boat with a lot of extra weight. The unloaded weight of my boat is 4,325 lbs. I got these figures from a boat dealer. Most dealers have a book with all this good information. The base weight of my boat is around 6,160 pounds. When I need to be extremely accurate with my predicted speed such as during a predicted log race,

I use the following checklist to ensure that my boat's base weight is the same as when I ran my speed curve.

___ Fill the fuel tanks.
___ Fill the water tank.
___ Fill the head water tank.
___ Carry one extra gallon of oil as a spare.
___ Fill the oil reservoir.

___ Carry 12 cans of soda and 2 bags of ice.
___ Carry one food cooler.
___ Set trim angle to one bar on indicator.
___ Pump bilge dry.

CORRECTING PREDICTED SPEED FOR DEPTH OF WATER

Oddly enough, I have discovered that the depth of the water can have an effect on your piloting predictions. Depths under 18 feet will change your boat's speed. The effect depends on whether your boat has a planing hull or a displacement hull. Planing boats increase in speed over shoal water, while a displacement boat's speed decreases. The rules of thumb for the depth element are as follows:

- Boat speed changes approximately 0.125 knots for each foot difference of depth under 18 feet of water depth.
- Displacement vessels are dragged deeper in the water by the bottom so that they slow down.
- Planing vessels are pushed up by the water so that they increase in speed.

Here is a simple technique for correcting your boat's predicted speed for water depths under 18 feet.

Step 1. Determine the depth of water along your course from a nautical chart (e.g., 12 ft).

Step 2. Calculate the height of tide for the time period when you will be transiting along your course line. A simple method is to draw a tide graph. Refer to Chapter 15. Assume the depth change is 3.5 feet.

12 ft + 3.5 ft = 15.5 ft

Step 3. Determine the depth below 18 feet by subtracting the height of tide from 18.

15.5 ft – 18 ft = 2.5 ft

Step 4. Compute the speed change due to depth by multiplying the depth below 18 by 0.125 kts.

$$2.5 \text{ ft} \times 0.125 \text{ kts} = 0.313 \text{ kts}$$

Step 5. Correct your predicted speed. If you have a displacement vessel, subtract the speed change from your planned speed because your boat will be slowed.

$$12.3 \text{ kts} - 0.313 \text{ kts} = 11.987 \text{ kts}$$

Or, if you have a planing vessel, add the speed change to your planned speed because your boat will increase in speed.

$$12.3 \text{ kts} + 0.313 \text{ kts} = 12.613 \text{ kts}$$

Note that at slower speeds, every planing vessel operates in a displacement mode. When this occurs, treat your planing vessel as if it was a displacement vessel. A table is provided below to help you determine when your boat transitions from displacement to planing modes.

Computation of Start of Planing

Planing begins at a speed equal to 1.34 times the square root of the waterline length of your boat. A vessel is said to be truly planing at two times the square root of the waterline length.

WATERLINE LENGTH (ft)	START OF PLANING (kts)	TRULY PLANING (kts)
15	5.2	7.7
16	5.4	8.0
17	5.5	8.2
18	5.7	8.5
19	5.8	8.7
20	6.0	8.9
21	6.1	9.2
22	6.3	9.4
23	6.4	9.6
24	6.6	9.8
25	6.7	10.0
26	6.8	10.2
27	7.0	10.4
28	7.1	10.6
29	7.2	10.8
30	7.3	11.0
31	7.5	11.1
32	7.6	11.3
33	7.7	11.5
34	7.8	11.7
35	7.9	11.8

CORRECTING PREDICTED SPEED FOR WIND

A continuous wind can produce a current that is deflected about 20 to 30 degrees to the right in the Northern Hemisphere due to the Coriolis effect. As a rule of thumb, the drift of this current is approximately 0.2 knots for a 10-knot wind. The drift increases by 0.1 knot for each increase of 10 knots of wind speed.

Waves are the result of this wind effect. By noting the direction of the waves, you can determine the set of the current created by the wind. This current phenomenon is found offshore and is not generated in inshore locations due to lack of fetch. *Fetch* is the distance that the wind blows in a fixed direction without encountering any land masses to block its effect.

Since it is virtually impossible to predict wind in advance, you should learn to make wind speed corrections while under way. Your major problem will be estimating wind velocity. The best source is the national weather broadcasts on your VHF radio. (See Figure 16.8 in the next section for a method for reading current from buoys while under way.) Here is a quick technique to correct your speed for wind.

Step 1. Estimate the velocity of the wind (e.g., 15 knots).

Step 2. Determine the angle between your boat's heading and the direction of the wind. This is accomplished by using angles relative to your heading. Assume your boat is heading 000 degrees and then estimate the wind's direction from that point (e.g., 045 degrees relative to the boat's heading).

Step 3. Referencing the angle, look up the speed correction factor in Table 2 (0.500). (See Figure 16.5 Table 2— Speed Corrections for Current.)

Step 4. Look up the rate of drift in the wind drift correction graph (Figure 16.7) referencing the estimated wind velocity.

Wind speed = 16 knots – rate of drift downwind
= 1.18 knots

Step 5. Factor the rate of drift by the speed correction factor.

1.18 knots × 0.500 = 0.590 kts

Step 6. If the waves are striking on the forward half of your boat, decrease your predicted speed by the factored rate of drift. Recompute your ETA.

12.3 kts – 0.590 kts = 11.710 kts

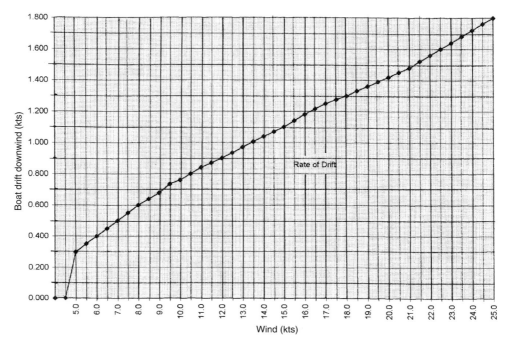

Fig. 16.7   Wind Drift Correction Graph for Small Cabin Cruiser. *(F. J. Larkin)*

Or if the waves are striking your boat on the aft (rear half), increase your predicted speed by the factored rate of drift. Recompute your ETA.

12.3 kts + 0.590 kts = 12.890 kts

Step 7.   If your boat is equipped with a tachometer that reads each RPM, you can decrease your engines RPMs to correct for the loss in predicted time, or you can adjust your predicted speed and recompute your ETA.

Note: The data used to make the drift correction graph of Figure 16.7 was taken from the *U.S. Coast Guard SAR Manual.* This data is the result of the compilation of many SAR incidents involving boats of various sizes which were grouped into this small cabin cruiser category. The drift correction graph may not fit your boat exactly. It is presented as a baseline only. Work out your own tables for your boat.

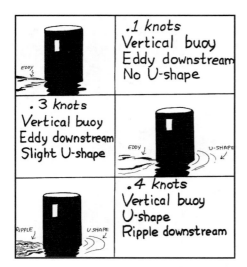

Fig. 16.8 Estimating Speed of the Current from Buoys. *(F. J. Larkin)*

ESTIMATING THE SET AND DRIFT OF A CURRENT FROM BUOYS

Figure 16.8 presents a series of representations of the action of water as it strikes buoys. The direction of the downstream ripple is the set of the current. The characteristics of the water as it strikes the buoy along with the attitude of the buoy provide an estimate of the drift of the current. Use these illustrations to double-check your current predictions. They will provide a reality check to your arithmetic and tabular calculations of set and drift. They are also very useful for those areas that have no published current predictions. Again, it will take practice to learn to use them quickly and efficiently.

SUMMARY

All of these calculations may be a lot to internalize at one time. It took me many years to figure out the effect of these elements on my boat. If you want to take up predicted logging, you will need to keep your predicted speed errors under 1%—that's under 36 seconds of error for every hour run. However, it doesn't take long to become an expert if you practice the art of navigation. I find that it takes away any boredom on long trips and makes each leg of the trip a game of competing against the clock. At some point along the way, you just may become a highly skilled navigator.

How to Check the Installation Accuracy of Your Compass and Install an Aiming Post

Compass installation errors are a common cause of steering problems on pleasure boats. For every degree of compass installation error, your boat will be approximately 250 feet or 80 yards off course for every nautical mile that you travel. Therefore, you want to be sure that your compass is installed correctly. Compasses are generally mounted in front of the helm or steering station on a boat. During installation, follow these simple steps to avoid steering problems later. Figure AP1.1 graphically explains the procedure.

Step 1

- Measure the width of your boat at the point where your compass is installed. You can use a tape measure. Divide the width by two.

- At this same point, measure from the same edge to the center of your compass.

- Subtract this measurement from the first to get the distance that your compass is installed from the center line of your boat. For example, the width of your boat measures 120 inches. Divide by 2 to get 60 inches. The measurement to the

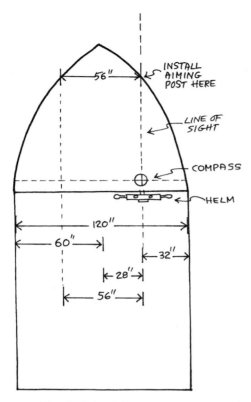

Fig. AP1.1 A Compass
Installation Procedure
Diagram.
(F. J. Larkin)

center of your compass is 32 inches. Your compass is installed 28 inches from the centerline of your boat (60 − 32 = 28).

Step 2

- Double the length that the center of your compass is located from the centerline of your boat (28 × 2 = 56).

- Set the tape measure or string to this width (56 inches) and find the point on your port and starboard bow rail that is exactly this width. It is important for this crossing line to be at a right angle (90 degrees) to the keel line of the boat. Check this by measuring back to the center of the rail at the bow. Place a mark on the bow rail side in front of your compass.

- This is the position for your aiming post. I placed a burgee staff at this position.

Step 3

- Sight along the center of the compass card and the lubber line that is scribed into the compass housing toward the aiming post or point. Your line of sight should be centered on the aiming post for your compass to be parallel to the keel.

- Make any adjustments to correct the alignment of the compass.

By performing this check, you have accomplished two objectives. You have corrected the installation of your compass and you have provided a proper aiming post for steering your boat. Many skippers erroneously use the center of the bow as a steering point when their helm and compass are installed off-center. This practice introduces steering error into their headings and causes their boat to move along an arc rather that a straight course line, which has an negative effect on their ability to predict an ETA accurately.

How to Check
Your Compass for
Built-in Error

Built-in compass error is a fault that is generated inside your compass and not from an outside magnetic influence. It is important to understand this type of error because it can usually be adjusted with a little work and planning. When a compass can't be completely adjusted free of compass error, you need to know the extent of this error in your compass so that you can compensate for it in your compass heading calculations.

This procedure applies to your boat's compass as well as any handheld or portable compasses.

Step 1. Find a convenient location ashore that fits the following standards:

- There is no local magnetic influence in the area. Stay away from large iron masses, metal rails, or large metal tanks.

- The location is positioned on a line of position (LOP) formed by two fixed objects that are charted on a nautical chart and form a natural range to your chosen accessible land position. Figure AP2.1 illustrates an ideal location.

Step 2. Using a plotting instrument, determine the true bearing of the LOP from your position toward the fixed objects that form the natural range.

Step 3. Using the TVMDC formula, convert the true bearing to a magnetic bearing. Record this bearing for reference on a Piloting Worksheet.

Step 4. Sight your compass along the range and record the compass bearing.

Step 5. Compare the magnetic bearing to the compass bearing.

Your compass has no built-in error when the magnetic bearing equals the compass bearing. When your compass bearing is *greater* than the magnetic bearing, you have westerly compass error. When your compass bearing is *less* than the magnetic bearing, you have *easterly* compass error.

If your compass has significant compass error (more than 3 degrees), you should:

1. Adjust it according to the manufacturer's instructions which are usually included in the literature that is packed with your compass when purchased.

2. Take the compass to your dealer and have it adjusted professionally. If you don't know what you're doing, this is always your least expensive alternative.

When a compass cannot be adjusted to read absolutely perfect, record the compass error near or even write it on your compass. Always show whether the error is westerly or easterly. This will remind the helmsperson to correct the course for the built-in steering error.

Since hand-held compasses should normally be used in a magnetic-free location on your boat, a deviation table is not required. Record any built-in compass error on the compass's housing to remind you to correct all readings taken with this compass for the built-in error.

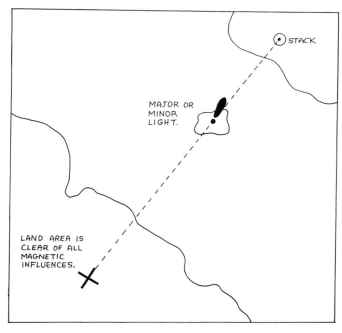

Fig. AP2.1   An Illustration of an Ideal Land Range.
(F. J. Larkin)

APPENDIX THREE

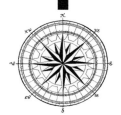

How to Develop Data for a Deviation Table Using Multiple Ranges and Your Boat's Compass

A deviation table is needed to correct your compass heading for magnetic influences found aboard your boat. These magnetic influences are caused by ferrous metal (iron) objects and their magnetic fields, which can be generated from wiring, transformers, electrical motors, and speaker magnets installed near your compass. You can minimize these influences on your compass by installing electrical equipment and wiring at least 3 feet away from your compass and by twisting all wires located near your compass. Twisting wires helps to offset their magnetic fields.

Evaluate the magnetic influence of each piece of electrical equipment mounted near your compass. Start by turning off all electrical appliances located in the area. Next, switch on each electrical device one at a time while you observe the needle of your compass. Record the number of degrees that the compass needle swings. Any electrical appliance with a speaker magnet or electrical motor can influence your compass. Isolate, shield, or reinstall any problem appliances. Windshield wiper motors should always be checked. You normally only use windshield wipers during poor weather conditions and you want to be assured that they will not cause compass error. Lay your radio mike beside your compass and observe how dramatically the needle of your compass is deflected. Mount your radio and microphone well away from your compass. Continue this checking process until you have eliminated all magnetic influences on your compass.

You will also want to review the handling procedures for portable appliances, especially portable radios. Visualize a globe, 3 feet in diameter, surrounding your compass. Establish the practice of not using this area for storage or the installation of any electrical appliances.

In some instances, you may not be able to remove the magnetic influence by moving or shielding the cause. If the error is small (less than 5 degrees), record it as part of your deviation table.

CAUTION: *Equipment-generated compass error changes when the appliance is in operation or off. Make special notes on your deviation table about this type of magnetic influence on your boat.*

Follow these simple steps to develop data for your deviation table:

Step 1.

- Using a nautical chart, find charted objects in your area that form natural ranges.

- Watch out for shoal areas along the LOP formed by the range.

- Discard ranges with shoals or other obstructions because you will need to operate your boat in these areas to complete Step 6.

Only use objects that are identified with the chart symbol of a circle with a center dot. These are surveyed positions and are accurate for use in obtaining position fixes in navigation. You need at least 10 to 12 ranges on various points of the compass to develop an adequate deviation table. An ideal deviation table will have 24 points.

Step 2.

- Using the Deviation Planning Sheet found in Appendix 7, write in the names of the charted objects that you have selected as your ranges on Column 1, Objects. For example, Stack and Tower.

Step 3.

- Using your plotter, determine the true bearing of each range.

- Record the bearing toward the object. You will use these bearings later in Step 7. For example, 065 degrees True.

- Write your bearings in Column 2, True Heading, on the Deviation Planning Sheet. You will have a different heading for each range that you select.

Step 4.

- Select the variation from the compass rose nearest to the range on the nautical chart.

- Enter the variation in Column 3, Variation, on the Deviation Planning Sheet. For example, 004° West.

Step 5.

- Compute the magnetic heading.

- You are proceeding from true to magnetic in the TVMDC formula so add westerly error and subtract easterly error in making your computation.

True heading	060
Variation	004W
Magnetic heading	064

Step 6.

- Take a trip on your boat and align your boat's keel line on a range line or LOP.

- Allowing time for the compass needle to settle, record the compass reading. It will be difficult to get accurate readings when the sea is up or when boating traffic is heavy in the area. For example, 065 degrees.

- Enter the compass reading in Column 6, Compass Heading, on the Deviation Planning Sheet.

Step 7.

- Compute the deviation for each entry on the Deviation Planning Sheet by comparing Column 4, Magnetic Heading, to Column 6, Compass Heading.

- If the compass heading is larger than the magnetic heading, you have westerly deviation error.

- When the compass heading is less than the magnetic heading, you have easterly deviation error.

Magnetic heading	064 degrees
Compass heading	065 degrees
Deviation	001 West

(Compass heading is larger than the magnetic heading.)

Magnetic heading	125 degrees
Compass heading	123 degrees
Deviation	002 East

(Compass heading is less than the magnetic heading.)

Refer to Figure 10.1 for a diagram that visually explains how this deviation calculation is accomplished.

How to Develop Data for a Deviation Table Using One Range and a Pelorus

The purpose of this procedure is to develop corrections to your compass for magnetic influences found at various headings of your boat. To perform this exercise, you need an instrument called a pelorus and someone to assist you. One person operates the boat and observes the boat's compass headings. The other person operates the pelorus and takes the relative bearings along a predefined range. You will need a calm sea to accomplish this task on a small boat. Don't forget your constant need for vigilance and lookouts while you are under way.

Set up the pelorus so that it is aligned along your boat's keel similar to your boat's compass. Aim the 000 degree point on the pelorus' compass card at the bow of your boat. Any reading on your pelorus will now be relative to the reading on your boat's compass.

Step 1.

- Find objects on your nautical chart that form natural ranges.

- Watch for shoal areas along the LOP formed by the range and reject them since you will need to align your boat on each range in Step 6.

- Only use objects that are identified with the chart symbol of a circle and a center dot on your chart. These are surveyed positions and are accurate for use in navigation.

Step 2.

- Using the Deviation Planning Sheet found in Appendix 7, write in the names of the objects on the range that you have selected.
- Enter this data in Column 1, Objects.

For this procedure, you are using a single range to complete your deviation table. All bearings will be taken along this single range.

Step 3.

- Using your plotter, measure the true heading for the range.
- Use the direction from your boat toward the range.
- Write the true heading in Column 2, True Heading, on the Deviation Planning Sheet.
- This heading will be the same for all entries planned in this procedure. This is the direction that your pelorus will be aimed in Step 6.

Step 4.

- Select the variation from the compass rose nearest to the range.
- Enter the variation in Column 3, Variation.
- The variation in this exercise will be the same for all entries.

Step 5.

- Compute the magnetic heading for each entry on your Deviation Planning Sheet and post in Column 4, Magnetic Heading.
- You are proceeding down the TVMDC formula so add westerly error and subtract easterly error.

Step 6.

- Take the range bearings with the pelorus. Maneuver the boat so that the pelorus is aligned along the range.
- Figure AP4.1 illustrates this technique.
- The pelorus operator calls out "Mark" for each reading and records the relative bearing from the pelorus.
- The boat operator, upon hearing the "Mark" command, reads and records the boat's compass heading.
- Record the compass bearings in Column 7, Boat's Heading, on the Deviation Planning Sheet.

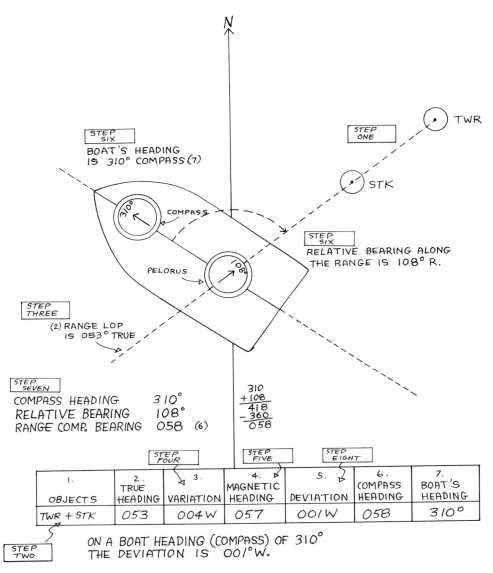

Fig. AP4.1 How to Determine Compass Deviation Using a Pelorus and Relative Bearings. *(F. J. Larkin)*

- The deviation that you calculate with this procedure is associated with this compass direction on your boat (not the direction in which the pelorus is pointing).
- Repeat this process until 12 to 20 readings are obtained as the boat is maneuvered around the 360-degree arc of the compass.

Step 7.

- Convert the relative bearings to range compass bearings.
- To convert a relative bearing to a compass bearing, add the relative bearing to the compass bearing:

Compass bearing	090 degrees
Relative bearing	+ 030 degrees
Converted relative bearing	120 degrees

- When your answer is larger than 360 degrees, subtract 360 to obtain the correct converted relative bearing.
- Record the converted relative bearings in Column 6, Compass Heading, on the Deviation Planning Sheet.

Step 8.

- Compute the deviation using the TVMDC formula.

What you have calculated is the deviation for a single compass heading on your boat. Continue this same procedure through 12 to 20 points of the compass and you will develop the data for plotting a deviation table for your boat.

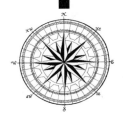

How to Plot Deviation on a Deviation Plotting Sheet

The purpose of the Deviation Plotting Sheet is to graph your deviations prior to the finalization of the deviation table for your boat. A blank Deviation Plotting Sheet is provided in Appendix 7 for use in this procedure.

You need to plot two graphs: one for magnetic headings and one for compass headings. Plot one category at a time so you won't become confused by an excess of plotting points on your graph. I suggest that you use different color pencils for each deviation curve.

The Deviation Plotting Sheet has two scales:

1. *The vertical scale:* The vertical scale (at the left-hand side of the graph) is divided to reflect easterly and westerly error by a zero error line. Plot easterly error below the zero line. Plot westerly error above the zero line.

2. *The horizontal scale:* The horizontal scale (at the bottom of the graph) is divided into 10-degree segments and is labeled in 30-degree intervals.

HOW TO PLOT MAGNETIC HEADING DEVIATIONS

Deviation on this graph refers to the magnetic headings found in Column 4, Magnetic Headings, on the Deviation Planning Sheet and will be the reference point for the heading column on your deviation table.

Step 1.

- Referencing your Deviation Planning Sheet, plot all the data found in Column 5, Deviation, in the Deviation Plotting Sheet's vertical scale (left side of the graph) in relationship to your magnetic headings found in Column 4, Magnetic Heading, in the graph's horizontal scale (bottom of the graph).

Note: If you are using relative bearings, as explained in Appendix 4, you must calculate the magnetic heading for the boat's heading using the TVMDC formula.

T	
V	
M	Calculate using TVMDC formula rules.
D	Take from Column 5, Deviation.
C	Take from Column 7, Boat's Heading.

Step 2.

- Draw a line through all of the points that you have plotted so that you approximate a curve.
- In other words, round the line through the plotted points rather than just connecting the dots.

Step 3.

- Develop your deviation table by reading the data from the deviation curve you drew on your graph.
- Read up the scale from a selected compass heading on the horizontal scale to the place where your line intersects with the deviation curve.
- Read across to your left from this intersecting point to the deviation error scale.
- Record the deviation error for the selected compass heading on a Deviation Table form supplied in Appendix 7.

HOW TO PLOT COMPASS HEADING DEVIATIONS

The reference point for your compass graph is Column 6, Compass Heading, on the Deviation Planning Sheet.

Step 1.

- Referencing your Deviation Planning Sheet, plot all the data found in Column 5, Deviation, against the vertical scale in relationship to the headings found in Column 6, Compass Heading, on the horizontal scale.

- Note that if you are using relative bearings as explained in Appendix 4, use the data from Column 7, Boat's Heading, to complete the horizontal scale.

Step 2.

- Draw a line through all of the points that you have plotted so that you approximate a curve.

- In other words, round the line through the plotted points rather than just connecting the dots.

Step 3.

- Develop your deviation table by reading the data from the deviation curve you drew on the graph.

- Read up the scale from a selected compass heading on the horizontal scale to the place where your line intersects with the deviation curve.

- Read across to your left from this intersecting point to the deviation error scale.

- Record the deviation error for the selected compass heading on a Deviation Table form, which is supplied in Appendix 7.

APPENDIX SIX

How to Develop a
Speed Curve

An integral part of any navigational package is an accurate speed curve. The smaller your boat, the more difficult it is to develop and use a speed curve. The principal problem will be the weight that you carry on your boat. As explained in Chapter 16, small boats are greatly affected by any weight difference compared to their base weight. The more frequent weight problems are related to fuel consumption, number of guests aboard, and changes in the amount of equipment that you carry on a trip. Your speed curve is only valid for the weight aboard your boat at the time when you ran the speed trials to develop your speed curve. I call this the boat's *base weight.* For accuracy in your piloting predictions, you must compensate your predicted speed for any change in weight from your base weight. Otherwise, your predictions will be invalid. Note that this is not as serious a problem on heavy displacement cruisers.

Here are a few of the main reasons that can invalidate a speed curve:

- Fuel consumption on a trip or half full fuel tanks. These computations are explained in Chapter 16.

- Additional guests.

- Extra equipment aboard. It's amazing how much junk accumulates aboard a boat as the season progresses. You will get a strong feeling for this situation if you can remember back to the day that you unloaded your boat last year.

- Marine growth on your hull. Any grass growing on your hull will slow your boat considerably.

- Bilges full of water. Remember to pump the bilge before you start out on any trip. Excess water slows your boat and sometimes can change the stability of your boat.

- Hull weight. If you have a wooden boat, let your boat sit in the water for a week or two before you calculate your curve. This allows time for the wood to absorb water. This water absorption adds weight to your boat. A wooden boat is much heavier at the end of the season than at the start if it is hauled annually. Wooden boats will be much slower at the end of the season.

EQUIPMENT YOU WILL NEED

Tachometer.   Your boat must be equipped with a decent tachometer. Most standard analog and digital tachs read in 100-RPM increments. This means that the tach is averaging the readout to 100-RPM increments. Note that 50 RPMs can have an effect on your speed predictions.

When your boat has twin engines, use only one tachometer as your primary controlling instrument. Synchronize the other engine to your primary engine. Rarely will two tachs agree precisely, even when the engines are synchronized.

Stop Watch.   Your watch should have the ability to time multiple legs.

Speed Table Worksheet.   A copy of a suggested speed curve worksheet is provided in Appendix 7, Navigation Forms.

Tide Graph.   A copy of this form is available in Appendix 7, Navigation Forms.

HOW THE DATA COLLECTION PROCESS WORKS

This simple step-by-step procedure will help you to develop a speed curve for your boat.

Step 1.   Find a natural or measured mile range on your chart. Be sure that the water depth is over 18 feet and that current influence is minimal. If there are no measured mile runs in your area, try to find two fixed aids to navigation. Measure the distance between the fixed aids. The distance doesn't have to be exactly a mile (see Figure AP6.1).

Step 2.   Approach the starting point of your selected measured course with your engine set at a planned RPM setting on the tachometer. As you pass the starting line, start your

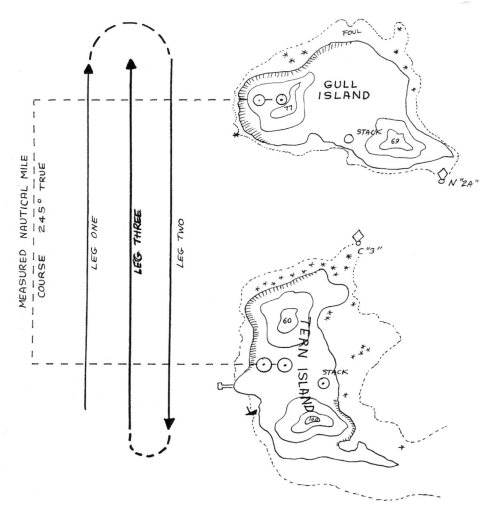

Fig. AP6.1 An Illustration of a Speed Curve Run. *(F. J. Larkin)*

stop watch. Hold this RPM setting for the entire run. Steer as straight as possible. It is best to make these timing runs when boating traffic is light, the weather is calm, and the current is at slack.

Step 3. As you cross the finish line, stop the watch. Record the running time on the Speed Curve Worksheet (Appendix 7). Make a triple run, repeating steps 1, 2, and 3, down (S1), back (S2), and down (S3) the measured course.

Step 4. Compute the speed made good for each of the three runs at each selected RPM, using the DR formula: $60 \times D = S \times T$.

Step 5. Average the speed of the runs, not the times. Average S1 to S2. Average S3 to S2. Then, average the speed of your two answers. It is more accurate to use seconds than minutes in your formula. Here is an example of a triple run with calculations. Use either the regular DR formula $(60 \times D = S \times T$ in minutes) or $(3600 \times D = S \times T$ in seconds).

RUN	TIME	SECONDS	SPEED @ 3,000 RPM	AVERAGE SPEED	SPEED
S1	4 m 28 s	268 s	13.432 kts		
				14.033 kts	
S2	4 m 06 s	246 s	14.634 kts		14.150 kts
				14.267 kts	
S3	4 m 19 s	259 s	13.900 kts		

Repeat this process at different RPM settings. Use intervals of 500 RPM. Record all the data on a Speed Curve Worksheet for future reference. Allow yourself plenty of time to complete all of the runs needed to finish the speed curve.

Step 6. Using a Tide Graph sheet (Appendix 7), label the vertical and horizontal scales. The vertical scale is on the left-hand side of the graph. Starting at the bottom, label upward at 500-RPM increments. The horizontal scale is at the bottom of the graph. Starting at the left, label to the right in 1-nm increments.

Step 7. Plot the data from your Speed Curve Worksheet onto the graph. Figures AP6.2 and AP6.3 provide an illustration of speed curve data and a plotted speed curve.

Note that displacement and planing boats will have a different curve. The displacement boat's speed curve will be more linear (a straight line), while a planing boat's curve will look more like an "S." The planing boat starts out as a displacement boat. As speed increases, it starts to come up on plane. As it reaches plane, the curve will flatten—smaller increases in RPMs cause larger increases in boat speed. As you apply more speed, it tends to become linear again. Figure AP6.3 shows a typical speed curve for a planing boat.

USE OF A SPEED CURVE OR RPM TABLE

The primary purpose of a speed curve is to predict the speed you intend to travel on a leg of a trip. For example, you may want to travel at a speed of 15 knots. You would use the DR formula to calculate your ETA.

Speed Curve Worksheet

Date:	15-Aug-98	Boat: Idyle Time			Run Length:		1.0
	Time (min)	(60 x D)/T					
RPM 0500	Leg 1	60	1.00				
	42.30		42.30 =	1.418	Avg Leg 1 & 2		
	Leg 2	60	1.00		1.480	Avg Speed	
	38.90		38.90 =	1.542	Avg Leg 3 & 2	1.5	
		60	1.00		1.466		
	43.20		43.20 =	1.389			
RPM 1000	Leg 1	60	1.00				
	21.00		21.00 =	2.857	Avg Leg 1 & 2		
	Leg 2	60	1.00		2.967	Avg Speed	
	19.50		19.50 =	3.077	Avg Leg 3 & 2	2.9	
	Leg 3	60	1.00		2.927		
	21.60		21.60 =	2.778			
RPM 1500	Leg 1	60	1.00				
	13.10		13.10 =	4.580	Avg Leg 1 & 2		
	Leg 2	60	1.00		4.899	Avg Speed	
	11.50		11.50 =	5.217	Avg Leg 3 & 2	5.0	
	Leg 3	60	1.00		5.088		
	12.10		12.10 =	4.959			
RPM 2000		60	1.00				
	7.00		7.00 =	8.571	Avg Leg 1 & 2		
	Leg 2	60	1.00		9.841	Avg Speed	
	5.40		5.40 =	11.111	Avg Leg 3 & 2	9.7	
	Leg 3	60	1.00		9.503		
	7.60		7.60 =	7.895			
RPM 2500	Leg 1	60	1.00				
	6.10		6.10 =	9.836	Avg Leg 1 & 2		
	Leg 2	60	1.00		10.687	Avg Speed	
	5.20		5.20 =	11.538	Avg Leg 3 & 2	10.7	
	Leg 3	60	1.00		10.769		
	6.00		6.00 =	10.000			
RPM 3000	Leg 1	60	1.00				
	5.20		5.20 =	11.538	Avg Leg 1 & 2		
	Leg 2	60	1.00		11.652	Avg Speed	
	5.10		5.10 =	11.765	Avg Leg 3 & 2	11.3	
	Leg 3	60	1.00		10.967		
	5.90		5.90 =	10.169			

Number of people aboard:	2	Equipment Weight	2300.0
Gallons of fuel:	120	Gallons of water:	20.0

Fig. AP6.2   A Speed Curve Worksheet with Data. *(F. J. Larkin)*

However, you must use your speed graph (RPM table) to determine which RPM setting to use to achieve the 15-knot speed on the leg.

Another typical reason is the need to travel at a certain speed in order to reach a destination point at a specific time. Your speed graph tells you the RPMs needed to attain the desired speed.

Things are constantly changing on your boat so you will need to check the accuracy of your speed curve. By using a Trip Log (provided in Appendix 7) for recording information about your trip, you will have the data necessary to validate your speed curve. Make checking your speed curve a standard practice after each trip.

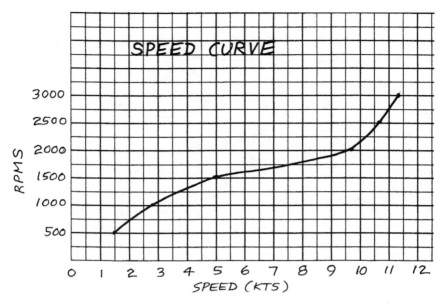

Fig. AP6.3 A Speed Curve Graph Showing the Plots from Figure AP6.2. *(F. J. Larkin)*

If your boat is slower than your speed curve:

- Did you have fewer people on board when you calculated your speed curve?
- Were you carrying any extra equipment?
- Were you towing a dinghy?
- Is there marine growth on the hull?
- Were you experiencing heavy weather or adverse currents?
- Did you have anything in your propeller, or is your propeller slipping or damaged?

If your boat was faster than your speed curve:

- Did you have more people on board when you calculated your speed curve?
- Have you taken any heavy equipment off your boat?
- Have you recently tuned up your engine(s)?
- Were you experiencing favorable currents or winds?

As you can see, nothing's perfect in the game of navigation. You must constantly observe what is happening to your boat versus what you are predicting will happen. I find the fun of navigation is trying to figure out what has gone wrong when things don't turn out exactly right and why.

Navigation Forms

Eight forms you will find useful as you work with this book or in actual practice on your boat are provided on the following pages:

Piloting Practice Chart

Piloting Worksheet

Tide Graph

Deviation Planning Sheet

Deviation Plotting Sheet

Deviation Table

Speed Curve Worksheet

Trip Log

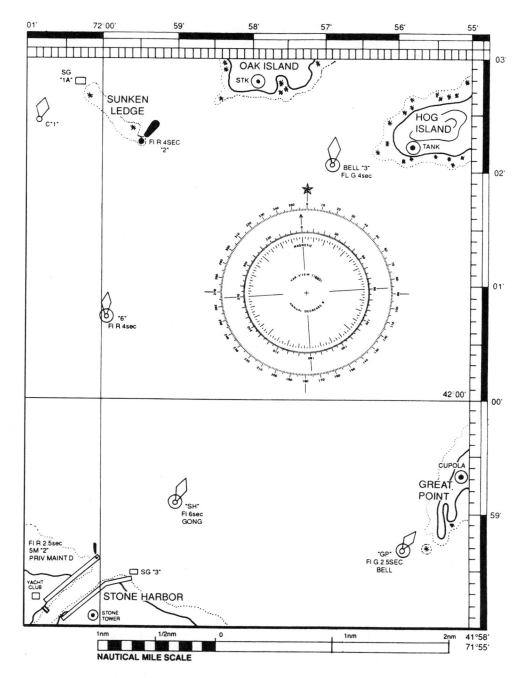

Piloting Practice Chart *(F. J. Larkin)*

PILOTING WORKSHEET

60D=ST   **TVMDC** ADD WEST DOWN

DATE	TRIP

Piloting Worksheet *(F. J. Larkin)*

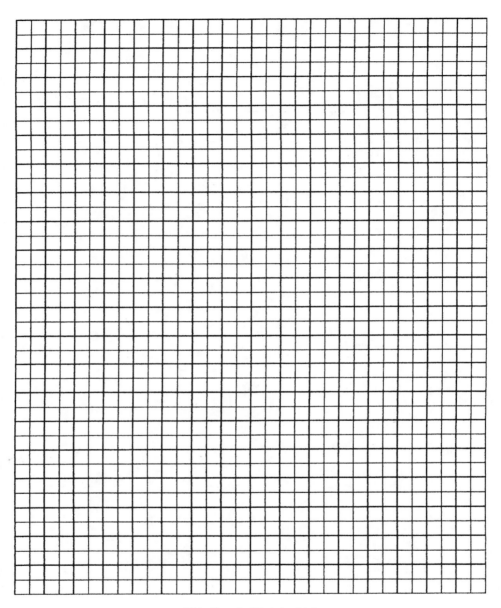

Tide Graph *(F. J. Larkin)*

```
                    DEVIATION PLANNING SHEET

DATE_____ BOAT NAME_____PREPARED BY_____
```

1. Objects (Range)	2. True Heading	3. Variation	4. Magnetic Heading	5. Deviation	6. Compass Heading	7. Boat's Heading

Deviation Planning Sheet *(F. J. Larkin)*

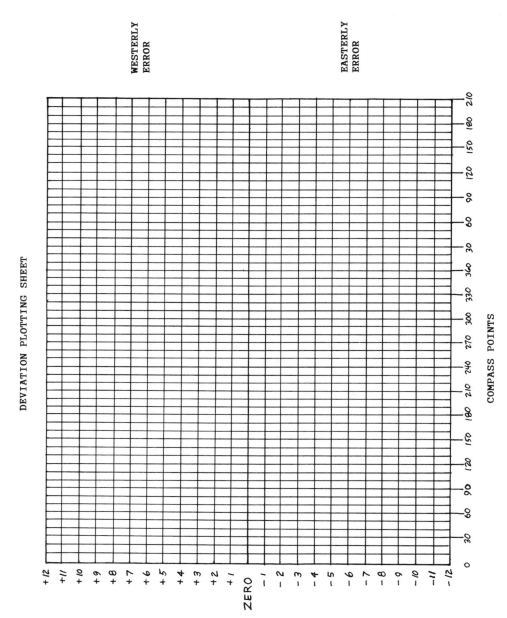

Deviation Plotting Sheet *(F. J. Larkin)*

DEVIATION TABLE

BOAT NAME _____ **DATE** _____

PREPARED BY _____

Heading	Magnetic Deviation	Compass Deviation	Notes
000			
015			
030			
045			
060			
075			
090			
105			
120			
135			
150			
165			
180			
195			
210			
225			
240			
255			
240			
255			
270			
285			
300			
315			
330			
345			

Deviation Table *(F. J. Larkin)*

Speed Curve Worksheet

Date:		Boat:	Run Length:

		Time (min)	(60 x D)/T		
RPM	Leg 1	60			
			=	Avg Leg 1 & 2	
	Leg 2	60			Avg Speed
			=	Avg Leg 3 & 2	
	Leg 3	60			
			=		
RPM	Leg 1	60			
			=	Avg Leg 1 & 2	
	Leg 2	60			Avg Speed
			=	Avg Leg 3 & 2	
	Leg 3	60			
			=		
RPM	Leg 1	60			
			=	Avg Leg 1 & 2	
	Leg 2	60			Avg Speed
			=	Avg Leg 3 & 2	
	Leg 3	60			
			=		
RPM	Leg 1	60			
			=	Avg Leg 1 & 2	
	Leg 2	60			Avg Speed
			=	Avg Leg 3 & 2	
	Leg 3	60			
			=		
RPM	Leg 1	60			
			=	Avg Leg 1 & 2	
	Leg 2	60			Avg Speed
			=	Avg Leg 3 & 2	
	Leg 3	60			
			=		
RPM	Leg 1	60			
			=	Avg Leg 1 & 2	
	Leg 2	60			Avg Speed
			=	Avg Leg 3 & 2	
	Leg 3	60			
			=		

Number of people aboard: _____   **Equipment Weight** _____

Gallons of fuel: _____   **Gallons of water:** _____

Speed Curve Worksheet *(F. J. Larkin)*

Leg/ WPT	To	DIST NM	SPEED/ RPM	COMP Heading	TIME (min)	Planned DEP	ETA	Actual DEP	ETA
TRIP LOG Date:	Boat:					Page	of		
Start									
Notes									
Notes									
Notes									
Notes									
Notes									
Notes									
Notes									
Notes									
Notes									
Notes									
Notes									

Trip Log *(F. J. Larkin)*

APPENDIX EIGHT

Coast Guard Districts and Addresses of District Commanders

Coast Guard Districts and Addresses of District Commanders

DISTRICT	ADDRESS	WATERS OF JURISDICTION
FIRST	408 Atlantic Avenue Boston, MA 02110-3350 PHONE: DAY 617-223-8338 PHONE: NIGHT 617-223-8558	Maine, New Hampshire, Massachusetts, Vermont (Lake Champlain), Rhode Island, Connecticut, New York, to Shrewsbury River, New Jersey.
FIFTH	Federal Building 431 Crawford Street Portsmouth, VA 23704-5004 PHONE: DAY 804-398-6486 PHONE: NIGHT 804-398-6231	Shrewsbury River, New Jersey to Delaware, Maryland, Virginia, District of Columbia and North Carolina.
SEVENTH	Brickell Plaza Federal Building 909 SE 1st Avenue, Rm: 406 Miami, FL 33131-3050 PHONE: DAY 305-536-5621 PHONE: NIGHT 305-536-5611	South Carolina, Georgia, Florida to 83°50'W, and Puerto Rico and adjacent islands of the United States.
	Commander Greater Antilles Section U.S. Coast Guard P.O. Box S-2029 San Juan, PR 00903-2029 PHONE: 809-729-6870	Immediate jurisdiction of waters of Puerto Rico and adjacent islands of the United States.
EIGHTH	Hale Boggs Federal Building 501 Magazine Street New Orleans, LA 70130-3396 PHONE: DAY 504-589-6234 PHONE: NIGHT 504-589-6225	Florida from 83°50'W, thence westward, Alabama, Mississippi, Louisiana , Texas, Mississippi River System, Illinois River north of Joliet, Illinois and the Tennessee-Tombigbee Waterway below Mile 411.9 (Bay Springs Lock and Dam).
	Director Western River Operations U.S. Coast Guard 1222 Spruce Street St. Louis, MO 63103-2832 PHONE: DAY 314-539-3900 (x285) PHONE: NIGHT 504-589-6225	Western River System.
NINTH	1240 East 9th Street Cleveland, OH 44199-2060 PHONE: DAY 216-522-3991 PHONE: NIGHT 216-522-3984	Great Lakes and St. Lawrence River above St. Regis River.
ELEVENTH	Building 50-6 Coast Guard Island Alameda, CA 94501-5100 PHONE: DAY 510-437-2940 PHONE: NIGHT 510-437-3700	California.
THIRTEENTH	Federal Building 915 Second Avenue Seattle, WA 98174-1067 PHONE: DAY 206-220-7280 PHONE: NIGHT 206-220-7004	Oregon, Washington, Idaho, and Montana.
FOURTEENTH	Prince Kalanianaole Federal Bldg. 9th Floor, Room 9139 300 Ala Moana Blvd. Honolulu, HI 96850-4982 PHONE: DAY 808-541-2317 PHONE: NIGHT 808-541-2500	Hawaiian, American Samoa, Marshall, Marianas, and Caroline Islands.
SEVENTEENTH	P.O. Box 25517 Juneau, AK 99802-5517 PHONE: DAY 907-463-2262 PHONE: NIGHT 907-463-2000	Alaska.

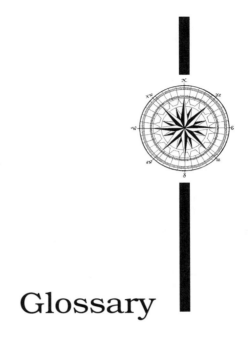

Glossary

Absolute accuracy: A term used to describe LORAN and GPS position accuracy when traversing an area for the first time. In LORAN-C, absolute accuracy decreases as a boat approaches shore and coastal bays.

Adrift: Afloat but unattached in any way to the shore or seabed.

ATON: Aid to navigation.

Bearing: The horizontal direction of a line of sight between two objects on the surface of the earth. *Beam bearing:* A beam bearing is a relative bearing, which is taken at a 90-degree angle from the heading of your boat. (It is assumed that your boat is traveling along its plotted DR track line.) *Relative bearing:* A bearing taken in relation to the heading on your compass. Relative bearings are usually taken with an instrument called a pelorus.

CMG: Course made good, the net direction of the actual path of your boat.

Coast Pilot: A nautical publication that enhances and expands on the data provided on a nautical chart.

Compass: A magnetic navigational instrument used to measure the heading of a boat.

Compass card: A card showing a 360-degree arc on a compass.

Compass rose: A printed compass card found on a nautical chart that indicates the direction of true north and magnetic north, shows the variation error for the area and the rate of change of this error.

Current: The movement of water. Usually, it is expressed in terms of direction (set) and speed (drift).

Current triangle: A graphic using a triangle where one side represents the set and drift of the current, one side represents your boat's DR course, and the third side shows the actual track of the boat.

Datum: A reference point for data. A vertical datum on a chart could be mean low water. A horizontal datum for a chart could be NAD27.

Dead reckoning: Deduced reckoning. A procedure for calculating your position from a known starting point using time, speed, and distance.

DECCA: An electronic navigational system.

DEP: Depart or departure point.

Deviation: Deviation is a magnetic influence on your compass originating on your boat. This error is solved by developing a deviation table.

Deviation table: A curve or list of compass errors for the full arc of your compass due to magnetic influences aboard your boat.

Dividers: A two-armed instrument used in navigation to measure distance on a nautical chart.

DMAHC: Defense Mapping Agency Hydrographic Center.

DR: *See* Dead reckoning.

DR position: A position calculated by dead reckoning procedures.

Draft: The measurement from the lowest point protruding below your boat up to the waterline.

Drift: The speed of current.

ETA: Estimated time of arrival.

Fix: A position obtained by two or more LOPs. Considered to be more accurate than an estimated position and a DR position.

Flashing: A light characteristic in which the total duration of light is shorter than the total duration of darkness.

Geographic range: The greatest distance at which an object can be seen due to the curvature of the earth from a particular height of eye without regard to luminous intensity or visibility conditions.

GPS: Global Positioning System.

GRI: Group repetitive interval. The length of a LORAN-C signal pulse time interval measured in microseconds.

Heading: The direction in which your boat's bow is pointed.

IALA: International Association of Lighthouse Authorities.

ICW: Intracoastal Waterway.

ISO: Isophase light characteristic. The duration of the light and the darkness cycle are equal.

Junction: The point at which a channel divides when proceeding seaward. The place where a tributary separates from the main stream.

Keel line: A line drawn fore and aft along the center of your vessel.

Lateral system: A system of aids to navigation in which the characteristics of buoys and beacons indicate the sides of the channel or route relative to a conventional direction of buoyage (usually upstream or from seaward).

Latitude: The lines that run horizontally across a nautical chart. Latitude is measured north and south from zero degrees at the equator to 90 degrees at the poles.

Leg: A single segment of a trip. The distance between two buoys.

Light: The signal emitted by a lighted aid to navigation. The illuminating apparatus used to emit the light signal. A lighted aid to navigation on a fixed structure.

Light List: A publication of the U.S. Coast Guard that lists all of the aids to navigation in an area.

LLNR: *Light List* number reference.

LNM: *See* Local Notice to Mariners.

Local Notice to Mariners: A written document issued by each U.S. Coast Guard district to disseminate important information affecting aids to navigation, dredging, marine construction, special marine activities, and bridge construction on the waterways within the Coast Guard district.

Longitude: The vertical lines that run north to south on a nautical chart. Longitude is measured east and west of the prime meridian at Greenwich, England.

LOP: Line of position.

LORAN-C: An electronic aid to navigation system that measures the time differences (TDs) of radio signals from land-based transmitters to a LORAN receiver on a boat to determine position.

LORAN-C chain: A series of LORAN-C transmitting stations.

Lubber line: A mark scribed on a compass housing to indicate the direction in which the bow of the boat is heading.

Magnetic north: The position on the earth's surface that attracts the needle of your compass.

Mark: A term for a buoy or day mark. An aid to navigation.

Mercator projection: A charting technique that projects the earth's spherical shape on a cylinder. Most nautical charts on the East Coast of the United States are Mercator projections.

Meridian: Vertical line on a nautical chart. Also called a meridian of longitude.

MHW: Mean high water.

NAD27:   North American Datum of 1927.

NAD83:   North American Datum of 1983. The newest horizontal datum for nautical charts of the United States and its territories.

NOAA: National Oceanic and Atmospheric Administration.

NOAA-NOS: National Oceanic and Atmospheric Administration–National Ocean Survey.

Nominal range: The maximum distance that a light can be seen in clear weather (meteorological visibility of 10 nautical miles). Listed in the *Light List* for all lighted aids to navigation except range lights, directional lights, and private aids to navigation.

NOS: National Ocean Survey located at Rockville, MD.

Occulting: A light flash in which the total duration of light is longer than the total duration of darkness.

OMEGA: An electronic navigational system.

Parallel: Horizontal line on a nautical chart. Parallel of latitude.

Parallel rules: An instrument for measuring course angles in navigation.

Pelorus: A nonmagnetic navigational device for taking bearings relative to your compass heading.

Pilotage: A Coast Guard term for the rules of using a pilot in a port.

Plotter: An instrument for measuring course angles in navigation.

Port: The left side of a boat when facing forward.

Prime meridian: Vertical line on a nautical chart that traverses Greenwich, England. Assigned the value of zero. Longitude is measured east and west from this point.

RACON: An electronic signal that is activated by radar.

Reference station: A fixed tide station where daily predictions of high and low water are provided in the *Tide Tables*.

Repeatable accuracy: Using LORAN or GPS, it is the navigator's ability to return to a position where prior electronic position readings were taken.

Retroreflective: A material that reflects light.

SC: Small craft. Used as a suffix on Small Craft Charts, i.e., 12345 SC.

Scale: Usually refers to the standard to which the distances on a nautical chart are referenced, i.e., 1:2500 where one inch on the chart refers to 2500 inches on the earth's surface.

Set: The direction of current.

SMG: Speed made good, the net rate of travel along a track.

SOA: Speed of advance, the planned rate of travel along an intended track line.

Sounding: A depth of water.

Speed curve: A series of measurements of speed over the ground in relation to the RPMs of the boat's engine plotted on a graph in the form of a curve.

Starboard: The right side of a boat facing forward.

Substation: A fixed location referenced in Table 2 of the *Tide Tables* for which corrective data are supplied in relation to a reference station.

Towage: A term used by the Coast Guard that indicates the rules and/or the availability of resources that supply boat towing services in an area.

TR: Abbreviation for track.

Track: The direction of your calculated track line using a current triangle.

True north: The north at the top of the nautical chart. The point where the earth spins on its axis at the North Pole.

TVMDC: Formula for converting true courses to compass courses.

Variation: Variation is a predictable magnetic influence on your compass, which is directly related to the position of the magnetic North Pole, the true North Pole, and the position of your boat.

USWMS: Uniform State Waterway Marking System.

WGS84: World Geodetic System of 1984. A horizontal datum used for the Pacific Island territories of the United States.

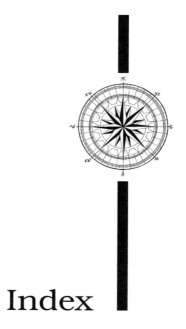

Index